T0339802

THE NEW
COMMON WEALTH

THE NEW
COMMON WEALTH

FROM
BUREAUCRATIC CORPORATISM
TO
SOCIALIST CAPITALISM

Claudiu A. Secara

Algora Publishing
New York

Algora Publishing, New York

© 1997 by Algora Publishing

All rights reserved. Published 1997.

Printed in the United States of America

ISBN: 0964607344

Editors@algora.com

Library of Congress Cataloging-in-Publication Data 97-70615

Secara, Claudiu Adrian

  The New Commonwealth, From Bureaucratic Corporatism to Socialist Capitalism / By
Claudiu A. Secara

    Edition: 2nd

    p. cm.

Includes bibliographical records and Index

  ISBN 0-9646073-4-4 (alk. paper)

1. Capitalism—History. 2. Socialism—History. 3. Bureaucracy—History. 4. State, The—
History1. I. Title: The New Commonwealth. II Title.

  HB501.S49 1997

  330.12/2 21—dc21

97-70615

Back cover quotation: from Nicholas Colchester, "Goodbye, Nation-State. Hello. . .
What?", *The New York Times*, OP-ED, July 17, 1994, Copyright © 1994 by The New York
Times Company. Reprinted with permission.

Manufactured in the United States of America
Second Edition

". . . to define it, is one person, of whose acts a great multitude, by mutual covenants one with another, have made themselves every one the author, to the end he may use the strength and means of them all, as he shall think expedient, for their peace and common defence.

As he that carrieth this person is called SOVEREIGN, and said to have sovereign power; and every one besides, his SUBJECT.

The attitude to this sovereign power, is by two means. One by natural force; as when a man maketh his children, to submit themselves, and their children to his government, as being able to destroy them if they refuse; or by war subdueth his enemies to his will, giving them their lives on that condition. The other, is when men agree amongst themselves, to submit to some man, or assembly of men, voluntarily, on confidence to be protected by him against all others. This latter, may be called a political commonwealth, or commonwealth by institution; and the former, a commonwealth by acquisition."

Thomas Hobbes (1588—1679)

"When I run in my mind the various commonwealths flourishing today, so help me God, I can see in them nothing but a conspiracy of the rich, who are fattening up their own interests under the name and title of the commonwealth. They invent ways and means to hang on to whatever they have acquired by sharp practice, and then they scheme to oppress the poor by buying up their toil and labor as cheaply as possibly. These devices become law as soon as the rich, speaking through the commonwealth — which, of course, includes the poor as well — say they must be observed."

Sir Thomas More (1478—1535)

"You, too, are a good member of the commonwealth."
William Shakespeare (1564—1616)

By the same author:

Post-Soviet, Euroslavia
Judeo-Christian Egotheism and the Anglo-Saxon Industrial Revolution

CONTENTS

FOREWORD

For anyone who has followed closely the events in Eastern Europe for the past thirty years, the systematic absence of one possible scenario from the mainstream media dialog is baffling – namely that today's Russian troubles may be only a shield behind which a more powerful regeneration is in progress. *The New York Times Magazine*, August 10 1997, brings up one of many questions to which modern history awaits a convincing answer. On the occasion of former Defense Secretary McNamara's revisiting Vietnam, it reminds us of one such unelucidated inconsistency: "If the reason [for the war in Vietnam] was to fight communism, why did the U.S. not help China in 1949, or why did the U.S. not help the Batista regime in Cuba in 1959?"

There are indeed significant and puzzling inconsistencies in the story of the Soviet Union's "collapse." Consider the artfulness, bordering on the Machiavellian, and the lengthy effort that went into its demise and one has sufficient grounds for a different tale. The process of "collapse," basically from 1983 on, came about as the country's establishment applied blow after blow to the highly coherent and resilient Soviet system. The most intriguing aspect of this incredible series of events is that behind it was the political will of the elite – the Soviet elite who had decided that the Soviet system must be dismembered, while the so-called disgruntled masses played a minor role. That amounts, but only on a superficial look, to the impression that the elite itself might have voluntarily decided to dismantle and demobilize its own lines of defense and submit to a condition of servitude to the rest of the world. On the contrary, I am not only in agreement those who ascribe perestroika and the collapse of the Soviet system to the Soviet elite, but I suggest that today's troubles are not a result of a failed perestroika but are only Phase II of a highly successful perestroika.

From socialism to capitalism and back to a superior form of socialism is how the old Marxist dialecticians would phrase it. By compromising both models – the old communist orthodoxy as well as the newer aspirant, casino capitalism – the power establishment makes it possible to bring the country safely back to socialist capitalism.

But if one accepts this hypothesis, then it becomes the premise of an unsettling line of reasoning. The elite of the second most powerful corporation in the world, the Soviet Union, must have had a self-serving reason to take such risks and must as well have had the opportunity to reformulate its modus operandi.

If this is so, the further implication would be that the "collapse" was possible not in reaction to a stronger U.S. but precisely because the other superpower also showed every sign of weakness and crisis so that it could not mount any credible offensive, economically or militarily, while the Soviet Union went through its own version of the Great Depression en route toward economic restructuring and political modernization.

The most plausible interpretation of the series of international issues of the 1980s (the new economic assertiveness of Western Europe and Japan, the war in Afghanistan, the Iran-Iraq craze, the Solidarity movement in Poland, the world debt crisis, etc.) is that they were already setting the framework for a future covenant – "the new world order" – between the former superpowers, to their mutual advantage. That presupposes an early, even pre-1980, agreed armistice and rethinking of the exhausting confrontation.

If Russia was in a position to let down its guard to the extent that we are witnessing today, it was only because it found itself not in a weak position but in the strongest military-strategic position in its history, free from imminent outside threat as enshrined at Helsinki in the 1975 Final Act of the Conference on Security and Cooperation in Europe. Given its control of the world's richest reserves of oil, gas, nuclear material, and raw materials, together with its educated professionals, an unmatched nuclear arsenal*, space technology leadership, etc. – all Russia needed was to repackage its system as a benevolent system, to make it into a soothing and attractive social and economic model, to launch a successful public relations scheme. To succeed at that would be worth the costs and the risks!

From such a strategic viewpoint one may infer that the dismantling of the Soviet Union was only the first step of the former Soviet elite's new policy of Soviet "market" outreach to the West as well as to the South.

In the west, Western Europe today seems at its zenith; however, its fate may well have been determined by (1) its military emasculation (by the Treaty of European Conventional Arms Reduction, the 1988 Soviet-U.S. Intermediate Nuclear Forces agreement and START II) and (2) its dependency on Russian-controlled oil and gas. In the south, oil producing Iran and Iraq, isolated by the United States' Middle East diplomacy, are quietly and slowly sliding further into the deadly embrace of the northern bear.**

The centuries long Russian-Anglo-American love-hate relationship has been evolving dramatically from late 1978 until today, that is clear. However, one might notice that it is being redesigned in such a way as to accommodate in the long run a more assertive, more successful and more powerful Russia overlording its European and southern

---

* According to *Komsomolskaya Pravda* on August 7, 1997: "More than $12.8 billion has been allocated for funding our programs for the creation of new types of weapons this year (the entire military budget amounts to $19 billion)." According to sources from Rosvooruzheniye, a military related consortium, the present high-priority strategic programs include: "Topol-M2 mobile intercontinental ballistic missiles (an upgraded version of the SS-25 missile, which was put into mass production at the end of last year); a new tactical nuclear arms system capable under combat conditions of firing nuclear warheads over a distance of 400 kilometers (the system was tested successfully at the end of 1995); ultra-small nuclear warheads weighing less than 90 kilograms, which are already being manufactured; seven Borey-class submarines armed with the D-31 new ballistic missiles.

In addition, Russia's military laboratories are developing laser and radio-frequency weapons."

** Notice the events taking place unremarked in the mainstream press:
– In March 1997, the Iraqi parliament ratified a 23–year oil contract with Moscow allowing a Russian oil consortium headed by LUKoil to develop reserves estimated at 7–8 billion barrels in Iraq's southern Qurna oil field, Iraqi media reported. Russia is to spend $200 million on activities related to the project and extend credit worth $100 million to Iraq.
– In August 1997, Interfax reported a joint venture between Russia and Iran to construct a major trade port in the village of Olya in Astrakhan Oblast, in the Volga delta, 95 kilometers from Astrakhan and 45 kilometers from the Caspian coast. On completion, the

peripheries.

A first sketch of such an analysis I presented in 1992 at the ISA conference in Atlanta. For a more detailed analysis of the historical background, of the economic, military and political circumstances of such a probable scenario, you are invited to read the following pages.

New York,
August 21, 1997

port will handle 10 million tons of freight annually. The first new facilities, scheduled to be completed by 2000, will have an annual capacity of 2 million tons.
– In August 1997, Russian oil companies concluded a series of deals with Baghdad to buy more than 30 million barrels of Iraqi oil under the UN's so-called "food for oil" arrangement. Among them, Zarubezhneft, LUKoil, Rosneft, and Alfa-Eko led the way; each will buy more than 5.5 million barrels of oil.

INTRODUCTION

The initial objective of this book was to examine, in a historical perspective, the forays of Eastern Europe and the former Soviet Union toward a capitalistic economic restoration following the abrupt demise of communism in the late 1980's and 1990's.

The goal of introducing free-market economic mechanisms over centrally planned structures captivated economists and scholars in the East as well as in the West, awakened the opportunistic instincts of the business community and attracted floods of free-market zealots from around the world. But, while this prospect brought delight to champions of Western superiority, in an era of deep instability it also raised fears of coming convulsions in the West itself. Needless to say, in the absence of any reliable signs and clear directions on the map of history, journalists fabricated ad hoc theories which the mass media disseminated across the new open borders.

As events unfolded, narrated and analyzed on the run by panelists *cum* media stars, the author's original goal was enlarged by the broader implications that called into question the beliefs and theories found at the very heart of industrial society. The desire to redefine such concepts as State and Public Capitalism, Social Market Economy, etc. became less academic and more a practical necessity. This redefinition demanded exercise in imaginative thinking, the reinventing of our rational discourse on the grand scheme of things, the refreshing of stale ivory tower charts of organizational management and the creation of new concepts of entrepreneurial individualism, resulting in our own manifesto of *intellectual perestroika.*

The events taking place in Eastern Europe at the end of the twentieth century did indeed engender a disruption of the old order on a profound scale. They were not merely radical steps on the way to economic reform, and they were not simply political or social reforms either. What, then, was the actual nature of the *generic reform* sweeping over Eastern Europe?

(1) Was it primarily a political revolution in which a distinct group overthrew the governing elite?

(2) Was it a social reform generated by a grass-roots constituency disenchanted with the old order, now coming to reclaim its vigor and energy?

(3) Or, was it an invention of the high-minded, born-again elites, seeking to propitiate the populace – albeit at their expense – through the use of free-market competitive devices, private ownership of the means of production, stock market instruments for capital formation, and profit-oriented production? – What was the *generic* nature of the Eastern European upheaval?

Clearly, the dismantling of the bureaucratic Soviet war machine marked the end of the Cold War era. It also coincided with the dawning age of real-time information management and the debut of TV soap-opera entertainment-news, with 'real-life' images and live information which confounded as much as enlightened the viewer. What was really happening? What was the significance of such large scale social engineering and what will be the impact of its aftershocks on the global economic environment in the years to come?

Unenlightened to the workings of Hegel's 'Spirit of History,' the business community was ripped apart by the temptations of a new frontier of the *Wild East* and the vagaries of an as yet unassessed political risk environment. Political scientists themselves simply revised old theories to fit some plotted curves of quantitative intersections of time series of past events, without committing to any historical hard descriptions.

The author's main objective was thus to determine the significance of the unfolding events in Eastern Europe within the broad historical, economic, military and political contexts.

Historically, the book considers the relatively short-term communist model, in the context of earlier circumstances to which communism itself was a response.

The economic context deals with the specific economic elements that differentiated the communist system from its rival, free market capitalism.

The international economic and political environment should not be underestimated. By focussing exclusively on the "internal causes" of Comecon's dismemberment as an economic system, one would miss the real dynamism of international interaction. By any economic measure, centrally planned economies proved to be self-sustainable and viable entities and nothing within their own internal developmental curve could explain the sudden and dramatic halt.

Indeed, the ultimate fate of the socialist economies is best understood as a consequence of accumulated changes in the international balance of power. The emergence of new economic blocs centered around Western Europe, China, and Israel demanded a reordering of alliances and national priorities and a new global strategy for the former superpowers. In this view, the concept of a new world order could be seen as a concerted counteraction, a joint effort of the former rivals, against the real threats of a powerful German-centered Western European integration, of a China-dominated Pacific Rim and, no less, of an emerging house of Israel.

As with any writing, there are a number of limitations that should be noted. Given the contemporaneousness of the events described, this is less than an exhaustive analysis. However, its main objective is to gather together a comprehensive view of the 'causes' that should be considered when one faces the task of explaining recent European history. By putting together a set of historical observations, in fact, one determines also a *holistic* methodology.

Of course, as with any test, the closer to the empirical foundations, the more varied may be the interpretations. Any answer to the question: "What is the rate of productivity growth in one economic system or another?" is based on quantified empirical observations. Similarly, any answer to the question: "Is there a cyclical pattern in the succession of the historical phases of economic development?" is still based on observed data. A conventional distinction would label the first a *quantitative* approach, and the second a *theoretical* approach, when they both turn out to be recounting *history* as one's true *story*.

Historical narrative consists of intrigues, plots and subplots, violence, conspiracies, good and bad characters — dramatic and vaudevillian — endless sequels and, most of all, lost incriminating evidence. As Carroll Quigley, respected professor of the Anglo-American establishment, said of the true insiders and the pragmatic, "more likely they knew it, but, English fashion, felt it discreet to ask no question." Left to a few exemplary personalities, whether Englishmen, Russians, or Turks, who managed to see the invisible, to hear the unspoken, and to understand the contradictory actions (where state bureaucracies just marched with the regiment), history was made mostly outside of the imperial chancelleries. While the general public was left to its imaginings, the academically-oriented person lost himself in the hunt for scholarship and petty scraps of written evidence. In fact, and above all, "the ability of Englishmen [but not only] of class and background to leave the obvious unstated, except perhaps in obituaries, is puzzling and sometimes irritating to an outsider."[1]

This study is based mainly on secondary sources of data. The author's background and his firsthand knowledge of the region provided a valuable foundation for the interpretation of current events. Still, *circumstantial evidence* and reflective philosophy of history were critical in the writing of this book. The use of such old-fashioned methodologies helped compensate for the largely unrecorded or remanufactured facts of history, as available in the official codex of the day. Only from the highest plateau of rational interpretation of the obvious and of the counterfeit can one reconstruct, with some approximation, the underlying connections that bind together the submerged contours of lost history.

Chapter 1 analyzes the economic theoretical grounds of industrial capitalism.

Chapter 2 presents the historical context of the centrally planned economies' development.

Chapter 3 reveals the limitations of past attempts at reforming state markets.

Chapter 4 discusses the military aspects of the East-West confrontation and its implications derived from technological advances in the last decade.

Chapter 5 deals with changes in world economic interactions at the end of the twentieth century.

Chapter 6 introduces the reader to the pitfalls of free-market reform in its crude and inconclusive experiment in Eastern European countries before and immediately after the 1989 watershed.

Chapter 7 examines the underlying invisible transformations of capitalist economies toward a modern social rationalization.

Chapter 8 elaborates on the subsequent conclusions on the nature of the emerging post-industrial commonwealth.

Acknowledgement

I wish to thank my editor, Andrea Sengstacken, without whose language sense and tenacity as a reader and critic of a much too often obscure text, this second, revised edition would not have been possible.

Chapter I

The Social Market

SOCIAL MARKET CAPITALISM

There is an inescapable self-evident meaning in the notion of *system* and that is its dual nature as one of *many*. Even when, in some tendentious viewpoints, the totality of the unity is supposed to predominate or, in some other extreme views, the distinctive attributes of the constituent parts are thought more relevant – any intellectual construct originates in the answer to this simple, culturally biased, cognitive archetype. And, although the generally agreed intuitive sense is that there is some sort of parity between individual identities and their ensemble, the uncritical dispute is always over the interaction of the ensemble.

Furthermore, there is a largely shared conviction nowadays among the modern public on the prevalence of free movement over static unity, which conviction unmistakably reflects the biased nature of the fashionable solution to the conundrum. The current relentless process of reformation and reorganization of the basic rules of the equation imply the absence of agreement on the optimal prescriptions. But it also excludes an all-encompassing social compact that would make dissent unsustainable.

The notion of a social covenant is central to any attempted social design. Yet even subtle shifts within the balance of relative importance among the components often reverberate into ominous consequences. Take, for example, the notion of *democratic centralism*. Intrinsically, it aims at creating the ideal of unity under democratic rule. However, in practice social centralism proved to be not a corollary of social unity but an exclusion of the majority. By the same token, the notion of *representative democracy* stands for the ideal of democratic participation in the implementation of a genuine system of social checks and balances. However, in practice, it develops its own particular kind of disease that comes with decision-making paralysis caused by the constituent special interests centrifugal tendencies.

Whether one brings under scrutiny the broad socio-political forms of organization or the micro-subdivisions that constitute the cells of economic activity (the enterprise unit, or the cluster of interactive industries or countries in their international intercourse, et cetera) the conceptional frame of analysis is bound by the same rules of systems analysis. Free-trade principles versus protectionist trade regimes within international settings are the equivalent of free-enterprise versus socially interventionist policies from a domestic viewpoint. One attitude emphasizes the interests of the constituent *individuals*, the other derives its validity from the imperatives of the *social contract*. Moreover, at the international level, whether one considers political regimes, trade, or multi-national corporations, the analytical framework does not differ from the underlying *modus operandi* of a smaller social entity. They rather might illuminate on a wider scale the uncritical practices or habits perpetuated by local mores and render out their method-ologically flawed elements, and vice versa.

In this sense, a business contract between enterprises is only a part of the social contract between economic entities and society that they serve, between the business community as a whole and its customer, society at large.

These are all common sense general principles, but as axiomatic truths they point to more exigent conclusions. Free-market competition is easily identified as a form of unbalanced bias in the belief of the importance and the relevance of the elements, by themselves, within an economic compound. The opposite is the appeal to rule by collective interest.

The optimal ground rules for both individual enfranchise-ment and a socially designed consensus can be derived from the rationalization of the social symbols and from the eradication of their intrinsic distortions. Social conflicts among groups of people, whether corporate-based competition among organized private armies, class-based warfare, ethnic or religious-based divisions, are all forms of social alienation. A truly integrative social system implies *proportional representation* by, and democratic dialogue, among various social groups (professions, economic interests, affiliations, associations, trade unions) rather than conflict. In this sense, open participation of all relevant social or economic constituents is accommodated on an equitable basis and in a competitive forum. The system is as old as Solon's democratic Athens and is as practical as the German guild system. It is known under various names and labels, as *social market capitalism, social-democratic capitalism, the welfare state, mixed economies,* or *socialism.*

THE ACCOUNTING NATURE OF CAPITALISM

The first question is: in what fundamental way does *social market capitalism* differ from *social market socialism?* Is there such an antinomical system as *socialist capitalism,* or perhaps *capitalist socialism?*

Ever since Marx made the distinction irreconcilable, we have believed that socialism is the deliberate negation of capitalism. The dichotomy is based on the supremacy of either the collectivist spirit or the individualist drive, vague as these notions are. It is, therefore, tested in practical terms through the nature of the ownership of the means of production: collective (i.e., state, public) ownership versus private.

At this purely conceptual level, it follows that the capitalist character of an economy would be radically altered by changing the character of the ownership of the means of production. This subversive act, advocated for over 150 years in the name of Marx, would make capitalism cease. Over this issue of ownership alone were drawn the social battle lines of the twentieth century.

Marx's criticism of capitalism starts by analyzing the

commodity nature of production, and its purpose of serving the market. "The wealth of those societies in which the capitalist mode of production prevails, presents itself as 'an immense accumulation of commodities,' its unit being a single commodity. Our investigation must therefore begin with the analysis of a commodity,"[1] is the opening line in the book *Capital*. To become a commodity a product must be exchanged for another product. Hence, "division of labor is a necessary condition for the production of commodities."[2] Furthermore, "only such products can become commodities with regard to each other, as result from different kinds of labor, each kind being carried on independently and for the account of private individuals."[3] The small scale and artisan character of the Adam Smith/Jefferson type of market capitalism is immediately apparent. "In a community, the produce of which in general takes the form of commodities, i.e., in a community of commodity producers, this quantitative difference between the useful forms of labor that are carried on *independently by individual producers, each on their own account* [emphasis added], develops into a complex system, a social division of labor."[4] In this sense, in a factory, for example, "although the labor is divided according to a system" since no exchange takes place between individual producers, there is no "production of commodities."

The 'independent, individual producer' has long since been limited in scope and relevance. The operations of the modern factory system fully integrate producers, processes and transactions. In this way, the factory system has become a potential replacement for the marketplace itself.

Says Marx: "This division of labor is a necessary condition for the production of commodities, *but it does not follow* [emphasis added], conversely, that the production of commodities is a necessary condition for the division of labor. In the primitive Indian community there is social division of labor, without production of commodities."[5] It is in this sentence that one finds the theoretical premise for the revolutionary idea of abolishing the capitalist economy. According to this logic, if it is true that the division of labor can be managed in the absence of a commodity exchange, then the market economy is no longer the condition of modern industry.

The model closest to such a vision, apart from the primitive Indian community, is the factory system in which large groups of working people share through their division of labor, in the production of a complex output. A factory system at a national level in which work is done without market exchanges either within or among the national assembly lines of production, vertically integrated from raw material extraction to the finished products was thought of as just such a practical possibility. An economy run by engineers rather than by businessmen would be able to rationalize the ensembled structure of industrial society. This fantastic enterprise would solve social ills and be highly efficient, humane, and egalitarian. The popularity of the idea of a floating island, as designed by Jules Verne in his fantasy novel of that title (written at about the same time as Marx's *Capital*), was proof of many people's conviction of the merits and the powers of human engineering – which was founded on about the same level of literary delusion.

Yet, but for the primitive Indian community, the world moved to validate the converse: Indeed, *the production of commodities became the necessary condition for the division of labor*. Which means that the extension and amplitude of the division of labor inter- as well as intra- factory, industry and community, only enlarged the character and the magnitude of the commodity-based economy.

As we will see, it was precisely the continued enlargement and subdivision of factory units of work into new sub-lines and spun-off enterprises, independent contractors, subcontractors, and franchises, all connected through the vast network of market exchanges, that extended the reach and the forms of the commodity economy.

This exchange of materials, products, services, and information only demands a medium of measurement, i.e. expression in monetary values. A money economy is an economy described in terms of a monetary quantifier, an accountant's economy.

One need not attach a value judgment to the bookkeeper's use of such tools as accounts, balance sheets, ledgers, prices, credits, and rates of interests. However, since the invention of writing, the profession of accounting has evolved as a more and more specialized subdivision of record keeping: inventory tallying, input/output tabulation, asset reckoning, and so on. Its profane simplicity notwithstanding, the arithmetics of accounting implied something secretive in the minds of the industrious and of the carefree alike, suggesting inside knowledge and exploits. It was the prime target of every revolutionary zealot.

Yet, by proclaiming war on capitalist brokers and agents, the movement for radical reform denounced capitalism's effective tools and not its imperfections, rejected the commodity exchange, not its distortions, outlawed private ownership, not the excesses of unequal distribution. It was anti-capitalist when it meant to be, rather, pro-accounting. It dispensed with the capitalist secular record-keeping and its professional accountants in the name of community-based accountability.

CLOSED VS. OPEN CAPITALIST SYSTEMS

The division of labor necessitates the concurrent exchange of produced goods, whether *consumable supplies* or *finished aggregates*. In Marx's formulation: "The circulation of commodities is the starting-point of capital. The production of commodities, their circulation, and that more developed form of their circulation called commerce, these form the historical ground-work from which it rises. The modern history of capital dates from the creation in the 16th century of a world-embracing commerce and a world-embracing market."[6]

The division of labor, commodity exchanges, capital circulation and, ultimately, the fully developed capitalist mode of production were the logical successive incremental phases of the economic development predominant since the beginning of the industrial age. A certain advanced level reached in the division of labor demanded that barter exchange also to be moved up to the level of commodity exchanges, i.e., value exchanges. A certain volume threshold acquired by commodity exchange activity, subsequently, brought up the capital accumulation and the ensuing capital circulation. Ultimately, it expanded to the full-fledged capitalist system of social relations of production based upon the capitalist profit-making mechanisms. The pursuit of the surplus value for the benefit of private interests based on private ownership of the means of production, rents, and capital, is the simplest expression of capitalism (in the eyes of its critics).

The key element here is the central role played by private interests. Capitalist production, without the lopsided and destabilizing forces of private interests, equals socialism.

This growing tension between the ever-increasing

socialization of production and the private character of the distribution of social output unmistakably indicated its terminal contradiction. Capitalism in its classical, metropolitan, nineteenth-century form, a closed national system, seemed also to be the only existing world system. Its limits were therefore the limits of the national marketplace. A labor market with a relatively limited scope for expansion faced the unlimited technological expansion of the industrial revolution. The result seemed obvious. Common sense suggested that productivity would increase at an ever faster rate, in tandem with a stagnant labor pool; this suggested the possibility of equally shared social prosperity in a socialist economy.

Nevertheless, two novel and fundamental developments related to the workings of the capitalist world system became apparent only later on:

(1) In the first place, there was the national nineteenth-century capitalist circumstance which Marx pointed out and which one can rephrase in Keynesian terms as follows. Whereas in the short-term the maximization of profit requires maximizing the withdrawal of surplus from immediate consumption of the majority, in the long run the continued production of surplus requires a mass demand which can only be created by redistributing the surplus withdrawn.[7] Within a confined system, these two tendencies move in opposite directions, which sets them in 'contradiction;' the system either becomes unstable under crisis or it alleviates the crisis by altering its class-based formula, in the long run.

Yet, a dissimulating acceptance and co-opting of socialism through the back door, on a short-term basis, was thought to lead inevitably to a virtual surrender to its demands in the long term. Whenever the tenants of privilege sought to co-opt an opposition movement by including it as a minority share into the circle of the privileged, they might no doubt have eliminated opponents, in the short run; but the privileged themselves also become identified with their enemies. The costs of 'co-option' rise even higher as the advantages of co-option result only in leading toward the inevitable changes.

(2) However, it was the opening of the European capitalist system to worldwide expansion that turned around the 'historical tendency' and infused new life into the moribund social arrangement. The spirit of economic imperialism rejuvenated the sclerotic metropolitan capitalism and gave it new purposes and new energies. The stalemate over the diminishing rate of profits

among national social interests was replaced with the notion of a metropolitan nation set against the periphery of the world proletariat. At the same time, over the social battle lines in the metropolis itself, there was an undisputed reallocation of the relative profit share among former social enemies in a truly capitalist celebration. It was a reallocation decidedly to the advantage of the new generation of capitalists, but still it allowed for a relative increase in the profit share of the ordinary working men and women.

Ironically enough, as Hirschman[8] and Gilpin observe, this happened to be entirely consistent with Marx's *Weltanschauung* and proven methodology. "In Hirschman's view, Marx focused on European capitalism as a closed rather than an open economy and thus he failed to develop a theory of imperialism even though one would have expected this of him as an assiduous student of Hegel. As Hirschman points out, Hegel anticipated all subsequent theories of capitalist imperialism."

Whether Marx purposely suppressed Hegel's theory of capitalist imperialism because of its disturbing implications for Marx's own predictions concerning the survivability of capitalism is not apparent from his writings. However, speculation on why Marx himself turned away from considering capitalism in its evolution as a world-system is not necessarily conclusive. First of all, Marx did refer constantly to world capitalism already as a 'world-embracing market' in existence since the sixteenth century. In this sense, Marx followed Hegel's outlook for a world-embracing system, which was the Western system, his day's only world system. Second, he maintained that no social system is displaced by another until it exhausts its inherent productive potential. The idea of a capitalist expansion going well beyond the Western world, thereby invalidating his theory, was quite inconceivable in his time. Certainly, in hindsight, it was the unforeseen expansion of the world system into the vast overseas markets, providing access to new foreign outlets for financial investments, and to cheaper and competitive labor, that was the secret exit from the seemingly inescapable collapse of the capitalist system. "Indeed, if such a collapse must await the elevation of the developing world to the economic and technological levels of the most advanced economy, then in a world of continuing technological advance, the requisite full development of the productive capacities of capitalism may never be reached."[9]

Indeed, the perspective was truly disappointing to those seeking the coming of the messiah, yet there were always a few skeptics among the hard-core socialists who questioned its historical timetable. Gilpin views Rosa Luxemburg as the first major Marxist theorist to give due importance to the open/closed variable involved in setting a deadline for the end of laissez-faire capitalism. She argued that as long as capitalism remains an open system and there are underdeveloped lands into which the capitalist mode of production can expand, Marx's prediction of economic stagnation and political revolution would remain unfulfilled.

At the turn of the nineteenth century, the New World frontiersmen gave increasing credibility to such an eventuality, as the sudden enlargement of capitalist space shifted its expansion from Europe to the United States, emerging Asia, and South-Africa, for the first time. It was these troublesome new signs that forced Lenin to search for new theoretical avenues of capitalist inner conflict. Now the prospect of international conflict of interests would override the diminishing national tension. Lenin argued in *Imperialism* that, "although capitalism does develop the world and is an economic success, the closing-in of political space through rising and declining capitalist powers leads to international conflict, which would undermine the system as a war-prone political rather than as a failed economic system."[10]

The inherent conflict among nations' capitalists did indeed fan the flames of social war. World War I and especially its aftermath of waves of revolutionary movements proved that analysis to be right. Professional cadres of Russian revolutionaries lost no opportunity to breach the ranks of the world's capitalist system.

Individualistic vs. Communitarian Capitalism

Lenin exposed and hammered away at the solution to the classical capitalist-engendered social disintegration. It is time again at the end of the twentieth century to face up to the logic of the market economy as a system inherently in collision with itself as well as with the requisites of a modern welfare state.[11] Lenin's *Imperialism, the last stage of capitalism* is alive and well. It describes the fundamental class conflict of capitalism in international terms as a conflict among national corporate owners. Only, yesterday's malignant Leninist rhetoric is replaced by the benevolent university professor's lecture warning everyone that: "Looking backward, future historians will see the twentieth century [rather, its second half – n.a.] as a century of niche competition and the twenty-first century as a century of head-to-head competition. Niche competition is win-win. Everyone has a place where they can excel; no one is going to be driven out of business. Head-to-head competition is win-lose. Some will win; some will lose."[12] Lenin spoke about carnage among the leading capitalist barons. In *The Coming Economic Battle Among Japan, Europe, and America*, Lester Thurow speaks of the declaration of economic war among the leading nations, a prelude to a world of national self-interests locked in irreconcilable economic conflicts. Sharper and uninhibited by the need to preserve cold war military alliances, economic conflicts are no longer restrained. "On one level a prediction that economic warfare will replace military warfare is good news. Vigorous competition may spur economic growth. There is nothing morally wrong with an aggressive invasion of well-made, superbly marketed German or Japanese products."[13] Actually, economic warfare could as well lead to military warfare as replace it.

> The economic competition between communism and capitalism is over, but another competition between two different forms of capitalism is already under way. Using a distinction first made by George C. Lodge, a Harvard Business School professor, the individualistic Anglo-Saxon British-American form of capitalism is going to face off against the communitarian German and Japanese variants of capitalism.[14]

Individualistic capitalism is awaiting the final act of abrogation and dismissal. This is evident to Lester Thurow, as well as to many of the members of the American National Council on Competitiveness. "The American system of allocating investment capital is threatening the competitiveness of American firms and the long-term growth of the national economy," their report unapologetically admits. And, although America's system has many strengths including efficiency, flexibility, responsiveness, and high rates of corporate profits, "it does not seem to be able to be the most effective in directing capital to those firms that can deploy it most productively and, within firms, to the most productive investment projects." Market efficiency is unequivocally dismissed since "as a result of this system, many American firms invest too little in those assets and capabilities most required for competitiveness, while others waste capital on investments with limited financial or social rewards."[15]

The Report avoids the self-deception of so many who blame the shortcomings of U.S. industry on a 'short time horizon,' ineffective corporate governance, or a high cost of capital, without seeing that these concerns are just symptoms of a larger problem. "What is at issue is a much broader problem, involving the entire system of allocating investment capital within and across companies. This system includes shareholders, lenders, investment managers, corporate directors, managers, and employees, who make investment choices in a context determined by government regulations and prevailing management practices."

The depth of the systemic deficiencies of capitalist individualist business practices is obvious to the Council's leading academic and business executives. "The American system of capital allocation creates a divergence of interests between owners and corporations which impedes the flow of capital to those corporate investments that offer the greatest payoffs. American owners, investment managers, and employees are thus trapped in a system in which all are acting rationally, but none is satisfied. The American system also has difficulty aligning the interests of private investors and corporate with those of society as a whole, including employees, suppliers, and local educational institutions."

A radical change in the nature of the ownership base of the United States' publicly traded companies caused institutional investors such as pension funds, mutual funds, and other money managers which act as agents for individual investors to increase their holdings from 8 percent of total equity in 1950 to almost 60 percent by 1990. In this new investing environment, the inherent inability of the dominant market players to outperform the market itself proves the 'ultimate absurdity' of the system. "Some institutions (as of May 1991, approximately 12 percent of all equity held by institutions) have moved to invest as much as 70 to 80 percent of their equity holdings in index funds, which involves no company-specific information in investment choices at all."

And the study goes on listing international competition, investment behavior, the determinants of investment, capital allocation mechanisms, comparative capital allocation systems, regulatory influences on the American system, the need for systemic reform, and the directions for reform. In unequivocal social-democratic overtones, it notes that "the optimal rate of investment for society may differ from that of an individual firm because of the presence of externalities (or spillovers) from private investment." It rediscovers that: "These spillovers create benefits for the economy as a whole (referred to as social returns) that exceed the private returns that accrue to a firm's shareholders. Social returns include such things as potentially higher wages for employees or the benefits to local suppliers that result from productivity-increasing technology investments." Indeed, it is refreshing to find out that "an important test for [a] national capital allocation system is the extent to which these social benefits are created and captured."

This unprecedented candid analysis made by the American corporate elite is highly rewarding to the discredited social economist. The report, chaired by Michael Porter and undersigned by a host of leading academics, and corporate CEOs,[16] states the revolutionary proposition that "overall, the American system for allocating investment capital works at cross purposes to appropriate investment behavior and competitiveness in a large part of the economy"; that the *competitive advantage of nations*, although closely related to the presence of specialized skills, technology, and infrastructure; of sophisticated and demanding local customers; capable local suppliers; competitive local companies in industries closely related by technology; and a local environment that encourages sustained investment and vigorous competition it is still, ultimately, a function of public policy. It is the government whose actions can support or inhibit those conditions. "*Government plays a decisive role in creating a nation's system for allocating investment capital.* Government policies, laws, and regulations influence the macroeconomic environment and both the external and the internal capital markets." In the light of this, the leading business community of the United States reports in a consensus already publicly reached by the early 1990s that "the emerging weakness of the U.S. system and the importance of regulation in defining that system suggest that those policy areas that affect investment behavior (and corporate performance) be reexamined."[17]

As it evolved in the late twentieth century, the American system of capital allocation "runs grave risks of undermining the very corporate sector that it is supposed to benefit." Ironically, only in the most recent decades, when exposed for the first time to international competition, America discovered that all major constituents had reasons to be dissatisfied and bitterly complain that:

American managers see owners/agents as not having the company's long-term interests at heart. They complain about the pressure from investors to achieve high short-term profits. Institutional investors see management as self-serving, receiving excessive compensations, and undermining shareholder value as they measure it. Owners are dismayed that many institutional investors underperform market averages. Small shareholders feel vulnerable and powerless. Employees are fearful of the way which the system may affect their livelihoods. Communities, and the elected representatives who serve them, are worried about takeovers and control changes that could threaten jobs and local revenues.[18]

The pattern of American investment practices reflected a set of regulations dating back to the 1930s intended to (1) avoid the concentration of economic power; (2) separate investment and control functions; (3) preserve equal treatment of all investors, big and small, by providing for equal disclosure of material information and protection against abuses from insiders; and (4) protect small investors, pension holders, insurance policy holders, and bank depositors. While hardly assuring a climate for the principles of free markets, the cumulative pattern of regulations encouraged "frequent trading and heightened the influence of accounting earnings on buy/sell choices."

As the external markets have become more and more dominated by "temporary financial owners," their pressures for "underinvestment in many companies especially in intangibles" (increasingly important to competitiveness) provided the explanation for the high American corporate returns, coupled with lower shareholder returns. *"The American system favors discrete, stand-alone investments that generate leaps in position over ongoing investment required to build capabilities, those whose pay-offs depend on complementary investments in other forms, or those that create an option value for the future."*[19] And because acquisitions are far easier to accomplish than complex patterns of complementary investments whose returns can be assessed only as "a group," and not by some "conventional budgeting techniques," this leads to an economy in which "new firms and emerging fields thrive, but difficulties arise when businesses mature."

That sits well with the overriding stated goal of American corporations, which is increased shareholder value measured by stock price, but the dominant German and Japanese goal is to ensure the perpetuation of the enterprise. As a consequence, while an estimated 74 percent of the directors of the American Fortune 1000 companies are outsiders "with no direct ties to the corporation," in Germany the supervisory board consists of 50 percent representatives of banks, significant owners, customers and suppliers, and 50 percent employee representatives (33 percent in companies with five hundred to two thousand employees). American senior management "lacks technical background needed to understand the substance of products or processes," exerting its control infrequently and exclusively through "*by the numbers*" system and financial reporting, while its counterpart, in Germany or Japan, advanced from highly technical backgrounds with a deep knowledge of the company's line of business.

The American system might serve better to provide some "short-term private returns," yet the German and Japanese systems "appear to come closer to optimizing long-term private *and* [emphasis added] social returns." Less regulated overall, their accounting rules provide far more discretion to management to plan long-term cash reserves and avoid speculative abuses. And more important, while showing lower short-term profit rates, "they have been able to sustain their competitive positions through higher levels of investment and to grow sales and earnings over time."[20]

Accordingly, it would be up to the government as regulator and social policy maker to overhaul the inefficient American capital allocation system. **Table 1.1** lists these recommendations.

The individualist ethic is set against the values and the strengths of business associations, social responsibility, team-work, firm loyalty, industrial strategies, labor partnership, shareholders' commitment to long-term goals as stakeholders, profits shared by labor, commitment to training for superior skills. The armies of the economic war thus were lined up for the twenty-first-century confrontations.

Defeated on the battleground of the past two world wars, the *new* capitalism, whether one calls it communitarian, social-democratic or socialist, overcame its ideological infighting and trappings and the open-world system. With nine of the ten most advanced nations organized on such principles at the end of the twentieth century, it can assuredly reclaim the leading position among the forces of world economies. In 1994, among the world's ten richest nations, the United States ranked at the lower end according to World Bank data[21] and stood a poor chance of advancing unless a dramatic reassessment of its own brand of economic system was to take place. In order of economic output per person, the world's success classification was the following: Luxembourg, $35,850; Japan, $31,450; Denmark, $26,510; Norway, $26,340; Sweden, $24,830; U.S., $24,750; Iceland, $23,620; Germany, $23,560; Kuwait, $23,350. Among them, Japan, Germany, and Sweden are the show-cases of the new capitalist concept.

Table 1.1
Recommendations for the U.S. Capital Allocation System

Improve the macroeconomic environment:
- Increase private and public sector saving
- Create a stable macroeconomic environment

Modify corporate ownership structures:
- Remove restrictions on share ownership
- Lower tax barriers to holding significant private ownership stakes
- Encourage long-term employee ownership

Shift the goals of owners and lenders:
- Create a long-term equity investment incentive
- Extend the long-term equity investment incentive to currently untaxed investors
- Eliminate restrictions on joint ownership of debt and equity
- Reduce the extent of explicit and implicit subsidies for investment in real estate

Improve the information used by investors:
- Modify accounting rules so that earnings better reflect corporate performance
- Expand public disclosure to reduce the cost of assessing true corporate value
- Allow disclosure of "inside" information to significant long-term owners, under rules that bar trading on it

Improve the relationship between owners, lenders, and management:
- Loosen restrictions on institutional board membership
- Encourage board representation by significant customers, suppliers, financial advisors, employees, and community representatives

Shift corporate goals:
- Codify long-term shareholder value rather than current stock price as the appropriate corporate goal
- Limit tax incentives for stock options and stock purchase plans with restrictions on selling
- Improve corporate investment incentives:
- Provide investment incentives for R&D and training

Capital Choices, Changing the Way America Invests in Industry, A Research Report presented to the Council on Competitiveness and co-sponsored by the Harvard Business School (Washington, DC: 1992).

The new word for it could be *communitarian capitalism* but, in the books of nineteenth century visionaries and agitators, it was called by its own name: *socialism*.

FORMS OF SOCIALIZED CAPITALISM

The gradual transformation of the nature of ownership of the means of production at the close of the twentieth century is unparalleled in historical significance and unprecedented in size. In every other reassignment of social ownership, there was a shift from one minority group to another, essentially preserving the class alignment within society. This quiet revolution, however, nullified all the previous economic wisdom.

In America, the percentage of the national wealth owned by the top one-half percent of families had dropped to its lowest level ever, about 14 percent in 1978, from over 30 percent in 1930. The temporary change of course brought by the Reagan administration after 1981, as a conservative backlash against the loss of economic power by the upper classes, served only to postpone for a decade or so the full-scale historical process of the socialization of the American economy.

Despite the 1980s rhetoric on the merits of unregulated capitalism and the corresponding excesses of paper entrepreneurship, merger and acquisition mania and junk-bond schemes, the American private enterprise system underwent the inexorable growing pains of economic socialization. It worked out its own set of revolutionary changes within a genuinely free-market framework.

The desperate attempt made by the Reagan conservatives to arrest this historical trend succeeded to the extent that, by 1992, America's richest recovered more than half of their loss. The top one percent of American families increased their share of wealth from 31 percent in 1981, to 37 percent in 1992, representing more than the total share of wealth owned by the other 90 percent. [24]

At this point, however, once more history repeated itself. The similarity with previous cycles in the dynamics of wealth distribution is unambiguous. There were other eras of great inequality in wealth distribution: before the 1860s, before World War I, and before 1929. Each of these climaxes of economic polarization was followed by a major social upheaval. In 1860s it was the Civil War and slave emancipation; the years of the robber barons were followed by World War I; the years of the Great Gatsby ended in the great Depression; and the years of Reagan neoconservativism were followed by the collapse of the cold war order and the beginning of *mutual fund socialism*.

In the Reagan years, while the largest military buildup in America's history gave a sense of security against the enemy from without, a bewildering invisible socialist revolution was taking over corporations from within. The very financial tools of capitalist economic policy and capital markets actually paid for the collective ticket to *mutually funded socialism*.

Here are some of the most successful capitalist instruments at work for the benefit of socialized markets.

(1) The significance of *Employee Pension Funds* was revealed by Peter Drucker in 1975 in his book *The Unseen Revolution: How Pension Fund Socialism Came to America*. In that year, according to the author, pension funds' total ownership of American equity broke the 30 percent level, with the expectation that by 1985 the pension funds of American employees would own over 50 percent of all businesses. An additional 10 to 15 percent from Individual Retirement Accounts would have brought the total up to 65 to 70 percent equity ownership of American businesses in the name of American employees.

> The American pension fund represents a bigger shift in ownership than any that occurred since the end of feudalism. In fact, one could argue that it represents a more radical shift in ownership than Soviet communism. It is not only, according to orthodox Marxist-Leninist theory, "ownership *by* the masses," which characterizes the "first stage of socialism," it is also "ownership *for* the masses" – the Marxist-Leninist slogan for the second and final stage of the "perfect Socialist society," which even Soviet Russia does not promise to reach for a long time.[22]

That prophecy was not entirely fulfilled, as studies made by Carolyn Kay Brancato in 1992 showed a mere 20 percent equity level owned by pension funds in that year (more about that in Chapter 7.)

Still, for the first time in modern history, an economically valid entity, embodying both the worker and the owner, was created. The typical conflict of interests between the wealth producers (workers) and the wealth possessors (owners) was being resolved in an unforeseen way. "The shift to an economy in which the 'worker' and the 'capitalist' are one and the same person, and in which 'wage fund' and 'capital fund' are both expressed in and through 'labor income,' is radical innovation and at odds with all received theory. . . At the same time, ownership of the economy's productive resources by the employee pension funds maintains both the mobility of the employer and the mobility of the capital, both individual freedom and the rational allocation of resources to productivity."[25]

(2) *Employee Stock Ownership Plans* (ESOPs) have seen a growing trend in the promotion of self-management and in the number of employee-owned corporations. According to Severyn T. Bruyn, by the mid-1980s over ten thousand firms with more than 11 million workers had ESOPs or the equivalent. Most of these workers were employed by companies with less than 15 percent worker ownership, but about one million were employed by companies with 15 to 50 percent worker ownership, and about a half-million worked in some one thousand companies with 51 to 100 percent ownership.[26]

By 1994, workers owned "at least 15 percent of more than one-quarter of the nation's publicly traded companies"[27] which amounts to $150 billion in stock value, according to a 1994 report by the Labor Department.

(3) The *Value-Adding Partnership* (VAP). The VAP is a new type of vertical structure most successfully developed in Europe. It is based on the concept of the 'value-added chain' that takes advantage of new communication and information systems. It deconstructs the corporate entity into several independent entities and assigns each one to a set of independent firms acting within a system. Italy's textile industry is a prime example. Since the mid-1960s the large vertically integrated mills of the Prato area have been broken into more than 15,000 smaller companies.[28] In the United States, the McKesson corporation, a $6.67 billion distributor of drugs, transformed itself into a VAP.

(4) *The Nonprofit Sector* represents another growing type of business in open rejection of profit as the business purpose per se. In 1929, according to Eli Ginzberg and Dale Hiestand, the nonprofit sector (including government institutions) accounted for 12.5 percent of all goods and services purchased; by 1963, it accounted for more than 27 percent. In the same period, its share of the labor force climbed from 9.7 percent to about 20 percent.[29] "By 1980, those in the private sector alone accounted for 5.5 percent of national income, and 9.2 percent of total employment."[30]

Table 1.2
Distribution of Private Wealth Owned by the
Richest Households in the U.S.[23]

Year	Richest Households (percent of population)	
	0.5%	1.0%
1922	29.8	31.6
1929	32.4	36.3
1933	25.2	28.3
1939	28.0	30.6
1945	20.9	23.3
1949	19.3	20.8
1953	22.7	24.3
1958	21.4	26.6
1962	22.2	26.6
1962	22.2	28.2
1965	25.4	31.3
1969	21.8	27.4
1972	21.9	27.7
1976	14.4	27.7
1981	20.0	31.1
1983	26.9	n.a.
1992	n.a.	37.2
1995	n.a.	>40

(5) *Associations* are alliances of companies established for the purpose of overseeing a whole range of business interests. One of the newest hybrid forms of economic entity, both at micro and macro levels, associations are determinant players in the life of their members from setting prices to agreements over production quotas, labor policies, and representation before government.

> When you belong to one of these associations, you are a "member" rather than a stockholder or an owner, and you are given voting rights attached to your membership. So it is significant that as today's executives look at the Japanese corporation, with its quality circles and life long membership for employees, they have begun to replicate it, describing their own employees as "members of the family.[31]

(6) The "technostructure corporation,"[32] the "managerial enterprise,"[33] the highly structured, bureaucratic organization suc-ceeded almost entirely in replacing free-wheeling patronage that was common from the early twentieth century to the mid-1960s. Al-though in popular belief large industrial enterprises were still prime examples of bureaucratic inadequacy, even ineptitude, all serious data support the conclusion that big organizations were in fact the center, the driving force of the success story of American business .

The impressive level of production concentration and asset accumulation is undeniable. "In 1976, the five largest industrial corporations, with combined assets of $113 billion, had just under 13 percent of all assets used in manufacturing. The 50 largest manufacturing corporations had 42 percent of all assets. The 500 largest had 72 percent."[34] The work force was employed in an equally disproportionate way by the top few hundred corporations. "The largest five manufacturing corporations in terms of employment employed 11 percent of the working force engaged in manufacturing."[35]

The resourcefulness and competitive advantage of corporations, in terms of the economies of scale and scope, were unrivaled. Nevertheless, risk aversion was built into their structural philosophy, requiring genuine inventiveness and symbiosis with the small, noncompetitive firms. As "invention was largely left to individuals or groups outside of the enterprise, often working in universities and institutes," and as "many times even the initial commercialization of the product and the process was left to small entrepreneurial firms,"[36] the large, managerial corporations themselves developed as self-promoting quasi-social institutions. In the end, largely insulated from stockholder accountability through a system of executive management, they evolved into a model of industrial phalanstery.

The aggressive profit-maximizing multinational corporations, feared all over the global market in their heyday of the 1950's, were indeed domesticated by early 1970's into communitarian institutions, subservient to joint management/employee interests.

One can only sympathize with the new underperforming American corporations under siege by foreign competition of the late 1980's, struggling under the pressure of profit rates diminishing from as high as 10 percent in the 1950s down to 1 to 2 percent. Their dual nature – nominally, money-making enterprises; actually, acting as socialistic institutions – explains why their economic effectiveness was so minimal. The proudly stated goals of free competition, inscribed on the frontispieces of their headquarters, were, in fact, a cover-up for backdoor compromising socialistic arrangements: military subsidies – Boeing, Lockheed, McDonnell Douglas, IBM; direct subsidies – Sun Microsystems, Silicon Graphics; outright bailouts – Chrysler; trade protectionism.

Under the unbearable burden of carrying heavy social costs on their own, while on a collision course with their international competitors, the American hybrid corporate structure was counting its growing losses. "In 1790, the Tariff Code consisted of a single sheet of rates posted at U.S. Custom Houses; now (1991 – n.a.), our tariff code occupies two hefty volumes with 8,753 different rates, a blizzard of arbitrary discrimination against and among products. This is equivalent to over 8,000 different industrial policies – and 8,000 different entitlement programs for protected domestic industries."[37]

The days of orthodox laissez-faire were long gone. "As the historian Karl Polany explained it, laissez-faire, or classical liberalism, required three interrelated tenets: 'that labor should find its price on the market; that the creation of money should be subject to an automatic mechanism; that goods should be subject to free flow from country to country without hindrance or preference; in short, a labor market, the gold standard, and free trade.' . . . This model more or less operated between the mid-nineteenth century and World War I, at least as an ideal."[38]

Capitalism, understood as "the restless never-ending process of profit-making *alone* [emphasis added],"[39] in the sense of Marx's famous formula M-C-M (money-commodity-money), was beginning to have a hard time. The once socially hot issue of capital's "appropriation of ever more and more wealth in the abstract," and the "sole motive of his operations," was finding its limits. While still acting in the external world as a representative of the 'bottom-line' league, its socialized internal structure was already making the revolutionary leap ahead.

A hundred and fifty years of slow conviction-eroding, depression-fighting policies, the refinement of the science of economics, the spread of affluence and the public's emancipation, cold war *realpolitik* imperatives and international competitive experimentation, all amounted to an invisible but steadily advancing pressure for reformation of the ground rules of the traditional free-market system.

Classic Hobbesian capitalism has been reformulated and weakened in its basic tenet: the unregulated nature of market competition. In this sense, Marx's record is mixed. The concentration and centralization of production into monopolistic organizations confirmed the trend toward a socialized economy. This socializing undercurrent, however, did not exclude the market environment in which it functions. On the contrary, it made possible the participation of new, untraditional actors as it opened its turf to all conceivable forms of ownership and entrepreneurship.

Instead of developing through the predictable dialectic scheme of a sequence of distinct monadic stages of "social relation of production," a more complex metamorphosis of the nature of the relations of production itself has occurred. The emergence of the hybrid concept of *socialist capitalism* would be its best description.

THE PROFIT MOTIVE

The issue of profit over wage is as inseparable from the concept of capitalism as is the distinction between the capitalist class and the labor class. While anything else may be subjected to intellectual scrutiny, questioning profit appropriateness touches a raw nerve. The politicized nature of the debate over profits is far reaching: it goes from the argument over the true source of profits, their proper retention, their productive allocation, and their moral qualifications, up to the social bargaining process over their fair redistribution.

It would not be inappropriate to say that, absent his profit distribution-related observations, Marx could be today the beloved capitalist's friend and counsel on topics ranging from political advising to macromanagement consulting, and would sit on some of the modern-day government/business policy study commissions. But he chose to side with the 'conservative,' 'conventional,' and the 'antiprogressive' Cartesian truth: *"Profit and wages remain as before in inverse proportion,"*[40] confessing his allegiance to the zero-sum rigor imposed by the equation that any shopkeeper thinks to know. Yet, at the same time, he remained inconsistent with his professed Hegelian logic and belief in the notion of dialectics. In his own words: "Let us sum up: *The more productive capital grows, the more the division of labor and the application of machinery expands* [correct – n.a.]. *The more the division of labor and the application of machinery expands, the more competition among the workers expands and the more their wages contract* [incorrect – n.a.]."[41] His error is thus the 'capital' error of orthodoxy.

The *iron law* of wages, as it remained known, was formulated in defiance of social progress, productivity growth and, more importantly, was based on the false premises of Say's Law. This alone was meant to provide the platform for the criticism of capitalism since it assumed that the increase in production output would always equate to a relative diminishing purchasing power. In other words, the supply side and the demand side would always find themselves in perfect correlation with one another as variables of the market equation. This would translate into the paradox that the richer the society as a whole, the more impoverished its labor. Says Marx:

> If capital grows rapidly, competition among the workers grows incomparably more rapidly, that is, the means of employment, the means of subsistence, of the working class decreases proportionately so much the more, and, nevertheless, the rapid growth of capital is the most favorable condition for wage labor [as capitalism's crisis increases – n.a.].[42]

But life after Keynes is not the same anymore.

First of all wages, although a cost to the employer, represent income to the employee. A cut in real wages is therefore likely to reduce workers' consumption and, via the multiplier mechanism, the incomes and consumption of other workers. Thus there will be a fall in the output of the economy and a rise, not a fall, in unemployment. (To put it more technically, the downward shift in the supply curve of labor represented by the cut in real wages may be offset, or more than offset, by a downward shift in the demand curve for labor, leaving the level of unemployment unchanged, or even lower than it was before.) With Keynesian techniques of demand management this adverse effect on incomes and employment could of course be counteracted by tax cuts or increases in public expenditure.[43]

After the 1930s, orthodox capitalism had to reinvent itself. Subversive talk about the redistribution of the surplus value moved from left-wing radical circles into the mainstream of social discourse. Kicking and screaming, on again, off again, capitalism's lords and labor leaders, academics and managers, political opportunists and street fighters – all, through collective effort, undertook the task of managing the conflict of interests. The apparently intractable formula of the redistribution of social profit had been redesigned in one nation after another, on an ever-more radical basis. The establishment of the Social Security fund, of the minimum wage rate, of unemployment benefits, of universal health care and, indeed, of the welfare system were each only incremental steps toward the massive transfer of social income in a socialistic direction.

Taxation and *government spending* were the financial tools for profit administration.

The predicament of ever-increasing competition among workers for ever lower wages came about unheeded. Ever-expanding productivity increases resulted in the growing abundance of aggregate goods. The corollary effect was that control over profits was taken away from individual hands and bestowed upon the political process.

* * *

The key word on the subject of profit is the politically charged notion of *exploitation*. One should approach this issue head-on and from a very pragmatic perspective. The simple fact is that slave owners, overlords, and sweatshop patrons were well aware of the arithmetic of their source of income, the unpaid work of their subjects. In this sense, Marx's own intellectual character is unique only in his facing that truth unadorned by the usual excuses of the conscience-stricken. In modern complex work establishments, it is confusing to try to identify the exact composition of a day's worth of work in terms of the composition of paid work and unpaid profit. It is only obvious in the case of one type of work performed by the serf under the obligations of corvées, which is out-right unpaid work separated from his paid work.

From early antiquity it was clear that one day's worth of work can produce more than necessary for one's own subsistence – and that surplus became the focus of the entire history of social warfare. A man can eat his extra bushel of grain or preserve it. He can sell it or he can let it rot. He can serve it as food to another less fortunate than he, or pay with it for another's hired-day of work. The crux of the social economic dilemma was and is still: by whom, how, why, and how much that surplus is to be *enlarged* and *used*. One can see it as an individual's right to the value of his own work. Yet, it is no less a question of social responsibility to the common good, as was pointed out by Marx.

> In the development of the richness of human nature as an end in itself. . . at first the development of the capacities of the human species takes place at the cost of the majority of human individuals and even classes. . . ; the higher development of individuality is thus only achieved by a historical process during which individuals are sacrificed; for the interests of the species in the human kingdom, as in the animal and plant kingdoms, always assert themselves at the cost of the interests of individuals.

Whether through the use of violence, through expedient arrangements of the powerful against whole communities, because of greed or idealist designs (all of which have been tried at one time or another), they all shaped a particular set of social relations around the question of *profit extraction and distribution* among the ordinary workers, owners, and rulers.

From slavery to more sophisticated forms of serfdom, labor for hire, the use of market labor allocation, or Communist bureaucratic administration, the main dispute over which position gives authority to regulate that precious social capital is still up for judgment. Whether profit is allocated to individual possession (a practical impossibility!) or to the discretion of one class of individuals in perpetuity, allocated on the basis of open competition among the ruthless, or allocated through a common budget to be decided by an elected body, and so on – these are all historical attempts to find the best practical solution to profit allocation in the face the fierce conflict of interests and the shifting rapport of social forces. They all have merits but they all have systemic shortcomings too.

Yet, there remains the central tenet that human beings, through their work alone, do produce a consumable surplus, the source of all accumulated (or squandered) social wealth. Its use by an idle class for absurd purposes is a measure of exploitative practices and can signal social decay and disintegration. Its healthy administration by conscientious classes for the purpose of an increase in general prosperity and betterment is the fortunate choice of a deliberate social organization. In one way or another, the latter choice is typically associated with democratic participation in the decision-making process.

The socially accountable (although easily manipulated) mechanism of public election renders the *social-democratic* capitalist pursuit of economic interests at once socially subservient and socially rewarding. The undemocratic corporate entity is ultimately questioned through the mechanisms of public institutions, themselves accountable to voters. Although corporate self-manage-ment and self-ownership has been introduced in some European countries, that arrangement has yet to be generalized. Only the generalized representation of labor on corporate boards and democratic councils will bring the final step in dismantling nineteenth-century patriarchal capitalism.

> The principle of federalizing can apply as well to whole industries. Some social economists have suggested that the corporate system can best be served by a model based on the concepts of a "republic" with "constitutional law." Scott Buchanan, for one suggests that the analogue of states' rights and the federal principle will provide a useful guide to the future of U.S. economy. He wants to see the private sector maintained, but with more attention paid to its democratic foundation.[44]

The new model of capitalism works both ways. It preserves entrepreneurial free enterprise as an everyday channel for upward mobility. It also makes room for market-sponsored universal access to social capital which is, by itself, as much socialist redistribution of resources as it is capitalist use of credit instruments.

On the one hand, the new model is based on equal opportunity principles, on continuously refreshed large-scale meritocracy, on prestige-enhancement incentives, as well as on publicly regulated union/association-type organizations. On the other hand, it involves risk taking and personal accountability, innovative entrepreneurship, private/stock ownership, self-management, and protection from direct state administration.

Furthermore, it is also in total compliance with the orthodox principles of capitalism. It is classic David Ricardo. It follows to the letter his "Principles of Political Economy *and* Taxation." It involves economic leadership in support of private energy and the pursuit of social good.

A man can be absorbed by the pursuit of accumulating profits as long as they are the only ticket to his self-realization as an individual, whether that is his personal survival, the raw exercise of power over other individuals, or the unrestrained pursuit of his be-loved liberal arts. But once the goals of his creative spirit are, for their own sake, attended to in actual entrepreneurial activity, the profit result is only a measure of his comparative success. Profit is a guarantee of further access to ever-increased resources, and it is the opportunity to reinvest in the ongoing venture. Profit is also a measure of the inherent augmentation of one's inheritance vis-a-vis his forerunners or his contemporaries. Says Drucker: "Profitability is not the purpose of but a limiting factor on business enterprise and business activity. Profit is not the explanation, cause or rationale of business behavior and business decisions but the test of their validity. . . The profit motive and its offspring maximization of profits are just as irrelevant to the function of a business, the pur-pose of a business, and the job of managing a business."[45]

When it comes to enlightened understanding of the profit motive, it is a matter of logic to equate cost/price quantification with the function of accountability, which is another name for not wast-ing one's day in the perennial hunt for one's labor yield. "The paradox of modern economic motivation is that profit maximization as a goal requires that the individual member of the technostru-cture subordinate his personal pecuniary interest to that of the remote and unknown stockholder. By contrast, growth as a goal is wholly consistent with the personal and pecuniary interest of those who participate in decisions and direct the enterprise."[46]

All along the curve of an enterprise's growth from a start-up to large-scale operations, profit maximization remains the test of truth. Yet, contrary to the traditional Adam Smith/Marx emphasis on the class nature of profit extraction and distribution, profit is not the cause or the explanation of capitalist enterprise. "If archangels instead of businessmen sat in directors' chairs, they would still have to be concerned with profitability despite their total lack of personal interest in making profits. This applies with equal force to those far from angelic individuals, the commissars who run Soviet Russia's business enterprises, and who [if they are to surpass them] have to run their business on a higher profit margin than the wicked capitalists of the West."[47]

Profit maximization, once seen as the earmark of capitalist exploitation, is more adequately described as the gauge of self-sustaining, self-financing, successful growth. To the extent that it is, ultimately, publicly allocated through the mechanisms of taxation and government spending, it is also socially consumed. And, subsequently, it puts to rest the radical Marxist class distinction and the conflict of interests on the question of profit's legitimacy, size, morality. It blurs the distinction between wages, profits, and rents through the means of social re-distribution and the dual nature of ownership.[48]

In truth, the measure of the socialized character of private profit is not related to economic descriptions, but rather is a function of the political process. The distinction between a profit-taking order and a socialized one is decided in the cabinet of the finance ministry, which is occupied through political competition. In its turn, the political process is bound to be democratic and truly representative only as long as one nation is inescapably challenged by other nations. The circumstance of international economic competition alone sets the character of the international-economic socialistic framework. It is inexorably derived from pitting one *economic team* against the others. But that is another story to be discussed in Chapter 5.

SOCIAL CAPITALISM

For all the stimulating effects that competition is credited with in terms of economic advancement, one might as well dismiss the rhetoric of the pursuit of *liberty, democracy and free enterprise* as purely bourgeois class slogans. The unavoidable issue of class cleavage of interests and the ensuing class conflict marks capitalism from its birth. All the more so, given that while class ideology permeates any social consciousness, a one-sided set of class-based ideas is presented by its advocates as representative of the society as a whole. "In considering the course of history we detach the ideas of the ruling class from the ruling class itself and attribute to them an independent existence."[49]

The violent nature of the history of class appropriation of wealth and of control over renewable sources, whether land, commerce, or industry, is indeed always denied on the basis of the same argument. "For each new class," says Marx, "which puts itself in the place of one ruling before it, is compelled, merely in order to carry through its aim, to represent its interest as the common interest of all the members of society, that is, expressed in ideal form: it has to give its ideas the form of universality, and represent them as the only rational, universally valid ones."[50] Indeed, the pursuit of liberty, democracy, and free enterprise is just an empty class slogan in the absence of the economic mechanism and of the social channels of distribution of rewards to ensure the universality of access and social participation of all players on the field.

Two observations are in order for dealing with the historical origins from which Europe had embarked on the road to wealth in the early years of capitalism:

The first observation is on the completion of a process of land settlement that has been going on in Europe for a thousand years and the growing population pressure inside the finite 'vital space.' European social consciousness – rooted in traditions of the manor and the guild – was patterned after the father figure, the family, the tribe, and the household. Coming out of the long-lived tradition of agrarian communitarian life, the authority and obligations of the seignior and the overlord were likened to those of the shepherd over his flock as much as to those of the father over his household. Its institutions reflected the undifferentiated mix offered by that fundamental human social organization, the traditional patriarchal family that stood on the borderline between communitarian interdependence and the hierarchical division of ownership. The head of the household was at once a member of the family and proprietor of its other members.

The slow erosion of that system, primarily due to its economic successes, occurred earliest in Holland, England, and France, and brought about a multitude of changes in the social covenant between lords and vassals. It also inaugurated the age of alienation. It ripped off the patriarchal social fabric, exposing one and all to the blatant and unmerciful capitalist division between the fortuitous and the superfluous.

The second observation is on the nature of the modern technological revolution, which was a direct consequence of an agricultural revolution that simultaneously opened the flood-gates of available labor and furnished the supplies for their subsistence. It gave way to a privately organized but socially aimed, innovative mode of industrial *employment*.

The new and crude act of organizing the ever-growing regiments of unemployed agricultural laborers into an industrial army was the first sign of things to come. Inexcusably inhumane in its early practice, the industrial enterprise emerged as an unlicensed prerogative of the minority class of venture capitalists committed to the better use of their private wealth at the expense of the rest of society. Later on, it evolved into a franchise for amassing unlimited profits. At that point, the eye-opening magnitude of the potential of the industrial powers made clear their tremendous social significance.

> In some ways, the most fundamental change in economic organization was the realization that the deeper function of a manufacturing enterprise was not simply to operate its factory (or, rarely, factories) efficiently, but to create or discover changes – in product, production, raw materials, distribution, or organization – that would increase the margin between costs and revenue. The concepts of an enterprise and enterprising became distinct from the concepts of a factory and manufacturing.[51]

As the industrial sector grew dramatically, it became concentrated in a few nations and, within them, into manufacturing branches. By 1870, two-thirds of the world's industrial output was provided by three nations: the United States, Great Britain, and Germany. By the turn of the century, over half of the employment in all three countries centered in the manufacturing industry. It was these *first movers*, large enterprise units, that provided the core for future national economies.

Their hierarchical expansion, vertically integrating first backward, to include mining and extraction branches, then forward to trade, distribution and service, was the key factor in creating the prototype of the modern industrial state. From private affairs involving a limited number of people, they evolved into large-scale works functioning as wealth-creating social enterprises.

> In order to benefit from the cost advantages of these new, high-volume technologies of production, entrepreneurs had to make three sets of interrelated investments. The first was an investment in production facilities large enough to exploit a technology's potential economies of scale or scope. The second was an investment in a national and international marketing and distributing network, so that the volume of sales might keep pace with the new volume of production.

Finally, to benefit fully from these two kinds of investment the
entrepreneurs also had to invest in management: they had to
recruit and train managers not only to administer the enlarged
facilities and increased personnel in both production and
distribution, but also to monitor and coordinate those two
basic functional activities. It was this three-pronged
investment in production, distribution, and management that
brought the modern industrial enterprise into being.[52]

From small-scale trade performed on the premises of a
household-factory, the enterprise entity turned into a national and
international oligopolistic technostructure. Employers and
employees were not only divided by skill level but also faced each
other over the barricades of social polarization. By 1977, at the
apogee of monopolistic concentration, two corporations alone,
"American Telephone and Telegraph and General Motors –
employed 2 percent of the United States employed civilian work
force."[53] From 1982 to 1992, the two hundred top corporations
enhanced their share of the United States' GDP from 24.2 percent
to 26.8 percent, with the leading ten taking almost half the profits of
the top two hundred.[54] This simple fact shows the inordinate level of
socialization of a formerly private undertaking.

In other words, the 1700's idea of investing one's personal
fortune in the uncertain venture of pin- or clothmaking, when one
could as well have saved his effort and simply have enjoyed the
fruits of his affluence, is obsolete in the modern industrial state.
Modern managerial enterprises are the equivalent of de facto
national establishments.

There are other ways to exemplify the changes in the institutional nature of modern industry. For one, since the early twentieth
century it is no longer conceivable to think of allowing private
money to decide on the merits of a national defense industry and
its priorities. Likewise, investing in the infrastructure sectors –
roads, airports, railroads, telecommunications, and education – is
not a private undertaking. Banks and other financial organizations
are, largely, institutionalized public agents under governmental
supervision. The bulk of the health-care industry is also of public
concern and is not an independent monopoly. Whether state-
owned, public stock-held, or merely publicly regulated, financed, or
technologically supported through R&D transfer and subsidies, the
days of the capitalist private sector's freedom of choice are history.
In 1990s America, a stand against socialized institutions is an
object of mockery for *New York Times*' columnists. "Get up a

neighborhood petition against socialized government. Demand an end to socialized street-lights, socialized storm drains, socialized road paving, socialized traffic signals, socialized police patrols, socialized firefighting and other such stuff that ought to be privatized."[55]

* * *

There is another dimension along which one is compelled to explore the realities of the socialization of capitalism. Technological developments during the last decades have had their own effects on the evolution of the corporate entity. What appeared to be an ever-expansionary course (whether through ever-more aggressive horizontal integration, merger and acquisition mania, or a first move into new territories of technological innovation) alternates at times with a process of cutbacks, divestment, and plant closures.

While the process of *mechanization* created the corporate giant, *automation and robotization* result in its dismantling and allow for a shift from labor-intensive industries to knowledge-based enterprises. In the long run, the net effect might be to make future manufacturing the equivalent of earlier farming. By themselves, household-based knowledge-manufacturing farms could provide timely, designer-made consumables. The 'economy of scale' concept dissolves into the 'economy of infrastructure.' The trend is a replica of the de-agriculturization of the last century and will follow its fate. "It is therefore highly probable that developed countries such as the United States or Japan will, by the year 2010, employ no larger a proportion of the labor force in manufacturing than developed countries now employ in farming – at most, one-tenth."[56]

The *entrepreneurial social economy* is now at hand.

Together with a supportive social-political-economic infrastructure, the technological mandate for democratic entrepreneurship dissolves the image of the ruthless, rugged individualist capitalist into a cheering crowd of socialized entrepreneurs. One can as well call the new class the *working capitalist class*.

The classical capitalist battle-cries of free enterprise, liberty, and democracy, which might have sounded cynical in the heyday of unrestrained capitalist exploitation, are here to stay. Reflecting their ideological call in the name of the *massive systematic innovation* imperative in the age of "creative discontinuity," their wake-up call to productive action and the duties of citizenship echoes far beyond class propaganda.

It is from this perspective that cooperation gains more meaning than competition. The management/labor divide, once class based, must answer the requirements of a function-based work structure. Also, the adversarial concept of competition among businesses is limited by the notion of interdependence and networking. Against the iron law of poverty where the winner takes all, here comes the tide of affluence that lifts all the boats. The prevailing nature of the commonwealth environment thus makes possible a government-business cooperation unbiased by the fear of a captive government pressured by special-interests in the act of picking winners and losers. As the provider of the consensual ground rules, capital disseminator, and keeper of the social knowledge bank – enhanced by the use of high technology information systems – the elected government becomes the glue, rather than the hammer, of the business system.

THE SOCIAL MARKET COMMONWEALTH

After a history of social and economic experiments, we might actually be leaving behind the bureaucratic form of capitalism. It is indisputable that we are invalidating the bureaucratic form of socialism.

The classical, class-*owned* society is unmistakably the converse of the bureaucratic-*controlled* industrial state, although essentially they are complementary. The former entailed heavy human costs and untenable inherent conflicts. In the words of Thurow, "left to itself, unfettered capitalism has a tendency to drift into either financial instability or monopoly. Tulip mania, the South Sea Bubble, numerous nineteenth-century financial panics, and the stock-market collapse of 1929 were all forerunners of the current mess in America's deregulated financial markets. The current consolidations in the U.S. airline industry are not unlike the great monopolistic trusts of the last half of the nineteenth century."[57] The latter are still being dismantled. However, the process of industrialization developed in the late twentieth century some extreme forms – superpower industrial states – which are still with us. Their unrivaled, all-embracing capacity for dominance was, not without irony, exercised by their wholesale subordination to the needs of the military-industrial complex.

Operating outside of ownership categories, unaffected by market forces, and unanswerable to social constraints, the hierarchical industrial technostructures had only contempt for capitalism. Administrative (Soviet-style) or monopolistic (American-style), they replaced money capital with *capital bureaucracy* as the instrument of the exchange production.

* * *

As we leave behind the industrial state, a practical middle-ground civil society can be imagined, based on a socially defined market commonwealth.

First, this vision requires rehabilitating the notion of the market economy functioning as a productive factor and not as a gambling establishment.

> One factor that inhibits this understanding is the paradigm of economics today, which is constructed to depict a market system devoid of social life; as a result, economic studies of the market as such are highly restricted and often inaccurate. This limited conception is also held by the general public, transmitted by the mass media's discussions of economic indicators, Laffer Curves, inflation rates, unemployment statistics, and the GNP. These economic categories keep people from seeing the patterns of human design and the cultural values that shape market life.[10]

Second, it invites the rewriting of the market's democratic rules to include universal access to education, to capital, to social services. In other words, from a form of elitist 'socialism' of the board of directors to a broad-based socialization of capital resources.

It also implies a multiform ownership redesign, as well as self-regulation. From the old-style proprietorship and corporate forms of ownership to a variety of franchising, trade unions and associations, Employee Stock Ownership Plans, vertical cooperation, et cetera, all forms of capitalist enterprises should stimulate work performance, a sense of responsibility, entrepreneurial innovation, and ultimately, overall social advancement.

The early English discovered the productive employment of idle human talent. If one's contribution is to be decided by his talents, then at least let him start from a higher level of skills and a sense of purpose.

Two competing models of the industrial-state most captured the attention of students of twentieth-century economics: the (American) *Anglo-Saxon technostructure* and the Soviet *centrally-planned*. In between two wars a *sui generis* third way was pioneered by the Germans and other Western Europeans, and by the Japanese. In a sense, the history of the twentieth century is dominated by the struggle between these models.

Their story is unfinished as yet, although a certain degree of finalization is coming. There is a fascinating similarity in the starting positions of each system, all exposed at the same time to global challenge as each one pretended to be the heir of England's world leadership.

They pursued divergent, national customization of the industrialization policy. They all produced impressive results – partially. But each one overplayed its strengths and initial successes. The analysis of how each tackled the conceptual question of social economy, as a deliberate economic policy, is a useful lesson. Some elements among the three role models are complementary. A few key features define the common trend:

- The prevalence of the business enterprise as the defining, socially productive cell;
- The redefining of capitalism as an accounting system; non-ideologic, class neutral;
- The socialization of ownership through capitalist instruments and the political, electoral decision-making process;
- The emergence of a new class: the worker-capitalist, or the entrepreneur;
- The change in business philosophy from adversarial competition to cooperative partnership: management/labor, government/private sector, national/transnational.

We call this new set of business rules the *social market*.

In the pages that follow this book aims to prove, through theoretical analysis as well as by comparative analysis of several national economies, the emerging trend toward a social market economy. Coming out of the (cold) war economies, both Russia and the United States are faced with the task of redefining their business rules. In the words of Arnold Toynbee, the 'times of troubles' in global balance of power politics are becoming the 'times of reinventing.'

While the Soviet Union's internal dismemberment was only the first phase of the implementation of the 'new world order,' its internal *economic* reform is the long-term challenge. Dismantling the war machine and replacing it with economic mechanisms demand imagination and foresight of historic proportions. Among the numerous competing models, social market capitalism is the most likely to impose itself.

In this view, and from a comparative analysis with the United States and German experience on the matter, we approach the subject of social market as a middle-of-the-road economic system that combines the best of government's vast resources and management power with the innovative and dynamic nature of free enterprise. The spectacle of a computer-driven Russian/American economic reinvention in accordance with some long overdue proposition for renewal is a most paradoxical possibility with unforeseen consequences for the twenty-first century.

Chapter II

The Historical Context

THE INTERNATIONAL POWER MARKET

At the turn of this century three nations were knocking at the door of the industrial club: Russia, Germany, and the United States. Totally different nations, they were confronted with similar acute internal strains, though derived from different blends of concerns. The alternatives for each one were to stick to a relatively regressive passivism, or to engage in active industrialization. The option of industrialization would achieve a two-tier set of goals: (1) fending off their internal social pressures; and (2) controlling the external challenges of other nations. For all practical purposes, the three countries were all junior partners, jockeying for a top position vis-a-vis the world's outstanding industrial metropolis, England.

Russia leaped ahead most dramatically. Following the 1917 Bolshevik Revolution and World War II's gun diplomacy, the entire area from Berlin to Vladivostok proclaimed itself a monolithic Communist bloc, a bureaucratic, centrally administered society. It encompassed a 270 million multinational population stretched across some 8,649,490 square miles. The Eastern European countries comprised another 110 million people inhabiting 450,043 square miles. In all, 380 million people living on one-fifth of the earth's land were enrolled in one unprecedented act of expansionism. They failed.

All three nations failed and rose again in one way or another.

The German Way

At the turn of the twentieth century, Germany was a most typical European countr y. Pushed into difficulties by its population expanding within a tightly circumscribed geographical territory, Germany was determined to channel its resources into creating a competitive industrial sector. Germany's answer, therefore, was to promote an open policy of war industrialization, a policy of 'blood and iron.' What England had achieved centuries earlier through its world-wide colonial conquest, German leaders aimed to accomplish in a shorter time span against England itself. This would bring about a dual outcome. Internally, it would mobilize the German population to achieve national objectives, and externally it would conquer Germany's competitors and enemies. As it happened, this grand policy, promulgated through two wars in one century, proved to be a resounding and a tragic failure.

The American Way

An opposite reality prevailed in the United States. While commanding a borderless stretch of land, underpopulated and remote from any source of employable manpower, the young rural nation, not yet homogenized, economically backward, with no capital or rec-ognized trademark and just recently emerged from a civil war, had to face the same needed industrialization. For that purpose, she traded the only trump card she had: her own shortages. If Germany invoked *violence*, the United States relied on her *charming attraction*.

Her enticements were many and free for all takers: land in the underpopulated West, a seat within the ranks of the economic establishment, civil rights. In the United States, the English *liberal individualism* enjoyed a hegemony so total that it was no longer a theory but close to becoming a fact of life. Immigration, free enter-prise, incoming foreign investment capital, unconstrained social mobility – it added up to a revolution every day, in the lives of new arrivals and the next generations of the newly arrived ready-made Americans.

Next comes Russia.

The Russian Way

By all standards, Russia was ailing at the turn of the century – but only relative to its competitors. It increased output by a considerable rate (during the 1890s, its industrial growth averaged 8 percent per year).[1] And, while Germany had reached the limit of its extensive agricultural growth, Russia was still colonizing new land. Large areas of unused land remained available to be inhabited and exploited by the increasing population. Driven by its own internal dynamics, the Russian economy was not utilizing most of its expanding labor force for industrial development. The inexorable change in the world's economic dynamics, the arrival of the industrial age, was understood only by its intellectual elite.

As is well known, the fate of Russia in those last years of the 1800s sparked a passionate national debate. The famous confrontation within the ranks of the Left, between Plekhanov and Lenin, is only one example. Counter to the Plekhanovist-objectivist approach, Lenin essentially argued that Russia, occupying a backward position in Europe, with a still feudal agricultural base, could not be left to develop at its own pace. Whether or not the people shared historical-materialist convictions, Lenin thundered, the intellectual elite first and foremost was responsible to its nation. The other alternative, the development of market driven capitalism, laissez-faire Russian-style, meant only a passive Oblomovist acceptance of defeat.

There were few real options in the climate of social crisis in Russia. To list the social movements briefly, there were (1) the *Narodniks'* anxiety to not lose sight of 'the people', which was taken with derision as so much Manilovist syrup; (2) the *anarchist* wing that proposed an economic solution that was unusable precisely because of its anarchic nature; and (3) the social-democratic *mensheviks* who were preoccupied with the redistribution of land and with humanitarian principles but very little involved with the nuts and bolts of industrialization. On the right side of the spectrum, there were no Western-type leading forces at work in behalf of capitalist interests. More than a few of the existing Russian entre- preneurs were in fact leftist sympathizers. The railroad tycoon Morozov and the financial magnate Mamontov, who personally financed the Bolshevik party out of conviction of the justness of its cause as well as out of a populist sentiment of guilt toward the *exploited masses*, are two examples.

In those circumstances, only one consistent and pragmatic program addressed the immense task of working out the Russian question. That was the Leninist revolutionary program. Essentially, it meant the forced dislocation of millions of people, forced redefining of social structures, forced reallocation of the nation's resources, and rethinking its values and purposes; in other words, an administrative, centralized, bureaucratic, and coercive if necessary, rationalization of the nation's entire economic blueprint.

Charismatic revolutionary movements, in the past and in modern times alike, tend to present their aims from a populist standpoint. Ostensibly, they set up against an unjust system, against the corrupted reigning elites, for the benefit of many. 'The proletariat in alliance with the peasants,' 'the workers' state,' 'people's democracy,' these were the catchphrases in the newly formed industrial Soviet Russia.

As is usual in a developing country, the composition of the Russian revolutionary elite also was made up of young anti-establishment intellectual men and women educated in the spirit of the best Western ideas and values, at the best Western institutions. "While only a very small fraction of the total population of undeveloped countries has received a higher education, has lived and traveled extensively abroad, or has served in a modern institution or profession, all or virtually all of the top revolutionary leaders in such countries have done one or more of those things."[2]

There is every reason to concede that the difficulties a nation confronts are understood and dealt with best by its most active elements, by its educated, intelligent, and patriotic young elite. "Sensitive to the discrepancies between distant ideals and contemporary realities,"[3] most often they are the sons and the daughters of the ruling class itself, as were the *decembrists* in Russia, or the sons and daughters of the old establishment in a broader sense: the large class of gentry, merchants, officials, and academics. They represent that faction of society most likely to come in contact with external influences through travel, higher education, or through cosmopolitan contacts. They were, in Russia as anywhere else, the source, the leadership, and the driving force of the 1917 revolution.

Bearing in mind these general observations, and the specific facts about Russia's troubles and their outcome, one can see the Russian revolution as a transliteration of Turgenev's novel *Fathers and Sons*, written some 45 years before the revolution. An unintended blueprint of events to come, it explains real history rather than offering a simple-minded ideological exercise in class struggle. Like the sloughing of a snake, the revolution is to be understood as a sacred social renewal rite committed by the 'sons' against the 'fathers" old-fashioned order.

In this sense, *perestroika* also grew out of a generational change. Former sons, now the entrenched old guard, were defending their own status quo. Sons against their fathers is a constant occurrence in Russia's long history.

THE INTERCONNECTED WORLD SYSTEM

The interconnected world system, from ancient times, continuing through the Western European gestation and the late expansion in parts of Asia, Africa, and the New World, appears to the historian as if "at different times different parts of the system have forged ahead of other parts".[5] Various centers of economic effervescence compete or precede one another, obscuring for the most part that single invisible hand behind it that Hegel called the Spirit of History. Yet some historians, after Marx, were trained to seek the engine of such leaps ahead in that unique dynamo called the *forces of production*.

The forces of production are us, the humans, and our means of production – our knowledge and skills along with our tools, machines and factories. Our work relations, i.e., the division of labor among individuals, make up the social *relations of production*. Changes in the characteristics and the performance of a productive tool have inevitable consequences and implications on the nature of work functions, responsibilities, and the roles of the participating individuals. Hence the inherent conflict between the need to develop the forces of production (in the interests of their future beneficiaries) and the tendency to preserve the social status quo (on the part of the existing privileged beneficiaries.) In Marx's still- Hegelian animist conceptualization, this is the contradiction between the 'forces of production' and the 'relations of production.'

In reality, it is the conflict between individual human beings over social roles and positions, when faced with the prospect of socially inequitable advances in productive capabilities. Our social attitudes, whether revolutionary or conservative, are built on the social nature of the division of labor, which engender a tension that is not necessarily related to specific class divisions.

Unfortunately, however, from such a primary and crude observation, more radical believers came to view the historical times of 'developmental crisis' as full-fledged episodes of social crisis. They sought to find all sorts of definitive solutions for human ills and miseries in social activism. Such was the basis of typical Leninist calls for social revolution.

Russians debated at the time the validity of such a rash course. For some, the question was: how many successful revolutions were rolled back by their inability to bring a lasting solution to the social class structure? None of the world's revolutionaries was remembered as having solved the problems of social inequality, poverty, and class exploitation. Was the ferment for revolution a cure – or a symptom – of a virulent social disease?

Marx's own revolutionary scope was more modest, yet still questionable. His assertion was that as production was undergoing a revolution of its own, this inevitably would be followed by a reordering of the social roles and functions among people. New forces of production called for new relations of production. While Marx focused on predicting change, Lenin went further. Accepting Marx's premises, he reasoned, why not reverse the order of events and speed up the process – set up new relations of production in order to unleash new forces of production now!

The trouble with this approach was that it assumed that the art of managing nature according to human objectives (in a teleological sense) could be mastered. Furthermore, it relied on being able to override the nature of things with seductive logical rationalizations. That turned out to be a bit optimistic. The development of electrical power, or the railroad or the telegraph, all were impressive technological achievements that certainly had an impact on the old social order. They created new professions, new skills, new functions, new organizations, and new social arrangements among the working teams, owners, producers and consumers. Yet simple ideological prescriptions could never provide for the ongoing genesis of unforeseen types of productive individuals, whether locomotive engineers, conductors, or switchmen, and their relations of production.

The Mediterranean Ecosystem

In ancient times the riparian agriculture of the Nile valley, spread over about 34,815 square km., supported a population of about 50,000 by the year 5000 B.C. (density: 1.4), some 6,000,000 by the year 2000 B.C. (density: 172), and 26,000,000 in 1961 A.D. (density: 750).[6] Obviously, while the growth of human population was technically unlimited, the arability and fertility of the land were defined by the sophistication of farm technology.

And so Egyptian society, the history of its human condition, its class division, and the degree of political participation modulated from peaks to valleys. The Pharaohs, the Christians, the Muslims, the socialists, the capitalists – all ruled in their own day. They brought new social relations and radical experiments in social engineering: from top-down command structures to the egalitarianism of the faithful, then feudalism, and up to the modern ideas of social justice and free enterprise. Yet they all faced the same critical challenge: how to cope with the ever-growing population on the limited economic base of the fading giant that was Egypt.

Meanwhile, a different turn of events took hold upon the surrounding world. Due to one technological invention or another – the iron plow, terracing – or rather their combined effect, the world moved away from the crisis of late Middle East antiquity into the open and endless land mass of 'dry arable lands.' Dry-land agriculture spread throughout the Mediterranean space, much as a fungus attacks a piece of cheese, up the waterways and then deep into the forests of the barbarian communities, until it eventually covered the entire slice, i.e., the Mediterranean ecosystem, through extensive/intensive economic exploitation.

In its heyday, the Mediterranean basin offered a unique combination of geographical circumstances, which was its peculiar interconnection of arable land and water communications. It was said that it was cheaper to bring grain by sail to Rome from anywhere on the Mediterranean coast than to have it hauled by cart from the port of Ostia.[7] Across the most diverse political forms of government and social relations, the development of the forces of production, based on dry-land agriculture and water transportation, took on a new life. Thus evolved the Greco-Roman civilization, until it gradually depleted its own ecological support system.

The simple demographic arithmetic of those years can tell a whole story by itself. The Greek *polis* was a limited, independent, self-governing community. Its emergence and character were a result of the geography of Greece which, like the whole region, was a mountainous coastal land studded with relatively small plains (only about one-fifth of it could be cultivated), separated by natural barriers whether impassable mountains or stretches of sea. Local trade facilitated by the water and the open plains helped to form natural political units, yet only very small: "few would have numbered their people in five figures."[8] Around the main center – often fortified (*acro-polis*) – farms and hamlets stretched as far as the mountains. In such a unique natural environment most of the communities, Athens even more so, were compelled, especially from the seventh century B.C. onward, to import the greater part of their food supply as well as all the timber and metals.[9] Ceramics, coinage, jewelry and metal working in silver and lead, manufactured textiles, wine and olive oil were shipped to districts as far apart as Italy, Thrace, Syria, Crimea, and southern Russia in exchange for corn, honey, and timber. This economic 'foreign policy' drove Greece toward a policy of 'naval imperialism,' in order to secure its supply routes. The time from the seventh to fifth centuries B.C. was certainly a period of economic expansion made possible by growing exports, an affluence that brought democratic stability, and unprecedented demographic growth. That was made possible by the regulating effect of outward colonization, the collection of imperial tribute and, no less, by the exceptional windfall of the newly discovered silver deposits of Laurian. (Those mines broughttogether the largest concentration of organized labor at the time, some twenty thousand slaves, all in support of and also supported by the large Athenian commercial and military fleet.)

As early as the beginning of the fourth century B.C., the tide in both economic and political spheres turned unfavorable, and a slow regression began. For reasons not completely agreed upon among historians, "there was a widespread and serious poverty among the mass of people, at the same time as the few were perhaps growing richer." Whether due to a contraction of the foreign market for Greek exports, as local production began to grow at the periphery of the Greek trading area,[10] or due to chronic crop failures which often happened in connection with increasing soil deficiency and over-exploitation, the end result was a growing social polarization between mass impoverishment and oligarchic concentration of wealth.

This desperate economic and social tension gave way in the end to a new approach to economic pursuit that succeeded beyond any previous experience. It was based on the 'international' alliance of the oligarchic elites in a merciless, intensive exploitation of the ancient outer world. "In the long run there could be only one satisfactory solution, from the point of view of the propertied classes in general: the acceptance of a powerful overlord who could quell by force any further attempts to change the existing scheme of things. . . which – it was thought – might provide land and a new hope for those who could no longer make a living at home."[11] This solution was ultimately adopted when Philip II of Macedon gained support from the oligarchic classes of the formerly independent *poleis*, virtually his 'fifth columns,' as de Ste. Croix points out, in building a regime of hierarchical and authoritarian alliance among the international elites.

His son Alexander brought this policy to military and political success. Then the Romans took over the methodical, skillfully administered task of total resource exploitation through the conquest and enslavement of larger and larger stretches of the neighboring populations and their accumulated wealth. This merciless looting lasted a few hundred glorious years. In its best days, the Roman Empire controlled a vast network of roads and protected harbors furnishing tin brought from Britain and even Norway, silver from Spain, copper from Cypress, iron from the Black Sea coasts, corn from Egypt, North Africa and Crimea, olive oil from Athens, dried fruits from Palestine, dried fish from Byzantium, linen, granite, and papyrus from Egypt, woolen goods from Asia Minor, timber from Macedon, Asia Minor, and Lebanon, marble from Paros and Athens, pepper and spices, pearls, and silk clothing from the Orient, ivory from Africa, and amber from Germany. Costs were paid, at the beginning, with the spoils from conquered treasuries, until quite soon chronic deficits began accumulating, combined with an exhaustion of new lands to plunder. "According to statements made by Pliny the Elder in two different passages, the trade in luxuries created an annual drain in cash of HS 50 million to India and as much again to China and Arabia combined."[12] In 374, a constitution was already issued that virtually forbade payments to barbarians in gold, particularly for slaves.

By that time, the Western Roman civilization had reached its limits of growth. At first, its unparalleled organization of systematic and large-scale exploitation of human labor was an enormous success. The otiose and apollonian pastoral inhabitants of the Mediterranean ranges, going deep into the hinterland west, north, east, and south, were now densely packed into labor concentration camps. The enslavement of readily available adult male laborers, at the cost of "not much more than what an artisan would earn in a year,"[13] on a massive scale (about half a million were enslaved in the conquest of Gaul alone by Caesar in about 50 B.C.) in addition to the plunder of those wretched people's treasuries (the treasure looted from Dacia in 106 was worth about half a million pounds of gold),[14] provided vast riches at a nominal cost, over a long period of time. Yet from the beginning of the Augustan epoch, the number of slaves that were appropriated or purchased cheaply from outside the Greco-Roman economy began to decline. That new phenomenon in conjunction with the great expenses of empire building (an army of 300,000 men was permanently deployed in the early days of the Augustan Empire) and with the gradual shift toward a domestic slave market signaled the inevitable beginning of the decline. The Romans had to face the unsavory reality that breeding slaves inside the economy, instead of bringing them in from the outside (either cheaply or virtually gratis), necessarily imposed a greater burden on the economy as a whole.[15] With a low average life expectancy (about 27) and a high infant and maternal death-rate, the overall rate of exploitation of the slave population must have diminished. The reaction of the propertied class, trying to preserve its standard of living, was likely to be a drive to increase the rate of exploitation of the still predominantly free population within the Empire. The nefarious effect was utter social disintegration and, ultimately, the institutional breakdown of the Roman Empire itself.

It was obvious by the third century that no innovative populist reforms could expand the social pie, already in slivers since the time of the Gracchus brothers. Only in the Eastern region "during the next three centuries, the financial, economic and military strength of the Byzantine state rested on the small holdings of the peasants and on the soldiers' holdings."[16] The demographically more stable Byzantium avoided the false economic dynamism and its ultimate resource-exhausting effects. Here, the ratio of cultivated land-to-settled population remained relatively constant for another thousand years. The Mediterranean and Balkan lands did not succeed in doubling their population in the next ten centuries and by 1450 had lapsed to only a little above their levels in 1000. The same appears to be true of the eastern lands of Russia, Poland, and central Europe. Yet in the West, France, England, Germany, and Scandinavia continued to expand their population. They trebled once before 1300 and despite bad temporary setbacks in the next hundred years still doubled again their populations, which had already been larger in the year 1000.[17]

The dynamics between these basic factors – natural resources and the human capacity to exploit them – was controlled always by the third element, which is the interaction with demographic growth. As it happens, our tendency to outstrip the relatively slow growth of available resources through exhaustive exploitation makes a good case for the perennial tension over the distribution of the *relative* scarce dividend. More so, when demographic pressure is compounded by recurrent natural disasters such as prolonged droughts, soil depletion, irreversible erosion and climatic changes, exacerbated social polarization and hence disharmony between social groups becomes a cause for further increase in social tension and division. The ensuing social strife becomes a barrier to the group effort needed to come up with a productive solution to the puzzle.

At this stage men's focus on the social question, i.e., group polarization, had only further obscured the real issues of their collective alienation by drawing their energies into political, ideological, even philosophical internecine fights over rights and distribution privileges instead of into a business-like assessment of the bottom line and a search for engineering solutions to the diminishing per capita output.

European Inland Farming

As it happened, the unexpected salvation of Mediterranean civilization came from precarious improvements in dry-land agriculture in the surrounding regions. This was truly a blessing for the troubled Europeans as no political power could have had the prescience to lead to such remarkable inventions. Their troubled economy was never far from the brink of collapse, still in spite of slow progress, the appallingly inefficient medieval agriculture was coming along. Farmers learned how to use more of the land – and managed to exhaust it at the same time so that less land was left to go around. As family holdings became smaller, most European households probably farmed less than eight acres by 1330. Above all, agriculture was vulnerable to weather; just two successive bad harvests in the early fourteenth century reduced the population of Ypres by a tenth.[18]

At this juncture the Western farmer made several discoveries of importance for his very existence. From the tenth century onward, such innovations as the observance of regular fallows and croppings, the enrichment of soil through the cultivation of beans and peas, and the introduction of the wheeple-tree and the shoulder collar for the traction horse kept accumulating and eventually had the double effect of increasing the food supply and of creating the embryos of a manufacturing sector serving farmers' increasing demands for better implements. Ultimately, this paved the way for the *industrial revolution*.

In the end, it was the history of food production that brought about the birth of modern technology. The cultivation of dry-lands in Europe demanded increased supplies of iron tools and implements: iron plows, iron scythes, iron components for carts and carriages, iron wheels for barrows and wagons, iron nails and hammers to build the needed warehouses and storehouses. It created a market for the first metallurgical establishments. By the fourteenth century the Rhinelanders learned to make cast iron; by 1600, the gradual spread of blast furnaces had begun to lower its cost. Finally, by the eighteenth century coal replaced wood as furnace fuel. Cheap iron was possible where ore and coal were plentiful.

By royal decrees, the first metallurgical establishments were founded across the beltway that runs from the Urals through Silesia, the Ruhr and Lorraine, up to the north of England and Wales. In the early eighteenth century, Russia's Ural foundries were leading the world in iron production. Eventually, international competition among metallurgical enterprises was the catalyst for a series of innovations. It was England who next took the lead by its invention and use of a new source of energy, the steam engine.

At the same time, European agronomy continued to make great leaps ahead. First, the turnip was found to help fix nitrogen in the soil, then the high energy potato was introduced, then corn, the three-field system and later on, industrial agriculture, each one in its time fabulously increasing output. This enlarged the viable living space and brought to the fore the industrial age and *industrial "overpopulation."* In this sense, technological progress was always multidimensional and on an eternal spiral, constantly providing, yet simultaneously causing an ever-increasing demand for, the basics of human life, i.e. of *social subsistence*.

Truly, the industrial revolution was first an *agricultural revolution*. In fact, the much overlooked turnaround of agriculture – from a struggling, existential toil into a food processing service – occurred on a grand scale that decisively transformed the basic condition of human life and its very purpose. Gradual improvements in land cultivation, undertaken from the Middle Ages to the beginning of the eighteenth century, made it possible to obtain about two and a half times the previous normal yield on seed cultivation. Yet this was only the beginning.

"From about 1800, it has been calculated, Europe's agricultural productivity grew at a rate of about one per cent a year, dwarfing all previous improvement."[19] The highest hour of triumph was reached on the American farm in the late twentieth century. Fully mechanized, it depended on petroleum as a source of fertilizer and also as a source of motor energy to such an extent that by the end of the century, the equivalent of about 140 gallons of oil were used for every acre of corn. "Modern agriculture was using land to convert petroleum into food."[20]

Once a convergence center of life and work, farms became more and more just the subservient provider of groceries in the

---

Table 2.1
Cereal Yields in Europe (1200-1820)[21]

A. Before 1200-49   *Yield of 3 to 3.7 from 1 seed*

1. England 1200-49	3.7
2. France before 1200	3.0

B. 1250-1820   *Yield of 4.1 to 4.7 from 1 seed*

1. England 1250-1499	4.7
2. Franee 1300-1499	4.3
3. Germany, Scandinavian countries 1500-1699	4.2
2. Eastern Europe 1550-1820	4.1

C. 1500-1820   *Yield of 6.3 to 7 from 1 seed*

1. England, Netherlands 1500-1700	7.0
2. France, Spain, Italy 1500-1820	6.3
3. Germany, Scandinavian countries 1700-1820	6.4

D. 1750-1820   *Yield above 10*

1. England, Ireland, Netherlands 1750-1820	10.6

service of a higher quest for industrial technology, the arts, military weaponry, and politics. Still, before any one country was to achieve supremacy in the world through its industry and trade, it had to win its prize at the country fairs.

By 1750,English agriculture was the best in the world. The most advanced farming techniques were integrated into a highly developed commercial market economy, in which land itself turned into a commodity. For the next century or so, European farmers went to England to learn new methods, buy livestock and machinery, and seek advice. Draining and hedging progressed replacing narrow individual peasants' strips with enclosed fields made up of a huge patchwork of different cultures operated in rotation. Field machinery could be seen by 1750 also, but only after 1800 were steam engines driving field threshers.

The results were remarkable, dismissing the peasant from the English social ranks and making possible the proclamation of the age of industrialization. "The transition from 3.1 to 4.0 [yield from one seed] represented a decisive step, the establishment (roughly speaking) of the first towns in Europe, or the revival of those that had not gone under during the high middle ages. For towns were obviously dependent on a surplus of cereal production."[22]

The changes, slowly and unequally, spread to continental Europe in the next hundred years. But the movement of modernization, throughout the continent, went in reverse order. The French formally abolished serfdom in 1789, the Germans a quarter century later, and finally the Russians by 1860. The Continentals started first with the revolutionary change of the social framework of what Marx called the relations of production. They changed the social order and the configuration of the rural village, but little was changed in the village's forces of production.

The rewriting of the social contract from the Urals to the Pennines meant an end to a social system that was passed from antiquity to Western christendom in the era of the barbarian invasions.[23] Yet the celebration over such a rapid social revolutionary success proved premature, for the most part, since it was not sustained by a similarly rapid economic revolution. What followed was a politically driven focus on industrialization at any cost despite the lack of a home-grown, internal, economic, grass-roots demand and source for it.

Especially in England, progress in agriculture made possible the expansion of social life (England's population increased from

Malthus' time of about 8 million to 22 million by the mid-nineteenth century alone). The population explosion meant a net multiplication in the manpower to be administered. A by-product of the English agricultural revolution's success in coping with this virulent explosion, the industrial revolution became an even more spectacular event that turned the peasant worker into a machinist, the farmer into a technician. The unrestrained pressure for more food led to developments in agricultural technology and induced the emergence of the industrial society. Iron foundries, nail factories, and textile enterprises multiplied. So did the needs of growing cities, for rapid transportation connections, sewage and water systems, for more and more energy, housing, health care in the crowded urbs, entertainment for the leisurely hours, politics, and mass management.

Ironically, the industrialization of agriculture ultimately meant the end of the primacy of agriculture as such and an end to the individual challenge to feed oneself and his close family as the primordial goal in life. Social life itself lost its existential condition and elevated its own pursuit to romantic and idealistic motivations. That created the romantic age in arts and philosophy and the modern intellectual wrestlings for life's higher meanings.

The Affluent Farming Societies

During all this time, as the relations of production, i.e., the social relations, were redefined with every new productive process, a state of permanent social revolution took hold upon Western societies. The age of entrepreneurial competition became possible as it proved to be beneficial for both the society as a whole and for the individual. At the beginning it was the class of landowners alone, in power for so long, that reaped the benefits. They were soon challenged by the next level of beneficiaries, the rich merchants and manufacturers. The big corn traders and textile manufacturers then came under pressure from the emerging professional class of lawyers, doctors, academics and technocrats. The working middle class had a strong voice, which it was eager to test on the streets of Europe's capitals. The petty bourgeoisie, the class of shopkeepers, mid-level traders, and smallholders were a force of their own, as they proved all too well through the strength of their rightwing politics. But for the disappearing group of peasants, the class character of the fight for a larger piece of the social pie was alive and well.

Yet in the long run there was little noticeable movement toward one predominant form of political government, or form of social relations, either toward an enlargement of democratic participation or toward a deepening of the stratification along rigid hierarchical social lines. In short, there is no proven historical correlation between the development of the forces of production and the associated social relations of production.

It was the rare commentator whose view was broad enough to be able to suggest that the whole world might be moving in any given direction. To the French intellectual of the eighteenth and nineteenth centuries, the world outside his castle window seemed to be marching inexorably to the tune of the masses empowered by their participation in the social enterprise. For the Russian literati, the iron law of capitalist exploitation ruled the world of the rich and the growing masses of the disenfranchised. The respectable small-town German professor timidly dwelled on questions of how freedom and liberty should be defined, uncertain over the direction of his destiny. For the American self-assured frontier patriot of the mid-eighteenth and nineteenth centuries, there were no limits to the individual freedom to pursue one's own economic prosperity.

The steam engine made the English establishment powerful enough to aspire to imperial world domination; it made the Russian landed aristocracy a foreign class within its own nation; it made the German burgher dream of the perfect social machine; it made the French into tempestuous revolutionaries and addicted them to social science fiction; it made the American farmer think of the dream-machine, the Holy Grail in profit making. The steam engine reinforced and strengthened aristocratic feudalism in England, empowered the urban middle class in Germany, brought political decadence and paralysis to the absolutist rulers of Russia, created the urban proletariat in France, and energized American entrepreneurs into assembling a giant industrial park.

In other words, the development of the forces of production was unrelated to the corresponding forms of social relations; and the forms of government that presided over various nations and their social composition were unrelated to the character of the productive forces.

Instead of bringing on the much-heralded proletarian/Communist revolution to end all revolutions, the inner dynamics of the industrial societies legitimized the existing social structures and amplified their national characteristics and their specific historical composition. Instead of leveling classes and national characters, nineteenth-century industrialization rather consolidated a more distinct national identity and differentiation among large national markets. Regions and populations that had only minor dissimilarities in the Middle Ages, under the common obligation to toil the land, now discovered, each in its own way, the creative opportunity of industrial entrepreneurship.

There was the automobile's manufacturing innovator, the airplane's flying hero, the fashion industry's connoisseur, the chemical composites' technician, the electrical machine's tinker, the steam train's engineer, the printing press's artisan – they all were ingenious first movers and the founders of national industries as much as of national social ideologies. Germany became famous as the source of state-of-the-art luxury cars, of chemical synthetics and of social democracy. France was known for its tasteful fashion, fast trains, and for its agitators for socialism. England remained the conservative center of trade and finance that gave the world its zealous belief in social liberalism. Russia made its name from its dedication to gigantic construction projects and immense white elephants,[24] one of which was the Communist system itself. The United States invented mass production and the assembly line as it sold around the globe the concept of individualism and of free enterprise.

There is another way to look at the social relations that a given country embraced and that is by taking a historical perspective. One expects to find a correlation between a nation's economic development and its social and/or political organization. Yet there is, again, little evidence to that effect in country after country. England preserved its constitutional monarchy from the Middle Ages to the modern information age with little change in the fundamental social definition of class structure, despite all the rhetoric and the turbulence of its early industrial years. France went a step further by replacing its landed aristocracy with a citizens' republic in 1789. Yet for the next 200 years it remained an essentially unaltered system as it centered on one strong president or another and one nominal party or another. Germany went from virtual feudalism through every other form of political government – monarchy, dictatorship, democratic pluralism, and socialism, to the current republican parliamentarism. Still, this does not confirm its political development since, among other things, major military defeats altered any sense of internal continuity and direction. Russia was believed to be the case study of political evolution, but with the hindsight of the post-Communist experience it no longer appears so. Its evolution from feudalism to absolute monarchism, War Communism and market socialism all preserved the same fundamental top-down command feature. Finally, the United States is the one nation with no political evolution at all for its 200 years of unparalleled economic growth tendered by its robber-baron free enterprise system.

Furthermore, even taking a historical view of a nation's social relations, one is surprised only by the extent of the elasticity of any one economic system. In Russia alone, in the years of landed aristocracy from the eleventh through the nineteenth centuries, under the same agrarian technological level of development, the relation of lord vis-a-vis peasant went from free-market farmsteads to master-slave, to landlord-tenant, to employer-salaried worker, to free enterprise, to employee-shareholders enterprise, in no consistent direction. In the sixteenth and seventeenth centuries, while over half of the landed farmers were state subjects – for all practical purposes, free small businesses – the other half shared in the most varied sort of relations of production from indentured servitude and the obligation of *corvées* (*barshchina*) to sharecropping serfdom, to head tax-based serfdom, a condition that could change radically from one individual to another or from year to year.[25]

Finally, there is one more paradox in the nature of the two extreme forms of industrialization of Russia and the United States. The fearful totalitarianism of the Soviet state dissolved itself, within a generation, into the economically inefficient but egalitarian, classless and unmanageable employees' democracy. The fiercely independent, self-made American farmer-entrepreneur evolved into a corporate employee enslaved under an unrestrained form of mandarin management.

The Emergence of Military-Industrial Corporations

As a consequence of technological changes, the framework of the social order developed in the twentieth century along two lines of social conflict: (1) internationally, nations entered into unprecedented economic competition; (2) nationally, internal competition among organizations fueled an ongoing corporate revolution.

Internationally, nation-state corporations disputed the international balance of power among themselves. One day England was the world's superpower, then France had her hour of glory. Russia was feared as Europe's gendarme following the defeat of France, then Germany controlled the continent as the United States made its own successful bid for world leadership, later to be challenged by the USSR and even Japan. The global scale of this process was made possible only by the development of the forces of production.

Nationally, the domestic corporate oligarchies challenged each other's reach. One day it was the cotton growers who set the rules, then it was the railroad tycoons, then the steel makers. For decades the oil industry magnates had the upper hand world-wide, while the telephone monopolies dictated pitilessly to peoples and to governments alike, as later did the deep-pocketed international financiers who kept the world economy running. From individual industries to whole sectors, the trend continued. The telecommunication lobby, the military-industrial establishment, the computer and information processing industry, and the exotic space technology all had their turns. The age-old cycle of monopoly-oligarchy-free-enterprise was played over and over again in each nation by the new protagonists, the corporate raiders. Small or large, the corporate organization came to act in the same manner as the earlier warlords of Medieval Europe. Whether the vintage East India Company or Hudson Bay Company, Standard Oil Co., I.G Farben, IBM, or SDPR (the Social-Democrat party of Russia), they all were the equivalent of minority privy clans, focused on plunder and social domination, to control and exploit the majority. The *corporate entity* itself became the outer extension and the organizational tool of its top self-serving individuals.

Strictly hierarchical and autocratic, secretive, exclusive, militaristic, aggressive, unaccountable, fraternal, uncompromising, unforgiving, the corporation – whether financial, political, commercial, manufacturing, or religious – was now the building block of the national body. The romantic concept of civic society as the place for urbane socialization was only an illusion in the world of competing special interest groups. The predatory spirit was now guest of honor in the salons of the boards of directors.

* * *

What makes matters more complicated throughout the last two centuries is the confusion over the coded political terminology in use. It was said that the forces of liberty were set against the forces of oppression, the liberals set against the conservatives, capitalism against feudalism. On a different level, however, it was England's private corporate imperialism versus the continental states' defense, the island-nation versus the multinational and divided Europe.

First, British industrialists undermined France, as their liberal envoys came upon the continental European stage disguised as progressive antimonarchists, the Voltaires, the Montesquieus, the Rousseaus, plus all the latter-day troublemakers-cum-dissidents. The immediate heirs of the progressives were the politically effective French revolutionaries, members of the infamous Jacobin club, widely believed to have been the conspiracy at the heart of the French 'revolutionary' suicide, the end of their 'empire of lights.' A comment by history professor Newt Gingrich sums up the role of British money and its superior economic machine: "I think equally useful is to look at the role of Pitt the Younger in the 1780s and 1790s, because Pitt the Younger, surrounded by the disciples of Smith, rationalizes British tax policy to create the commercial environment in which so much wealth is made that people are able to fight the Napoleonic Wars and Britain is able to carry virtually the entire financial weight of the Alliance against Napoleon in a way that would have been literally impossible without Adam Smith's intellectual ideas being transmitted into the tax policies of Pitt the Younger."[26] In fact, it was the British Royal Navy and its protection of good bases and maritime communications that created the wealth on which British financiers drew to eliminate their most immediate competitor, France. In 1815, the protected bases of Malta, St. Lucia, the Ionian islands, the Cape of Good Hope, Mauritius, and Trincomalee, were all key stones in the implementation of the tax policy that empowered imperial expansionism.

The second act in the spread of liberal ideas further inland was then perpetuated by the first European civil war that ended with the Vienna settlement of 1825. Once territorial questions were settled, in a sense that no continental European state was to be strong enough to mount a challenge to the unscathed new Rome-on-Thames, the seeds for the next move were laid down. As the continental ruling elites and their institutions were swept away, they were replaced by two new configurations of political guerrilla warfare: class war and national war. These were to have a long history that ultimately forced the large continent into submission.

Yet, with characteristic modesty and unparalleled self-restraint, the English still recall this period of glory over a tranquilized Europe as the happy years of the 'Concert of Europe'. The concept was to use the shabby Austrian house as the main force in central Europe, backed up from afar by the Russians. The Vienna system worked well for the next forty years, given the fact that France was still unable to recover – especially after the last drop of poison, which was the imposition of the Jacobin Louis Philippe of Orlans on her throne.

Not until 1848 did Europe show any sign of reemergence. And then the *Grand Nation* of France once again took the lead. Hers was intended to be the revolution of the newly formed middle class. As it happened, the subsequent civil and nationalist movements swept over all Europe's capitals with the notable exceptions of London and St. Petersburg. The Germans followed the French, then the Italians, the Hungarians, the Czechs, the Poles, the Romanians, and so on. Although they were all justified by different slogans and given different popular objectives, when Vienna fell, last, the cumulative effect of the revolution meant the complete dislocation of western, central, and eastern Europe. As always when widespread conspiracies are at work, things got complicated. Class and nationalist agendas interplayed. The net result, however, was a further breakdown of central and eastern European political structures , which were replaced with political weakness and economic market liberalism.

From this point on, for a long stretch of modern history, liberalism and nationalism were thought to be inseparable. Representative government, popular sovereignty, freedom of the individual and the press were considered basic national aspirations. Yet the outcome meant smaller and smaller political units of bickering communities, less centralized power, unprotected and smaller national markets, and, ultimately, weaker international economic competition.

Indefensible, continental Europe (less Belgium, already a British subsidiary) fell under the spell of high-class agents of destruction such as liberalism-*cum*-socialism and political emancipation as nationalism. The aura of respectability and prophesy of a French count, Claude Saint-Simon, and then the soothsaying virtuosity of a professional intellectual of the German-Jewish school, Karl Marx, sowed the seeds of rebellion and upheld the legitimacy of antigovernment activities throughout the continent. The subversive books of Marx and the nationalist romanticism of Mazzini were two masterful lines of mass propaganda. (Incidentally, Marx received protection and, ultimately, an arrangement was found for a comfortable existence among the respectable British middle class; his seditious ideas disturbed no one there. And while Mazzini seemed to embody the epidemic of nationalist frenzy, he lived an insipid life in London cool to the "Irish volcano of nationalism.")

European history in the second half of the nineteenth century was filled with intrigue, power jockeying, weakening of the stronger elements and a gradual advancement of English merchants' bridgeheads around continental seaports from the Baltics to Sevastopol. This was later on to be recalled, with unassuming irony, as the glorious years of *balance of power* politics. It simply continued a tradition of British foreign policy. "Under that old system, which Britain had followed since 1500, Britain should support the second strongest power on the Continent against the strongest power, to prevent the latter from obtaining supremacy on the Continent."[27] England and Austria-France defeated Russia at Sevastopol, 1856, England and France-Sardinia defeated Austria, 1859, England and the United States-Mexico defeated France, 1861, England and Prussia defeated Austria, 1866, England and Prussia defeated France, 1871.

And then there was Russia. The Russian question required a longer and more sustained effort. (It still does.) By now England itself has had to undergo an identity transformation. The British Empire had to yield its leadership to its bigger alter ego, the emerging second insular power, the English of the United States of America.

And so the Anglo-Americans and France defeated Prussia, Russia, and Austria in 1918, and the Anglo-Americans and the USSR defeated Germany in 1945. Thus, for the time being, was Europe defeated.

The Anglo-Saxons and the Slavs

Although the two wars that devastated most of Europe in the twentieth century involved a complicated web of alliances and participants, the real bone of contention was the control of Western Europe as a whole. The bidding for Europe involved two only marginally European protagonists that had outgrown their earlier inferiority complexes.

From a population of less than 500 in the British colony of 1610 to 250,888 (224,010 whites) in 1700, to 3,929,625 (3,169,890) in 1790,[28] the year of the first official census, the new nation of the United States was not even in the game. The 36 million-strong Russia, herself only remotely European, underwent her own successful power struggle across the vast Eurasian continent during her relatively isolated history from the eleventh century on.

At the time of the War of Independence and of the promulgation of their Constitution, the thirteen United States' population and economic power were somewhat similar to those of their spiritual forefathers, the Aegean Greeks. Almost a direct continuation of the same wave of migration initiated by the Helas, the modern colonies at the far western rim of the Atlantic reproduced a page from the earlier books of the legendary Aeneas. They themselves felt an unmistakable kinship with the old men in their pioneering settlement. City-states spread over the coast line, their communities resembled the 150 Hellenic polis and their inhabitants, citizens and slaves, ranging from about 20,000 to 300,000 souls at most. One finds a striking similarity with the history of the Peloponnesian League in the American union, two thousand years later, under the name of the Confederation of the United States.

In fact, the principal difference was based primarily if not exclusively in the reversal of that one special relationship between population growth and the elasticity of living space. For, while the Greek world had to confront a negative elasticity, the United States had the unique privilege of a favorable, positive elasticity. In other words, the population overgrowth that eventually brought ruin to the Mediterranean ecosystem and so to the Hellenic civilization, became the fuel for unlimited growth in the United States; the plenitude of land and a population explosion were the two fundamental coordinates of the American miracle for the next 200 years.

In this sense, the United States functioned as an absorption pump, drawing off the overflowing, ingenious juices of knowledge and visionary contradictions of Europe, fermenting creativity, people, technology, capital, and markets. The United States exercised its charm to attract and to employ the human capital bubbling up in the European biological soup. Richly endowed with natural resources – food in abundance, fuel, minerals, oil and gold, lumber, fish, cotton and furs, coal and iron ore, living space and open frontiers – the United States offered these in exchange for labor.

Acting as a counterweight to the Old World, the United States relieved Europe's extreme overcrowding and its depleted resources and became an eager supplier of needed manufacturing inputs from cereals to cotton[29] and steel. From the early 1800s, for the next two centuries, a peculiar sort of symbiosis evolved; an unprecedented cooperation between two worlds for the benefit of both. Piggy-backing on the European march toward industrialization, the United States had one hundred years to make up for its historical gap with Europe before it reached its own critical mass of forces of development.

Although the United States reached a population of 24 million by 1850, it jumped to almost double that, 40 million, by 1870. Still heavily dependent on European markets for its great agricultural expansion – which made North America virtually the granary of Europe and which brought back so much needed capital. By 1870 the United States was a decidedly agricultural economy with less than two million of her work force employed in manufacturing. One can point at this moment to her relative parity with imperial Russia – except that Russia was following a different trajectory.

* * *

Russia surged spectacularly from the early eighteenth century up to 1870, but not so much in terms of economic reinvention as in empire-building. For, economic theories notwithstanding, it was military superiority that ultimately set the social framework of economic comparative advantage in Europe.

All the modern contenders for world economic leadership, Great Britain, Germany, the United States, Russia, Japan, and China, were nations through violence, through an act of armed emancipation. Their founders set up what is called the national character – made up of the ruling class and its complex set of collectively defining rules, traditions, institutions, and language, governing an assimilated mass of followers.

It is from this nuclear founding ancestry that a nation derives its own self-identity, and it is the success of this elite group that is critical for the viability of the entire social entity. In other words, a state entity, a national being, an ethnic group, is defined and is upheld by its leading elite's conscience and skills. In Great Britain, William the Conqueror made the constitutional history of England since 1066 the story of his Crown. France since the tenth century

followed the success of the house of Capetians. The history of
Germany is a newer one that starts with the Prussian electors of
Hohenzollern in about 1415. Russia's founder is Alexander Nevsky,
who carved his principality out of the peoples of Eurasia in the
early 1200s. George Washington and his fellow independents
induced the birth of a new Anglo-Saxon nation in 1776.

The founding of a nation was as violent an enterprise as it was
a coercive operation to make it stand and grow. In all its
orientation, means, purpose, character, and discipline, the story of
a nation is most of all the epic of its leaders. Whether in ground
battles, in diplomatic maneuvers, in trade policies, in economic
wars, in ideological confrontations, or in industrial competition, the
under-lying quest was for victory over the other national elites.

There are two observations to be made here. (1) The first is
that an insurrectionist overthrow is always a clear harbinger of the
inevitable subsequent decline in that nation's international
immunity. (2) The second is that, notwithstanding 200 years of
sermons on class-struggle ideologies, the real social antagonism is
international as it cuts across the leading elites. The key to understanding the secret history is to see not national elites in a class
struggle with the national underclasses, but to see the *international
marketplace of elite power politics*. In this sense, seemingly
internal affairs such as civil strife, revolutions, and ideological
crusades are only reflections of the international balance of power,
of foreign manipulation of the internal social heterogeneity, the
international elites acting against the local, national elites.

Examples abound throughout modern history. France was a
case study. All of a sudden, in the late eighteenth century, word
went out throughout France that there was a long forgotten social
contract that for obscure reasons should be honored by the royal
court vis-a-vis its lower classes. (Rousseau was an instrumental
proseletyzer.) What was actually happening at the time was that
the superpower rivalry between France and England was taking a
new course (which, ultimately, brought France to ruin). The internal
civil war that took on more and more acute forms was rather an
extension of the external war carried on within one's enemy's borders. From an international perspective, a revolution may be
considered a successful infiltration of the external enemy in order
to tear it apart. It is the Trojan horse approach.

France was the greatest European power at the time of Louis
XIV, who saw no reason to hide his view that France's greatness

was the outcome of his great leadership, hence "*L'état c'est moi..*"
Under the *grand monarque*, politics were competently reduced to
administration, the royal councils together with the royal agents in
the provinces. The *intendants* and military commanders made up
the actual working government. The reign of Louis XIV, which "was
the triumph of hierarchical, corporate, theocratic society" and gave
France world renown, glory, and recognition as the model for
enlightened monarchy, brought an end to hardship for her people,
and set herself in the spotlight as the epitome of superior culture,
refined taste, creative arts, and philosophy.

Between 1715 and 1740 there were no important international
tensions capable of producing internal changes in states, nor were
there great ideological divisions, and everything seemed to be
settled in favor of the French notion of the European *belle époque*.
Yet, at that very high hour her fate was already sealed. The invisible army of liberals, Freemasons and intellectuals, the ambitious,
the dissidents, and the troublemakers were doing their best to
undermine the enlightened empire. Their celebrated success was
the modest publication of a short essay on the imaginary origins of
the primordial Edenic social contract, autographed by the
Genevan   J. J. Rousseau. In fact, as Ferdinand Lundberg notes,
"the idea of democracy, seemingly dead beyond recall, surfaced
again in revolutionary 17th century Britain, a time of civil war and
tremendous political turmoil." It was then, a hundred years before
Rousseau lived, that "just about every conceivable political idea
received some sort of written sponsorship in a great variety of
journals and pamphlets, among them a vastly romanticized version
of long-dead Athenian democracy." Indeed, it was in England that
the "concept of popular sovereignty exploded into modern view."
And only later on, it resurfaced in France and in the new-born
United States.[30] It was an other-worldly ideological platform and
the only corrupting alternative to the real prestige of the French
monarchy.

Life was beneficent and well administrated under the French
house of luminaries, yet, "although humanitarian, of course, the
policies of the 'enlightened despots' were not necessary politically
liberal [?]," according to the conventional English historiography.
Although modern and undermining traditional social and religious
authority, they "often cut across accepted [?] notions of social
hierarchy or legal rights [?], they tended to concentrate lawmaking
power in the state and assert its unchallenged authority over its
subjects who were treated increasingly as an aggregate [?] of
individuals rather than as members of a hierarchy of corporation

[?]." In other words, it was a "fascist," that is to say, nonliberal brand of government.[31]

Sound familiar? For the British propaganda machine it was a *politically incorrect* system, which is to say dangerously competitive, given its unmistakable success.

In a clever reversal of strategy, the British followed the dictum that defines diplomacy as a continuation of war by other means. That is to say that from their awkward insular location, which inherently narrowed the effectiveness of continued direct engagement on the battlefields of continental Europe, the British had to invent a subtler brand of international engagement. The centuries-old Franco-British rivalry and armed conflagrations had ended for a long time with the conclusion of the Aix-la-Chappelle peace in 1763. Yet, following the inconclusive Seven Years' War and the subsequent loss of India and Canada to the British, as well as the subsequent minor but costly success in the American Revolution, France's troubles were clearly in the making. And the internal virus worked out the rest.

International debt was at first a minor affliction coming from abroad, limiting France's independence in foreign affairs and establishing the increasingly unequal distribution of fiscal pressures on its classes.

Then there was demographic pressure. Since the second quarter of the century, France's population growth outstripped the growth of food production while underperforming the rate of fiscal demands and the insidious inflationary spiral.

Yet, in all its social frictions, France was no different than the average European country of the time. What made the difference was the symbolic agitation around such passionate yet impractical and imprecise ideas as reason against superstition, freedom against slavery, et cetera. Furthermore, at the beginning, "what did not exist was a party of revolution clearly confronting a party of reaction." The idea itself of social revolution was not home-grown, as the only two modern overthrows of a sovereign class in the Western world, Cromwell's in 1642–49 and the American revolution of 1776, were undertaken in the lands of Albion.

The shocking experience of the Revolution of 1642 was more than a metaphysical revelation for the British, especially since it was followed by the bitter sequel inflicted by their beloved American colony. Both those events clearly demonstrated the precariousness of the established social order when attacked and undermined from within. The rock-solid state power was demystified and the spirit of righteous revolution from below took hold in the consciousness of the British state chancellery. Once this spirit got out of the bottle, the modern strategy of making revolutions on order was devised, and it did its dirty work in faraway lands.

For the next 200 years, making a *social revolution* in another's political courtyard proved to be as valuable a British foreign political strategem as was the other English invention – the *industrial revolution*. The rule that assigns a net advantage to the *first movers* once more prevailed in preventing any second challenger from overcoming his laggardness in the field of intrigue as well as in the later domain of corporate competition – unless the challenger emerges from within one's own ranks. In this sense, the United States was to be the stepchild of the Anglo-Saxon school of international thought and to inhabit an island of strategic superiority to both the British Isles and the rest of the world.

Once the technique was mastered, first by the British political elites, then by the newer Anglo-American political class, this simple device of artful support from afar for divisiveness within a target society worked miracles on demand. It required only the willing broker's services, which was not a matter of insurmountable difficulty. In the multiethnic, multireligious European amalgam of old and new political tribal unions, one particular nation stood out as the most likely candidate for the new conspiratorial agency. The international character of Israel made it a God-given blessing to this enterprise, answering the requisites of an available and educated internationalist ally. The two together expected to be unrivaled. And they were.

Perhaps coincidentally, by 1720 the first English lodge of the international brotherhood of freemasons was introduced in continental Europe and "within a half-century it spread widely; there may have been more than a quarter-million masons by 1789."[32] Their main predilection for "discussions of new ideas, of circulating concepts and diffusing the written word through print and private gatherings" was of no little significance, if little publicized, for the history of modern Europe.

* * *

More revolutionary yet, in the long run, was the British approach to empire building through *targeted control of the elite*. The British influence was not exercised by acting directly on the masses of foreign nationals (or domestic for that matter) as one collective group. Instead, it shaped events by targeting "the opinions of the small group of 'important' people who could influence wider and wider circles of persons." The greater part of such influence would not come from its mass-appeal or mass-subjection but from a system of concerted action by several branches, seemingly autonomous, of a single group. "The unanimity of the various branches was believed by the outside world to be the result of the influence of a single Truth, while really it was the result of the existence of a single group."[33]

How would that work? Here is a rare documentation of such interactive opinion management from more recent times when the British establishment was acting through the agency of the Rhodes/Milner Group at the turn of the twentieth century:

> Thus, a statesman (a member of the group) announces a policy. About the same time, the Royal Institute of Foreign Affairs publishes a study on the subject, and an Oxford don, a Fellow of All Souls (and a member of the Group) also publishes a volume on the subject (probably through a publishing house, like G. Bell and Sons or Faber and Faber, allied to the group). The statesman policy is subjected to critical analysis and final approval in a 'leader' in *The Times*, while the two books are reviewed (in a single review) in *The Times Literary Supplement*. Both the 'leader' and the review are anonymous but are written by members of the Group. And finally, at about the same time, an anonymous article in *The Round Table* strongly advocates the same policy. The cumulative effect of such tactics as this, even if each tactical move influences only a small number of important people, is bound to be great.[34]

There were indeed no limits to the scale and the manipulative character of such concerted opinion storming, on local, national, and international centers.

> If necessary, the strategy can be carried further, by arranging for the secretary for the Rhodes Trustees to go to America for a series of 'informal discussions' with former Rhodes Scholars, while a prominent retired statesman (possible a former Viceroy of India) is persuaded to say a few words at the unveiling of a plaque in All Souls or New College in honor of some deceased Warden. By a curious coincidence, both the 'informal discussions' in America and the unveiling speech at Oxford touch on the same topical subject.[35]

A condition *sine qua non* of the success of such *soft pedaled imperialism* is the appearance of scientific objectivity and of rational and intellectual persuasion. Outright falsification and concealment of evidence was to be avoided. It rather foisted its self-serving agenda and interests by "interpretation and selection of evidence." It could easily topple a nationalist government with the help of just a few dozen well placed converted loyalists and avoid costly military engagement and bloodletting.

Yet, one such large-scale history-making disinformation exercise brought about the worsening of Anglo-German relations that eventually started World War I. By playing up all anti-English actions and statements and playing down all that was pro-English, by quoting obscure and locally discredited papers, by promoting anti-German incidents, and by encouraging the escalation of minor confrontations, *The Times*-guided propaganda orchestration "misled the British people and abandon[-ed] the good Germans to a hopeless minority position, where to be progressive, peaceful, or Anglophile was to be a traitor to Germany itself."[36]

The Battle over Europe

Brutal conquests, from the siege of Troy to the pursuit of modern war among fellow nations – from time immemorial, the history of the European race is that of total warfare. It bred and elevated arms professionials into the establishment class and identified its economic, social, and political functions with the morality derived from superiority in brute force. This concept came to be represented by the feudal lord, who was at once the private owner of the accumulated public wealth and the public leader of the people's community.

This long tradition of marriage of sovereign private interests to public affairs led to an understanding of community as something legitimized exclusively through the actions of its strong leader. In other words, the community becomes the manifestation, the outward extension, the arms and the organs of the individualized supreme leader.

Britain, however, was well secured from the threat of recipro-cated aggression and, given its insular existence, was able to preserve and develop that unique code of the Habeas Corpus Act that limited the power of the central authority, to the advantage of an oligarchic class.

By the same token, the notion of the separation between community as state and community as collective individuals found full support in the new 800,000-strong nation of the United States. Eminently secure, remote from European conflicts and surrounded by the breath-taking serenity of endless frontiers, the United States allowed for the elevation of an element of civility and a sense of primeval, community-based values into its social philosophy. The republican form of government that was chosen by the newly independent American elites was meant to ensure the spirit of private individuals sharing in the decision-making process that affected the community at large and that was to be the repository of the central authority. This unique set of circumstances set the United States apart from the rest of Western civilization from day one, and later on was to play a special role in the dynamics of the global community of the dis-united nations.

* * *

In a letter written to one of his friends toward the end of his life, Karl Marx admitted that for almost 25 years, his entire energy and effort were devoted to uncovering the high level of interventionist hypocrisy and brutality that czarist Russia had forced upon Western bourgeois democracies. Confident in the industrialized West's continued process of socialization, Marx had trouble finding any grounds for optimism connected to that Empire of Darkness. Yet, ironically enough, it was a Russian revolutionary adventurer that questioned Marx's own revolutionary credentials, challenging his very leadership of the Socialist International – and that was Mikhail Bakunin. His anarchic-aristocratic craze, in Marx's view, was just another diversion from the rigors of the proletarian organization. And he also, supposedly, lacked Western intellectual sophistication.

It was another Russian aristocrat-intellectual who really changed all the coordinates on Marx's revolutionary-theoretical guide map. Gheorghi Plekhanov lived in London, almost next door to Marx (who, nevertheless, never heard of him). Plekhanov, at the time, was following in the footsteps of the other London-based revolutionary educator – first among the future Russian dissidents – Alexander Herzen. By 1883, Plekhanov had already translated *Das*

Capital into Russian and set the first framework of the party 's conspiratorial work in Russia from which, ultimately, Lenin would emerge.

Plekhanov and Lenin, while they were united on their revolutionary zeal, differed on some details. Plekhanov sought to subordinate Russia's evolution to the Western European lead, while Lenin focused on revolutionary means rather than ends and skillfully pointed to the soft spots in Russia's czarist political armor. Whether to slowly undermine Russia's ruling class through the guerrilla force of radicalized lower masses, or to dynamite the entire state edifice by a concentrated and professional assault on its supporting institutions, that was the revolutionaries' dilemma.

Working at the grass-roots level with oversized zeal and commitment, they were the minuscule grain of sand caught between the empires' millstones. Their trivial travails were significant only in the context of the big powers' mortal struggle. England, foremost, looked to Russia with all the sympathy of a saboteur, helping Russia dampen any ambitions to extend her continental power and letting her knot herself in administrative impotence. The prospect of having their enemies slinging mud at each other in the pit of their own destruction must have pleased any privileged spectator positioned in the balcony of the murderous European theater.

* * *

At the turn of the twentieth century, England was under the threat of a critically mounting tide of industrialization from the two emerging continental nations, the Germans and the Russians. Russia was still backward but it was surging ahead at a rate of 8 percent a year. By 1910, it reached the level of about one-third of the pig iron produced by England and one-quarter of the steel produced in Germany. Reforms implemented under Stolypin helped Russian agriculture turn the corner and made her capable of producing a grain harvest that would grow faster than the population. By removing the last restraints on individualism imposed by the terms of the abolition of serfdom, a successful effort was made to provide Russia with a class of prosperous, independent farmers whose self-interest was linked to raising productivity.[37]

Russia's natural resources, her steadfast political structure, her large and expanding consumer market, the education and culture of the ruling class, her awakening middle class dynamo made up of managerial, entrepreneurial, and technical professionals along with the world-renowned intelligentsia, her low-wage labor pool, and her impenetrable geographic expanse, all were signs of ominous times ahead for England. True, the Germans were an immediate threat to be dealt with in the old-fashioned way, but the truly indigestible piece of competitive economics was amassing potence in the empire of the Romanoffs. It would require bold thinking, a radical political approach, exceptional orchestration and focus, and extreme fire power. To put all these ingredients together at the right hour with the right men in place would require genius and uncommon luck. It all came together as events unfolded under the catalytic conditions of the Great War. But by then the British power itself had vanished from pre-eminence as a result of a series of cataclysmic circumstances. She herself, then, suddenly found to be the smaller fish, would be swallowed by the United States.

* * *

As early as 1900, it was more than clear to the British business class that Germany was a major rival. There were plenty of signs that in technology and method German industry was greatly superior. And then there was the United States, an industrial machine of immense scale that by 1914 was producing twice more pig iron and steel than Great Britain and Germany together and coal equal to both of them.[38] Within this unhappy international context, the idea of a United States of Europe had a sinister ring to the ears of the newer nationalist interests.

The causes of the European civil wars of the twentieth century, from the First World War to the end of the Second World War, could be viewed as the result of diplomatic impasse, colonial ambitions, market share appropriation, overheated nationalist passions, an oligarchic conspiracy against a revolutionary threat, disagreement over the Ottoman possessions in the Balkans, boredom and fin-de-siècle malaise, and so on. Yet, given that all these elements had been present for forty years, the decision to gamble stability, status quo, and national existence itself, involved obvious risks. The decision to pursue the political equivalent of a gentlemen's duel could have come only as a consequence of a vital impasse. The Europeans were facing the same dilemma that the United States had experienced in the mid-nineteenth century – a domestic dispute over sovereignty in the house of the United States of Europe. There was a growing consensus among the leadership of Great Britain, Germany, and Russia that their own survival as well as the survival of the European entity itself, vis-a-vis the vast, expanding North America, depended on creating the equivalent of a unified and centralized European state.

The dispute was only over which leadership would take control and implement the founding of the new political entity. And, had it not been for the United States' outside interference – as it was she who stood to lose the most – there is little reason to doubt that the classical process of Hobbesian selection would have accomplished, out of the existing elite players, the crowning of the European sovereign.

The ultimate irony of the European tragedy in the twentieth century is that of continued continental weakness, once induced by England's balance of power games, now translated into a common misfortune as all of them faced America, untouchable in its remoteness. Tragically, their continuously unfulfilled moment of holy unity was to be further delayed as a curse of destiny. It was now the Anglo-American nation of the United States that presided over the troubled peoples living in the ravaged valley of Europe, the British included. The story was over. The Europeans were, for the first time in recent history, not in control of their own affairs. It would be up to the government in Washington to dictate the terms of the new European order, the same government that was "committed by the beliefs of its founders to the destruction of the whole pre-war European order."[39] From now on, events in the European nations were closely monitored, supervised and directed, through proxies and from afar, by that hybrid elite made up of the heirs of the Anglo-Saxons sanctimoniousness and predilection for rogue intelligence operations; projecting a mythology inspired by a Germanic spirit of assertiveness and scientific ingenuity; shielded behind a legalistic administrative apparatus; artists in show business – the nation of the Yankees.

The process of the unification of Europe practically spans the entire century. It was prolonged by the American effort to derail it in every possible way and by the indigenous mix of conflicting ideologies, social upheavals, superpower politics and nuclear threats, state and ethnic rivalries. A swirling collection of mad crowds brought together by the Darwinian play of forces guaranteed the collapse of all straightforward negotiations for the leadership that could generate a new European union. Yet the ultimate fate of integration could not be stopped. It continued, moving through back alleys and back doors, dealing in back rooms. The most uncommon marriages of interests were sufficiently confusing, throughout those years, to undermine the mental state of many simple-minded soldiers.

Blowing apart the Russian social order was blasphemous to the law abiding bourgeois but it made sense to believers in old-fashioned power politics, the British and the American masters, who saw it as the easy way to take out of the game the obtrusive threat of Russian domination of Europe. The idea of Britain, the United States and (Soviet) Russia encouraging Germany to take the initiative in two wars which it stood no chance of winning would find little credence in the eyes of newspaper-minded citizens. Yet the major diplomatic, economic, military and ideological struggle of the twentieth century was over the control of continental Europe, and it was waged primarily between Russian and American protagonists. The ultimate irony of ongoing historical clashes is to recognize them all as different scenarios of one and the same story.

In Russia's case, short-term discords, class divisions, ideological carnage, and party feuds notwithstanding, all positions on a long-term basis can be reconciled as variations of one and the same historical process. What seemed to be of enormous importance in 1917, the very survival and future destiny of the Russian nation, a merciless choice between capitalism and socialism – is proven to have been of absolutely no relevance a hundred years later. Either one would have led to the same destination, although by different means and through a different composition of cost distribution.

In hindsight, a few things seem to have been in the cards from the very beginning. For all her strengths and aggressive posturing, Germany had two main factors weighing against her bid for continental sovereignty – first, her underprivileged geopolitical location; second, her avowed state ideology of assertiveness and conquest. Positioned in central Europe in the open space between the sea power of Great Britain and the land power of Russia, relatively poor in natural resources, commanding a medium-size population ethnically unrelated to the rest of the continent, Germany's call for mobilization could only antagonize and coalesce against her the rest of the nations.

Great Britain was inherently limited to her seapower, which handicapped her direct involvement in the administration of Europe.

Russia, although looked down upon, was the European power that had, potentially at least, the greatest weight of all.

Between the bad and the worst – a German Europe, a British Europe, a Russian Europe, or a collapsed Europe – a keen American leadership sought to help bring about a Russian Europe. Reading again the events of the Great War, it appears that the United States, in order to undermine Russia, supported the Bolshevik takeover. Yet, at the same time, in order to wipe out the pretense of the Central Powers, it mobilized its influential and subversive call to revolutionary-nationalist upheavals that immediately after the war brought to their knees both the house of Austria and, of course, that of Germany. To limit the ambitions of Great Britain, it sowed the seeds of the Second World War at Versailles and then brought Britain to virtual bankruptcy.

What followed signaled the definitive write-off of Western Europe as a serious contender for world leadership. Europe's rich cultural legacy, its technological superiority now stood less threateningly between the remaining adversaries in the recurring battle of the West against the East.

Futhermore, the defeat of Germany as a European power also meant the defeat of a German ethnic ascendancy (a relative majority of 25 percent of the population) over the English-heritage minority (12 percent) in the United States. Anti-Germany war *agitprop* offered an excuse for an anti-German-American domestic crusade.

* * *

The outbreak of the Russian Revolution in St. Petersburg, on February 8, 1917, was indirectly supported by the United States through the commencement of hostilities against Germany on April 6, 1917. The future members of the first Soviet Communist Central Committee, Trotsky among them, found their way from the Lower East Side of Manhattan to St. Petersburg in time to apply the final blow to the imperial house of Russia, and had the second detachment of national-revolutionaries carry out the liquidation of Austro-Hungary and Germany herself a year later.

But the power struggle was not yet over.

It happened that, overcoming the initial debacle, Russia set out to pursue her own brand of development. Germany followed suit.

In 1921, Russian pig iron production was about one-fifth of its 1913 level, that of coal a tiny 3 percent or so, and manufacturing output only 20 percent, while the railways had in service less than half as many locomotives as at the start of the war. Livestock had declined by over a quarter and cereal deliveries were less than two-fifths of those of 1916. Exacerbating this impoverished economy was a drought that occurred in 1921 in southern Russia that left more than two million dead in the subsequent famine. Even cannibalism was reported.[40] Yet by 1927, both industrial and agricultural production were back to prewar levels. Two Five-Year Plans carried out an industrialization program that made it possible, by 1937, for 80 percent of Russian industrial output to come from plants built since 1928. By then, Russia was again a great power.

Thus something new had come to populate the landscape of the international big league. Essentially, a non-Western nation, brandishing non-Western communist economic institutions, unencumbered by indebtedness to the Western economic world or military structures, a militant and a full-fledged world unto itself, the Soviet Union turned the tables. This novel threat, the unresolved status of Great Britain and Germany (still revanchist after the 1918 defeat), and the potential revival of the rest of Western Europe itself, determined the ambivalent position of the United States in its design of the League of Nations and in its ultimate endorsement of a second Great War which was meant to be the last blow to the final vestiges of the European empires, with them doing the dirty work of mutual destruction.

Despite the enormous disruptions caused by the war itself as much as by the redesign of the economic map of Europe – new borders separating former trading partners, Russia, Germany, Middle Europe, the Danube valley and the Balkans – in the years after the First World War, from 1925 to 1929, a gradual recovery brought back to Europe the prospects of the prewar years. In 1925, the production of food and raw materials passed the 1913 figure for the first time, and a recovery of manufacturing was also underway. Currencies emerged from enduring inflation and reinstated their gold-standard rates. International trade reached a level in 1929 not to be touched again until 1954.

Nevertheless, though this was scarcely notice at the time, the source of this sudden bloom was not domestic. Huge investments from the United States, and the availability of American loans meant that the European economic recovery was artificially accelerated by an unsustainable reliance on foreign money. Its insecure foundations were dependent on the supply of American capital without simultaneous access to American markets. Those were the premises on which the origins of the next war were set. For it was the American-led economic down-turn of 1929 that dried up the flow of capital, closed up the limited overseas markets, even raised the demand to call in previously generous loans. The world plunged into the most ravaging depression on record. To help avoid such a development in Germany, given her long tradition of intellectual social-democracy, grassroots trade unionism, and corporate welfare-state socialism, a second internal front was also supported from afar under the vigilant eye of the Kremlin *apparatchiks*. In their view, a war with Germany would only help consolidate their own revolution. On orders from Moscow, enthusiastic Stalinists of the time (Clara Zetkin among them) unleashed an uncompromising opposition to the forces of bourgeois democracy and in "bitter political speeches in the 1920's and '30s helped divide the country and bring down the Weimar Republic, thus paving the way for the rise of Hitler."[43]

Riding on the wave of popular discontent brought by the economic crisis, Hitler came to power and the American corporations resumed their peculiar interest in the newly assembling German war machine. "U.S. investment accelerated rapidly after Hitler came to power," Christopher Simpson points out in his study. It increased "by some 48.5% between 1929 and 1940, while declining sharply everywhere else in continental Europe" and barely holding steady in Britain.[41] Even as late as 1937, the State Department saw Germany's rearming as the natural reaction of "the rich and middle classes, in self-defense" before the "dissatisfied masses, with the example of Russian revolution before them, [could] swing to the Left," so that it "must succeed or the masses, this time reinforced by the disillusioned middle classes, will again turn to the left."[42]

Of course, old Britain too had her own agenda. "By this date, certain members of the Milner group and of the British Conservative government had reached the fantastic idea that they could kill two birds with one stone by setting Germany and Russia against one another in Eastern Europe."[44] This idea of bringing Germany into collision with Russia found support as much from the earlier "experts on the American delegation to the [Versailles] Peace Conference who were most closely associated with J.P. Morgan and Company," as from the members of the British conservative establishment, as well as from Russian Bolsheviks themselves. Each of the old and new power barons was jockeying for supreme mastery of the much prized post-war Europe.

Against this background European easily fell victim to the spiraling march toward the final cataclysm. The Second World War was now ready to unleash. "Many Europeans still found it hard to see this, though, and they continued to dream of the restoration of an age when that civilization enjoyed unquestioned supremacy. They forgot that its values had rested on a political and economic hegemony which, for a time, had worked but was already visibly in decay all around the world."[45] This self-delusion was prevalent first in the 1930s, then made a comeback in the 1990s.

There was so much irony in the Indian summer extravaganza of the 1930s upper-class European *Dolce Vita* that it was hard for any sober mind to see that they were already gripped in the claws of destruction. But it would require yet another cycle of sad self delusion at the turn of the tweny-first century before the making of another *new European order*.

The Balkanization of the World

Sudden changes, revisions, and the complete rewriting of treaties among former rivals and allies alike have been the norm in the Balkans' long political chronicle. Borders have been moved and at the stroke of a pen, whole groups of nations forced to change citizenship, allegiance, and the law of the land, often even without leaving their ancestral home.

In the history of the Balkans, events set in motion close to home or in far away chancelleries were equally influential. As the fortunes of diplomacy and war shifted, the sense of large-scale social engineering accompanied every new political order, as each new international scheme had to be accommodated. Again and again, the tectonics of the world's balance of power cut across the private gardens of those seasoned peasant nations.

To them, at the bottom of the social order, collective wisdom deconstructed the terms 'international security' and 'strategic balance of power' as euphemisms for the new kid with a big stick. To them, the real question always was, who was to be feared next?

Now, what is new in world affairs at the turn of the twentieth century is the Balkanization of all of Europe. So the question arises: by whom? Who is to have the big stick now on the streets of the new Europe?

* * *

In political science terminology, the new world order in the post-Communist era was to be structured around the institutional framework of the Atlantic Alliance, based on collective security guaranteed by the United States as the sole remaining superpower. And this might have been valid, were it not for the exigencies of the world of *realpolitik*.

In fact, the idea of a single-superpower world invokes not so much the comforting image of one nation hierarchically sovereign above every other nation, but rather the re-enactment of the structure of a new bi-polarity, in which *one nation* faces *all the other nations*.

There are two principles in classical Machiavellian imperial politics: (1) the old-fashioned *divide et impera* philosophy, and (2) the *power-sharing* philosophy. Applied to these principles, the idea that 'all politics are local' means that what is valid in local politics is also valid in world politics.

The first approach suggests an empire ever at war with itself. The second approach rests on the duality of good and evil. Both means of political management have special strengths and inherent limits.

(1) The politics of division aim to undermine potential challengers by systematically stimulating competition among them. It is based on the glorification of particular sets of interests at the cost of corrupting the collective social being. Easy to exercise when applied to heterogeneous populations of various ethnic and religious backgrounds, its devilish workings appeal to the immorality of self-promotion, appease the visceral emotions of minority groups and serve to raise the insecurity, the fear, and the aggressive insensitivity of all others. Yet, for all its power in leveling down potential adversaries, this policy is unsustainable in the long run. Ultimately, it undermines the foundation of the powerful.

(2) For better long term results, wise superpowers resort to managing agents or proxies. The real power belongs to the benevolent arbitrator and moderator; yet he is to be surrounded by evil courtesans and sycophants. He rules through them, whether as

brokers, administrators, courtiers, minorities, party functionaries, or *nomenklatura*. The duality in governing is thus not merely a partnership between the powerful and the junior, it is also a source of moral display. While the powerful stands for honesty, generosity, and justice, it also highlights the *other*, which is mean, vile, and onerous. Yet, together, good and evil work for the common good of the community. Universal harmony prevails through administrative order in the name of supreme liberty. It also allows, from time to time, for exceptional bursts of revolutionary energy against the corrupted executive power that leaves the sovereign above the fray.

In its enlightened and glorious heyday, the nominal legitimacy of the Holy Roman Empire emanated from the graceful power of the pope. His supreme will was exercised through the work of his stewards, who were his feudal administrators. The vassal system brought a simple solution to the complicated task of ruling over the large territory of Western Europe. It applied direct rule through a mastery of principles akin to those used in the artesian gardens of the time; the admististrtive system was in essence a political artesian architecture.

Its vascular system of hydraulic politics provided a viable alternative to the socially level world of premedieval city-states. The result was the basis of the emerging social emancipation stemming out of the roots of the subsistence economy. This European innovation in social organization allowed for a vertical and also complex and flexible integration long before the European Steel and Coal Association reared its head.

Unfortunately, the feudal principles of European vassalage were replaced in the early market-minded age by national-based economic entities. The factory system and mass production required a mass consumer, leading to the uniformity of the corporate state. The medieval political picture gave way to states seemingly inspired by the art of cubism, run by boards of directors or party politburos. They were corporate structures operated from bureaucratic headquarters over the rows of marching subalterns. A century of total corporate rule and monopolist control of the markets stood for the capitalist system, while administrative party centralism stood for the Communist system. One can say that the recent century-long process of European political soul-searching was nothing more than an effort to reconstruct the lost unity of the Holy Roman Empire.

Less dramatic, since their direction of growth was almost

linear, the United States expanded from the *City on the Hill*, where their constitutional outpost was built by the founding fathers, down to their truly continental *downtown*. Starting from a clean slate, they had the unique privilege to think globally, across the geographic and demographic space of their open frontiers, and to implement a project designed both politically and economically from an original blueprint. They had their design in place from day one and had only to revise the arithmetic of scale and scope. It went on multiplying from coast to coast, community by community, until they became as a whole the *Nation on the Hill*.

Now, on the basis of their respective regional integration, the Eurasian and American commonwealths were positioning for the next stage of global power-sharing. Their mutual interdependence, to which they were resigned after years of painful adjustment, overcame their seemingly systemic incompatibilities and made them look more and more alike. Capitalistic in their thorough application of accounting principles and at the same time socialistic in the scope and the scale of their social management, they faced the need to overcome ideological divisions. At the end of this new global drama the new villains were the Asians, who began to press their claim to membership in the same exclusive league.

In the age of technological politics, the administrative bureaucracy is replaced by political management, the use of information systems and statistical supervision. It ushers in the reign of *virtual politics* in contrast to the political virtuosity of the ancient regimes.

Chapter III

The Question of Economic Models

The first round of the industrial revolution occurred in the aristocratic England of the 1700s, parented in a sense by that peculiar social system known as the English constitutional monarchy, a top-down feudal organization practicing a unique juridical system, identified as the common law, within the context of upper-class liberalism. It successfully combined inconsistent demands for economic freedom and labor discipline, private trade and state might. Few other nations were able to integrate these elements into a competitive replica in the decades to follow, although no efforts were spared. This system eventually became widespread under the name of *capitalism*.

At the opposite end of the developmental spectrum, Russian *theocratic communism*, called upon to usher Russia into the industrial age, resembled, rather, the Catholic Church's institutional approach of applying visionary imagery to the management of historically backward nations. But even so, the command system was based on the rudiments of "capitalist" economic mechanisms. Its guidebook, Marxist political economy, was indeed a short and basic course in *capitalist* concepts.

THE INTERVENTIONIST PHILOSOPHY

Before pursuing the latter-day efforts to reform communism-cum-socialism, let us take a look at what Marx himself has laid down as the basic principles of a socialized economy.

The collective ownership of the principal means of production was the essential element of such an economic model. It resembled the structure of an army, founded upon pooled social resources, aiming at a common goal and voluntarily submitting its individual wills to a central authority. The model is an ancient one. An echo of its failure comes to us from Aristotle's laconic comments. "A society is not like a military alliance . . . ; but the elements out of which a [social] unity is to be formed differ in kind."[1]

Needless to say, Marx himself was uncomfortable with the phraseology of egalitarianism as a utopian program and all but relegated its wonders to the mythical "higher phase of communist society" when "the enslaving subordination of the individual to the division of labor, and therewith also the antithesis between mental and physical labor, has vanished." The only real-life basis for the examination of socialist workings was the existing commodity exchange economy. But therein lies an inherent conflict. If the value law regulates the capitalist exchange of commodities, it follows that the same economic law of exchanges should regulate the 'socialist' exchange. But how can one design an equal exchange of unequal values?

> What we have to deal here with, says Marx, is a communist society not as it has *developed* on its own foundations, but, on the contrary, just as it *emerges* from capitalist society; which is thus in every respect, economically, morally, and intellectually, still stamped with the birth marks of the old society from which it emerges. Accordingly, the individual producer receives back from society – after the deductions have been made – exactly what he gives to it. What he has given to it is his individual quantum of labor . . . He receives a certificate from society that he has furnished such and such an amount of labor, and with this certificate he draws from the social stock of means of consumption as much as costs the amount of labor. . . *Here, obviously, the same principle prevails as that which regulates the exchange of commodities, as far as this is exchange of equal values.*"[2]

Furthermore, it is worth unearthing the once celebrated "Critique of the Gotha Program," of 1875, if only to find in it the implicit reasoning behind the modern reassessment and subsequent demand for restraints on the practice of laissez-faire economics. It also points out the common root of the interventionist policies of the social market, Keynesianism and *perestroika* included.

Although ideally the concept of socialism "recognizes no class difference, because everyone is only a worker like everyone else" still it has to tacitly recognize "unequal individual endowment and thus productive capacity as natural privileges."[3] Hence, this is only another way of replacing the property- and capital-mediated spread of inequality with a more insidious and pervasive inequality derived from nature's work. It would actually sanction a return to the cruder and unmitigated form of predomesticated *social-Darwinism*. It would restore the curve of historical development to its beginning. It would legislate, in the words of E.K.Trinberger,[4] the higher status of the beautiful, intelligent, radical, and attractive individuals. In economic terms, it is described by Marx as follows:

> One man is superior to another physically or mentally and so supplies more labor in the same time, or can labor for a longer time; and labor, to serve as a measure, must be defined by its duration or intensity, otherwise it ceases to be a standard of measurement. It is, therefore, *a right of inequality, in its content, like every right*. Right by its very nature can consist only in the application of an equal standard; but unequal individuals (and they would not be different individuals if they were not unequal) are measurable only by an equal standard in so far as they are brought under an equal point of view. Further, one worker is married, another not; one has more children than another, and so on and so forth. Thus, with an equal performance of labor, and hence an equal share in the social consumption fund, one will in fact receive more than another, one will be richer than another, and so on. *To avoid all these defects, right instead of being equal would have to be unequal.*[5]

And this was exactly what the centrally planned economy did for the first seventy years of its history. It basically distorted the application of fundamental economic laws for the purpose of employing radical administrative correctives to steer the Russian economy to a new direction away from its natural one, in a very Leninist sense.

It differed from reformist Keynesian Western state

interventionism only in its all-encompassing nature, in the absolute magnitude of its reign. But then one has to account for the distortions deriving from the uncommon history of the two nations. If Russia were inhabited by Martians, it would still have to factor in for the individual Martians.

* * *

Since the beginning, Soviet leaders, whether reformers or conservatives, were faced with the supposedly irreconcilable dilemma of choosing either economic strategic planning at the expense of market principles or upholding socialist principles (such as full employment, egalitarian pay scale, subsidized prices for essential goods and services) at the risk of economic performance.

But the choice had been made already by the Communist revolution itself, through its action of sweeping away all of the old economic structures. It chose the capitalist tools of development. The revolution brought its special brand of capitalist zest to the country. It abolished old-style private property – a petty private house, an inefficient strip of land, a paltry private business or a street-corner grocery. It suppressed the traditionally closed, paternalistic, autarchic, ethnic communities. It enlarged the market from village-wide to nation-wide. It actually opened the Pandora's box of capitalist economics: (1) It freed people from age-old concepts and traditional bonds on an unimaginable scale while educating them in the concepts of modern growth-oriented economics; (2) it instilled in them consumer-type aspirations; (3) it created an open border market-commonwealth area; (4) it established common standards. But more important, (5) it introduced the capitalist form of private property on a large scale, and its tool, which is money.

A Communist economy that outlawed private property coexisted with the capitalist ownership of money, its accompanying financial mechanisms (banks, savings accounts, interest) and its purely capitalist form of profit-making. While prohibiting a shopkeeper from operating so much as a kiosk or a contractor from employing a single apprentice, it encouraged large-scale exploitation of the proletariat through state-guaranteed interest on bank investments. The banking system allowed one to accumulate his life's savings in state financial institutions that guaranteed a collectible dividend, creating new paradoxes. "Excepting automobiles, household appliances, furniture and hoards of consumer goods, all private wealth in the republics of the former U.S.S.R. takes the form of currency or bank deposits held by the citizens. . . While the government negotiates with the West over $10 billion or $20 billion of emergency credits, it has virtually. . . 600 billion rubles of private wealth accumulated over decades in which the purchasing power of the ruble was roughly equivalent to a dollar."[6]

In fact, one can summarize Eastern Europe's past experience with communism with a Marxist truism that equated it with the "inevitable historical process of primitive accumulation of capital," which is *primitive* only "because it forms the pre-historic stage of capital."[7]

The *physiocratic-Communist* approach aimed to provide economic growth through cumulative administrative expansion. "Priority was given to industrial development, and within that sector to industries producing investment goods, and particularly to machinery. The emphasis was on capital-intensive technology, using large-scale methods of production. The necessary high rate of investment was sustained by forced savings. Agriculture, housing, and consumer goods industries were treated as shock-absorbing sectors."[8] It proceeded through unit and scale augmentation: a new, bigger factory, new land being cleared for farming. It was urban industrialization at the expense of rural resources, and was therefore naturally restricted by the limits of growth of agricultural productivity. Its disregard for growing industrial productivity as the main tool of economic policy meant that speed of industrialization would be inverse to the available pool of agricultural resources. To double labor capitalization from 10 percent to 20 at the expense of farm labor was one thing. To continue doubling it by the same extensive approach from, say, 80 percent to 160 percent national employment in industry, was a mathematical impossibility. At 100 percent labor industrialization, the process of industrial development and subsequently of the country's modernization would cease to advance by this means.

Yet, this economic disposition was still prevalent in the Soviet Union's bureaucratic deployment of forces up to the 1980s despite all the Western countries' examples to the contrary. Instead of replicating their low-efficiency industries, advanced Western nations have long since focused their energies on increasing productivity as the goal of industrial policy. Russia's long delayed and much-needed rethinking of her own economic mechanisms required in the end a more brutal reexamination and overhaul of her economic philosophy.

THE TRADITIONAL CENTRALLY PLANNED MODEL

The original central planning model was conceived in the Soviet Union in the early 1930s as a state-led economy of immense scale and scope. This was a reflection of the United States' own budding structural adjustment, as observed already in 1932 by A.A. Berle and Gardiner Mead in *The Modern Corporation and Private Property*. The Soviet Union's goal was to achieve rapid industrialization and military power by mobilizing its considerable natural resources and its plentiful skilled and unskilled labor. Its spirit was that of Taylor's *scientific management*, only its scale and aims were amended to serve social objectives as well.

The key features of orthodox central planning were already well established: *(1)* All the principal means of production were nationalized. *(2)* In agriculture, collective ownership under state supervision wsa the dominant form of ownership. *(3)* The system of economic organization was determined by a top-down decision-making hierarchy, and vertical channels of inter-enterprise relationship. *(4)* Production and distribution were planned in detail and measured in physical units. *(5)* Control over allocation of raw materials, capital, labor, and other resources, was thoroughly centralized. *(6)* Prices were set by administrative means at a cost-plus value that excluded self-financing capitalization but preserved the principles of revenue/expense accountability. Prices reflected thus a political rationale rather than an economic one, hence the pervasive consumer shortages. *(7)* The functions of money were limited to accounting uses such as taxes and credits. *(8)* Labor was managed through Stakhanovist-Taylorist methods of increased work intensity; and *(9)* The role of foreign economic relations was diminished, and mediated on a small scale through bureaucratic, specially designated foreign trade units.

The centrally planned system therefore lacked significant foreign trade, direct contacts with foreign customers or suppliers, and foreign import-export interrelations. Ironically, of all its design features, this was the only one that had no internal origin. It was in fact a Western imposed penalty on the perceived Soviet threat, especially in the years following World War II, and covering the Soviets and their subjugated dominions in Eastern Europe. This feature alone proved in the end to be the most handicapping of all in facing the economic challenge from the West.

Starting in the early 1960s, a certain shift was more and more apparent in the relative weights of the *extensive* industrial build-up vis-a-vis the depleted agricultural sector. During the period of de-Stalinization, discussions of the need for reform and of specific reform proposals were underway simultaneously in several of the peoples' republics. The limiting character of the system became evident sooner and more sharply in the relatively developed countries, such as East Germany, Poland, Czechoslovakia, Hungary, and later and less acutely in the less advanced countries. In a broad sense, the situation called for an adjustment of the instruments of development, a shift from an *extensive* to an *intensive* approach,. This would replace the emphasis on rapid structural changes and capital widening with a reorientation toward capital deepening, and more efficient production through technology and innovation, rather than capital accumulation. However, the response to this line of thought was only human resistance from both management and labor.

Managers and workers alike were in favor of reform in principle, it was reform in its details on which no one could agree. According to party ideology reform was incompatible with the notion of collective ownership. To central planning agencies, it would have brought an unmanageable level of uncertainty that would have rendered any planning models captive to disorderly effects due to inflation, unequal and therefore socially disruptive income distribution, unrestrained vagrancy and unemployment. In addition to damaging everyone's personal security, reform came to be seen, for good reason, as a sure way to national disaster. For the ministerial and financial bureaucracy, it would imply a loss of authority, but far more important was the lack of a replacement institution. In the absence of a parallel system:(a functioning banking structure, credit organ-ization, stockholding interest groups), it was feared that the simple abolition of the huge administrative apparatus would spell economic collapse despite all the reformist rhetoric to the contrary. (Dramatic proof came to reformers and conservatives alike in the days of *perestroika*.) For managers, the sense of independence and freedom in decision making was a day dream followed by a nightmare. They were production engineers, not businessmen, and the task of competitive salesmanship was never in their job description. And, finally, there were the workers. Customers of the social product, their demand for reform was always strong when it came to employing market principles... for others.

The call for reform was a daily staple in the gridlocked cabinet meetings of the Soviet nations. And some attempts were constantly made at various levels in every country. Yugoslavian tinkering with workers' management, the Hungarian 'managerial market social-ism,' and the Czechoslovakian 'self-regulated enterprise' were tempting ideas, but not self-sustaining, practicable, competitive alternatives, the abundance of optimistic literature in their support notwithstanding.

TO REFORM OR NOT TO REFORM?

Having been brought later under the grip of autarchic central planning, Eastern European economies were first to see the beginning of a continuous deterioration in their overall economic performance. Partly, because their economies had been for the most part dependent on Western technology until they were cut off from sources of goods and replacement parts, partly also because of their limited room for further *extensive* development. Sooner or later, from the most advanced (Czechoslovakia, Hungary, and East

---

Table 3.1

GDP-indices for six OECD countries, 1900-87
1950 = 100.00

	Greece	Ireland	New Zealand	Portugal	Spain	Turkey
1900	-	-	17.3	42.4	49.5	n.a.
1913	59.6	80.7[a]	29.9	52.9	66.8	47.1[b]
1929	101.4	80.6	53.7	58.1	97.3	52.1
1938	130.4	88.3	70.8	74.2	n.a.	85.6
1950	100.0	100.0	100.0	100.0	100.0	100.0
1965	264.3	143.9	160.6	197.1	238.3	233.4
1973	468.5	208.9	207.4	342.8	392.1	389.8
1980	593.0	282.2	213.1	428.0	452.9	521.5
1987	638.9	326.7	248.8	490.3	528.5	765.6

a) 1911.
b) Per capita product assumed equal to that of 1929.

Source: Angus Madison, *The World Economy in the 20th century*, (Washington, DC.: Development Center of the Organization for Economic Cooperation and Development, OECD, 1989), p.126.

Germany) to the least (Romania, Bulgaria, and the USSR itself), it came to light that growth deficits were chronic and intractable.

OECD statistics (see **Table 3.1** and **3.2**) confirm the official data that appeared between 1950 and 1965, showing that in Czechoslovakia, Hungary, Poland, and East Germany the aggregate growth rates of GNP were below average, as compared to Romania, Bulgaria, and Yugoslavia. Hence the pressure for reform was strongest in the first group of countries, the more so as their net rate of industrial output actually declined in the same period.

Some of the explanations that were proposed focused on a decline in the rate of growth of inputs (labor especially), a decline in productivity, and an "increased difficulty in substituting one factor for another"[9] – whatever that means.

Internal Factors of Decline

Calculations made by Alan A. Brown and Paul Marer show that "the rate of growth of nonagricultural labor inputs declined steadily in Czechoslovakia, Hungary, and East Germany, while Romania, Bulgaria, and the Soviet Union were able to maintain relatively stable rates of growth of labor input over the entire period."[10] According to the same authors, although capital grew

Table 3.2

GDP-indices for Eastern Europe, 1913-87
1950 = 100.00

	Bulgaria	Czech.	E. Germany	Hungary	Poland	Romania	Yugoslavia
1913	45.6	64.0	78.2	n.a.	54[b]	-	-
1929	48.2	97.4	95.4	97.1	76.8	-	-
1938	72.0	95.8	105.1	111.6	86.6	-	-
1950	100.0	100.0	100.0	100.0	100.0	100.0	100.0
1965	272.5	180.8	219.8	190.5	196.1	236.4	231.5
1973	393.2	236.6	279.7	248.3	294.8	377.1	358.1
1980	459.9	280.3	341.4	287.6	338.6	505.3	544.4
1982	486.6	278.8	351.4	293.6	307.6	521.9	557.3
1987	503.9	301.9	393.5	300.1	338.6	611.3	604.2

a) 1937.
b) 1909-12.

Source: Angus Madison, *The World Economy in the 20th century*, (Washington, DC.: Development Center of the Organization for Economic Cooperation and Development, OECD, 1989), p.126.

from 1955 to 1965 in every country except the Soviet Union, the "fastest rate of growth of capital input occurred in the least developed countries."

In the same vein, productivity had a decidedly uneven growth rate among the centrally planned countries of Eastern Europe. Based on a set of official data analyzed by the above-mentioned authors, from 1955 to 1965 labor productivity declined in every country except Romania (which showed a slight decline only in the 1960s). Also, data confirm that the highest productivity gaps were in Czechoslovakia, Hungary, and Bulgaria(?!), slightly less in USSR and East Germany, considerably less in Poland, and the least in Romania.

The Western solution to similar growth constraints encountered at this time[11] was even less successful in Eastern Europe. The minimum level of capital substitution for labor shortages shows that in Hungary, as an example, "the elasticity of substitution in the early 1960s, the crucial period for reforms," had "approached zero."[12] Reasons vary from plain capital misallocation and capital underutilization, to lack of imported raw materials and intercountry trade bottlenecks.

External Factors of Decline

Overall, in the 1970s, West-bound trade as a percentage of GNP showed a divergent pattern between the declining group (Czechoslovakia, East Germany, Hungary, and Poland) and the advancing group (Romania, Bulgaria, and Yugoslavia). "Hungary and East Germany followed far more incrementalist strategies. . . Both found their terms of trade with the West deteriorating sharply after 1973, and both incurred large hard-currency debts to cover the deficits created by expanding East-West trade. Neither used the occasion to pursue domestic economic reform; indeed, in the 1970s both countries turned away from earlier experiments that enlarge [d] the enterprise autonomy."[13]

An early shift in the balance between Comecon-directed trade and West-bound, again, is demonstrably cluster discriminatory between the first group and the second. Czechoslovakia, Hungary, and East Germany demonstrated a persistent regional distribution of trade (within Comecon), with chronic deficit balances of payment, while the opposite is true for the USSR, Bulgaria, and

Romania. This fact is accentuated even more by the large balance-of-trade deficits that Romania and Bulgaria incurred especially with the most developed industrial countries.

The uneven rate of development between the two groups of countries helps explain their different approach to the increased internal demands for one or another sort of reform. The experiments were multiple, sometimes short lived, and hailed with high expectations. Their actual impact on the competitive performance of the two groups appears to have been a great deal less significant than their intellectual supporters had given the public, in both the West and in the East, to believe.

There were, however, a number of incremental steps taken to bring the internal price system into line with world-market prices, to align currency values closer to real exchange values, and to restore the function of value measurements against physical taxonomy. They were most often related to foreign trade activity since that had to respond to real criteria, i.e., world prices, based on an objective two-way flow of commodities, and having to be expressed in value terms, irrespective of the quantitative denominations.

Worth mentioning were the efforts to forge a meaningful correlation between internal prices and world prices and to determine trade profitability:

1. At first, cumbersome 'adjustment coefficients' were introduced to account for the two sets of prices.

2. Later, there was a more sophisticated use of 'shadow exchange rates,' which consisted in two or more different exchange rates for specific international transactions, sometimes tabulated across countries and type of commodity. Modified and tinkered with for the next twenty years, the concept was in effect up to the time of the 'big-bang', *perestroika*.

3. A genuine attempt at wholesale price reform was a relentless part of the constantly invoked economic 'new thinking' of the 1960s and long thereafter. It was no more than an honest effort to bring domestic prices closer to factor cost and to align them in some meaningful way with world prices.

4. Highly regarded as a breakthrough in the reform process was the radical departure from managing foreign trade through central agencies and authorizing firms to make their own arrangements. Branch associations and specialized firms were introduced in East Germany, the USSR, Romania, Poland, and Bulgaria, but outright decentralized trade was allowed, starting in 1968, only in Hungary.

5. Foreign trade was marked also by the radical move from quantitative sales targets to more economic ones reflected as value targets. Again, Hungary took the lead when, in 1968, it abolished most compulsory plan targets and allowed market criteria to determine production and sales abroad.

A second tier of the gradualist approach to economic reform, started in the late 1960s, dealt with the central planning structures themselves. Sometimes this showed up as increased autonomy in a firm's foreign market exposure. Speaking more generally, the central planning mechanism gradually had been upgraded with an infusion of streamlining elements. One was a more expert use of econometrics by academic economists, in the name of 'scientific economics.' Another was the ongoing process of enterprise consolidation that went on through the 1950s up to the 1970s under various names, basically reproducing the Western pattern of production consolidation and restructuring upon the economy of scale and scope. A sense of this process is given in **Tables 3.3, 3.4,** and **3.5.**

The diminishing number of targets detailed by the central authority more often than not reflected internal streamlining within the newer, larger state corporations, the so-called combinats. Targets that used to be set in connection with other economic units, productive inputs needed by another enterprise, for example, were

Table 3.3
Index Numbers and Rate of Change in Number of Industrial
Enterprises in the GDR, 1955-70 (Selected years)

Year	Index of Number of Enterprises		Average Annual Rate of Change in Number of Enterprises	
	All Industry	Socialist Industry	All Industry	Socialist Industry
1955	100	100	-	-
1957	98	100	-1.0	0
1959	94	94	-2.0	-3.0
1960	90	88	-4.5	-6.0
1963	84	81	-4.5	-2.5
1964	81	74	-2.0	-8.5
1967	75	65	-2.5	-4.0
1968	72	60	-4.0	-7.5
1970	65	46	-5.0	-12.0

Source: Statistiches Jahrbuch der DDR 1971, p.99.[14]
Note: The definition of "industrial enterprises" has changed several times since 1955.

now accounted for as part of the firm's internal operation flows. Truly, this was a step ahead in decentralizing the national concentration of power, but only as far as it was deconcentrated along economically meaningful lines of operation. It would stand rather as a centralized 'rationalization' of the command economy, which, on the one hand, gave a higher order of responsibility to the supervisory ministries at the macro level and, on the other hand, forced a more hands-on, professional approach to the nuts and bolts of production and engineering processes at the corporate level.

In Pursuit of Capitalism with a Human Face

Reforming their centrally planned economies was the challenge facing the most advanced industrial group among the Eastern European countries. The mythology of reform shared by a large number of well-meaning intellectual hopefuls had little to do, however, with the political undercurrents that would jolt the bureaucratic ship off automatic pilot. By and large, one reform measure after another came with the intent of actually tightening control and removing the special niches and loopholes sheltering the clever few.

The simple fact that reforms were more needed and indeed 'granted' to the most-advanced/least-performing of the national

Table 3.4
Industrial Enterprises in Hungary,
1960-70 (selected years)

Year	State Enterprises	Cooperative Enterprises	Total Socialist Enterprises
1960	1368	1251	2619
1962	1283	1092	2375
1963	894	993	1887
1965	840	811	1651
1967	807	784	1591
1968	811	792	1603
1970	813	821	1634

Source: Hungary, *Statistical Yearbook* (Budapest: Hungarian Central Statistical Office, 1962), p. 121; 1963, pp.104, 120; 1968, p. 101; 1969, pp. 89, 133, 149. *Statistical Pocket Book of Hungary 1971* (Budapest: Statistical Publishing House), p. 93.[15]

Table 3.5
Industrial Enterprises in Czechoslovakia, 1957-68
(selected years)

Year	National Enterprises	Local Industry	All Cooperatives	Enterprises
1957	1445	247	575	2267
1958	935	210	544	1689
1059	923	163	508	1594
1961	818	196	399	1413
1965	715	183	338	1236
1967	713	183	331	1227
1968	743	185	338	1266

Source: *Statisticka Rocenka CSSR* (Prague: SNTL, 1958), p. 114; 1959, pp.137, 139; 1960, pp. 129. 131; 1962, p. 158; 1966, pp. 187, 379; 1968, pp. 216; 1969, pp. 119, 374.[16]

economies created a subtle confusion. Was reform a sign of success on the part of unrepentant anti-Communists? Or, rather, was reform an efficient way to enroll them, now defenseless, into the knowledge-working-class, in its socialist version?

Academic energy was not spared in either camp in arguing for the benefit of reform and applauding its step-by-step implementation. It was hailed as a liberating crusade, loosening the grip of state control, when the evidence shows that in fact reform aimed at strengthening control. As long as directives communicated from the supervisory ministers were inefficiently, insisting on production plans, with their product composition, material allocation, manpower, wage targets, and investments, one needed little imagination to figure out a way to get around the bureaucratic game, shoot for the bonus, and still come out clean despite the self-contradicting commands. The use of legal loopholes and extralegal manipulations of the cumbersome system was as widespread as one can imagine. "Changes in product composition toward higher-value commodities, disguised price increases, quality deterioration, obtaining materials outside official distribution channels, and increasing output without regard to costs"[17] were only a few of the common practices.

Whether managers and supervisors were intentionally squandering the nation's wealth, outsmarting the bureaucracy, or floundering in incompetence, the net effect was a slow-moving economy and a deteriorating standard of living. Finally, a last moribound attempt to get out of the deepening morass, known under the well-packaged, belt-tightening measures called the 'New Economic Mechanism,' came to its death in the 1980s.

The Soviet Union aside, all of the Eastern European countries were small and had under-developed demand for consumer goods, relatively scarce raw materials, and infant industries. Considering the task of creating and nurturing a dynamic self-driven economy – to overcome trade barriers, investment neglect, technological exclusion, and a host of other 'structural impediments' slapped on by the 'democratic' nations as well – and to attain the dream of harmonious integration within the Western economic circuit – well, there were very few managerial devices in place to do the trick. On top of the structural impediments, firms were for the most part un-competitively small, since their national market share hardly allowed the operation of a single firm of optimum size. Therefore, internal competition was an impossibility, and head-to-head competition with advanced industrial nations was nil.

> According to the results of the sample survey in 1968, 40 percent of the firms did not experience any competition from domestic firms, 48 percent experienced some competition, and only 12 percent experienced strong competition. The share of the latter group was 3 percent in the machine-building industry, 10 percent in the chemical and food-processing industries, and 23 percent in textiles, clothing, and shoes production.

> In response to the questionnaires, firms also provided information on the extent of import competition: 46 percent of the respondents did not experience any import competition, 37 percent felt the existence of some competition from imports, and 17 percent had much foreign competition. Foreign competition appears to be strongest in the machinery industry and weakest in the food industries. Still, nearly one-third of the firms in the machinery industry reported that they had neither domestic nor foreign competition.[18]

Besides the daily staple of calls for national self-sacrifice, more devilishly devised accounting schemes were employed in order to tie a manager's performance to some hard formula. Complicated mathematical equations were used to compute overall input on the part of management, worker employment, value-added gains, profit ratio, or any other set of variables used for the purpose of productivity stimulation. While the rank and file workers and floor

managers alike were still routinely given plan targets, as in any
Western corporation the focus of the new mechanisms was mainly
to preserve the class of upper-management. Once through the
gates of experimentation with sophisticated management devices
and with ever more optimized equations in place, the sky was the
limit for compounding bureaucracy. Here is an example:

> To reduce the adverse consequences of the incentive system,
> in 1969 the actual average wage replaced the wage norm for
> the purpose of calculating the share of the distribution fund in
> total profits, and the 4 percent ceiling on wage increases was
> abolished. But as wage increases were still calculated on the
> basis of the 1968 wage norm, and increases undertaken both
> in 1968 and 1969 were deducted from the distributive fund for
> 1969, the adverse effects of the incentive system hardly
> diminished.
>
> In 1970, increases in the working force also become taxable,
> with varying proportions of the increases in total wages
> burdening the distribution fund, depending on whether this
> represented a rise in average wages or in employment. Three-
> tenths of increases in average wages up to 4 percent
> compared to the 1970 level can be accounted for among costs
> while the remainder, as well as increases exceeding 4 percent
> and wage increases undertaken in 1968 and 1969, are
> financed from the distribution fund. Etc.
>
> The rules introduced in 1970 reduced the difference in the tax
> treatment of the rise in total wages due to higher average
> wages or to larger employment. Only increases in average
> wages compared in previous year will be subject to tax, with a
> rate of 50 percent applying to increases not exceeding three-
> tenths of the percentage rise in the sum of profits and wages
> per worker and progressively increasing thereafter.[19]

Too simple, right?

Reforms and Their Results

Historically, mercantilism stood for economic development
through one's own national forces. Its unapologetic pursuit as
economic policy by France helped make mercantilism into a
subspecies of applied political economy. Colbert, for one, advised
Louis XIV with relative success on the benefits of centrally planned
development. Under his leadership, imperial France of the

sixteenth century built its docks and shipyards, set up its port cities, foundries, its silk and glass industries. Another success was Germany under Bismarck. His savvy pragmatism helped him and Germany design the policy of social market that he launched in 1860 as a purposeful national strategy. His model helped the Meiji Japan of 1867 set its own course of development as a direct knock-off of the German prototype.

Having said that, how well did the ongoing experimentation with new forms of central planning, selectively borrowed from the national socialism of Germany, assist the Eastern European countries in their struggle to revamp their cumbersome Soviet-style administration? A quick look at **Table 3.6** and **3.7** reveals a rather mixed balance in judging their performance.

For the five-year plan from 1970 to 1975, the economic growth of reform-minded Hungary maintained an unenviable position among at the back of the pack of its six East European neighbors. For the second set of five years, Hungary improved its relative standing but only because of Poland's disastrous performance and the surprisingly weak growth achieved by Bulgaria. Romania and Yugoslavia were the unmistakable leaders throughout the Seventies, far ahead of the rest in respect to GNP rate of growth. Despite the overall slow-down of East European countries, their performance could be given passing grades for keeping up with the rest of the world.

The beginning of the 1980s showed the impact of rising global energy prices and of the accompanying financial crisis that was

Table 3.6
Annual Percentage Rates of Growth of GNP in
Six East European Countries, 1970-89 (constant prices)

Country	1970-75	1975-80	1980-85	1986	1987	1988
Bulgaria	4.5	1.2	0.9	4.8	-0.8	1.8
Czechoslovakia	3.4	2.2	1.4	2.1	1.0	1.4
East Germany	3.5	2.4	1.8	1.5	1.8	1.8
Hungary	3.4	2.3	0.9	2.2	1.0	1.1
Poland	6.6	0.9	1.2	2.7	-1.7	1.9
Romania	6.2	3.9	2.0	5.8	1.1	2.1
Total	4.9	2.0	1.4	3.0	0.1	1.5

Source: Thad Alton, "East European GNP's, Domestic Final Uses of Gross Product, Rates of Growth, and International Comparisons," in 101st Congress, *Joint Economic Committee Pressure for Reform in the East European Economies, Vol. 1* (Washington, DC.: U.S. Government Printing Office, 1989), p. 81.

ravaging the West as well as the East. Hungary proved again to be the least prepared, regaining its traditional last place in the race for development.

Romania's rate of economic growth outperformed its neighbors' on a continuous basis. Its benign form of national socialism was a special case, however. Romania's charismatic leadership borrowed from experience that went beyond the generally accepted economic guidelines of bureaucratic socialism. Romania's form of socialism called for a re-editing of nationalist state corporatism and its benign nationalist tendencies. Unrivaled in its magnetism, capable of mobilizing the masses of workers and efficiently coordinating them under a command structure, such a system also had to deal with drawbacks that came from its latent militant tendencies.

To the outside observer, given Romania's gentle and temperate national spirit, the fact that it was spared the fate of out-right violent policies was not sufficient reason to advocate using it as a model for more assertive nations. On the contrary, the mass media

Table 3.7
Indexes of East European Real GNP Per Capita
at Adjusted Factor Cost, 1970 and 1975-88
(indexed to 1975 = 100)

Year	Bulgaria	Czecho-slovakia	GDR	Hungary	Poland	Romania	Yugo-slavia
1970	81.1	87.5	83.4	86.6	76.4	75.9	83.9
1975	100.0	100.0	100.0	100.0	100.0	100.0	100.0
1976	102.6	101.0	102.4	99.8	101.5	109.7	102.1
1977	101.0	104.6	105.6	105.5	102.4	111.4	108.5
1978	103.1	105.5	107.7	107.5	105.1	115.6	113.5
1979	106.9	105.7	110.6	107.7	102.5	118.7	120.2
1980	103.4	107.7	113.0	108.7	99.1	116.1	125.2
1981	105.8	107.2	115.3	109.4	92.9	115.6	126.3
1982	108.9	108.8	115.1	113.4	91.2	117.2	126.4
1983	106.6	110.1	117.4	112.4	94.8	116.9	126.7
1984	109.9	112.5	120.9	115.6	97.4	123.5	128.8
1985	106.6	113.0	124.8	113.0	97.6	124.5	128.7
1986	111.8	115.1	126.8	115.6	99.6	131.2	132.7
1987	110.7	116.0	128.9	117.0	97.3	131.9	131.3
1988	103.0	108.4	98.0	104.1	101.2	126.3	130.7

Source: Thad Alton, "East European GNP's, Domestic Final Uses of Gross Product, Rates of Growth, and International Comparisons," in 101st Congress, *Joint Economic Committee Pressure for Reform in the East European Economies*, Vol. 1 (Washington, DC.: U.S. Government Printing Office, 1989), p. 82.

focused on discrediting the system, even by distorting its real successes, in order to support a largely shared opinion on the malefic character of authoritarianism. The media went so far as to produce a widely advertised public execution of its unrepentant champions, the Ceausescus, and their peasant spirit of nationalist missionarism.

Along any single economic indicator, as one can observe from **Table C-6,** Romania outperformed her sister centrally planned economies. The model did not produce uniform results, but neither did it indicate that the model was ineffective. However, given the history of national socialism in Germany, it wasn't politically correct to applaud even a more benign variant of socialism.

Yet, across the political divide, the same type of authoritative-presidential economic leadership operated by Taiwan, South Korea, Hong Kong, Malaysia, and Singapore were justified and praised as politically acceptable and as self-serving success stories of capitalism – notwithstanding their unmistakable affiliation in style and method with nationalist mercantilism.

Motivation vs. Management

Large economic organizations characteristic of the mature phase in the development of any mode of production throughout history, whether large-scale latifundia in the late Roman civilization, the feudal estates of the Middle Ages, or the national/transnational corporations of the industrial age – all were faced with the double-fold imperative of focusing large masses of individual employees upon a common goal. Their extended purpose, from the time of their genesis and self-sustained growth, was marked by their evolution in collusion with the rest of the surrounding economic and political environment. Nations themselves were such sociopolitical complex entities from the start; so were the states, and the multi-national corporations, all evolving as complex organizations faced with fierce competition from equally complex contenders.

Competitive, antagonistic, militant, defensive as much as offensive, fighting units of a vast concentration of human resources, they all thrived upon their generic motivation and their capacity for a fast, concentrated response to aggression. Their success is derived from their single-mindedness, their shared purpose and the internal identification of structure with function. The Catholic Church is a representative example. The Nazi economic system is another. The Japanese national corporate system is even more familiar these days.

Managing through motivation was always considered to be the unrivaled power tool in the service of governing the masses. Team competition in sports stands also as a benign test in collective psychology and its aggressive polarization. When corporations speak of the need for employee motivation, it should be understood as a call for corporate warfare. Moreover, as a manifestation of the collective killer instinct, it also finds its identity in the primary need for human immortalization through collective being. Religious fundamentalists know that better than any secular manager.

In its full deployment, collective motivation and its charismatic calls for selfless devotion to corporate entity demands collective subservience to an expanding and devouring idolatry. In this sense, collective corporate worship is ultimately self-destructive, due to the very nature of its perpetual conflict against other corporations, within the social whole of which they are constitutive parts.

Conversely, it is also true that lack of collective motivation is a sure sign of a moribund social animal and no techniques, market or otherwise, can replace the resultant soulless drifting.

This antagonistic nature of motivation was experienced throughout the last sixty or so years of European history. The weakly motivated socialist playhouse featuring the Hungarian, Czechoslovakian, and Polish New Economic Programs was no match for the national socialist house of Germany in the 1930s. Such programs just did not work since they were based on guaranteed equal outcome. Fearing no loss and having no world to conquer, firms and individuals had nothing to gain by joining the gladiators' market. Self-preservation replaced self-motivation, and safe play superseded risk taking.

In retrospect, the drama of the centrally planned economies was similar to that of the bureaucratic, large-scale corporate institutions of the oligopolistic market economies. They were confronted with a seemingly insoluble dilemma:

On the one hand, cheap talk on motivating employees always has to be moderated in practice, due to its savage logic – the truly aggressive raider-corporate entity, motivated by the take-no-prisoners philosophy, eventually becomes a form of extreme *corporate fundamentalism*, which is fascism.

On the other hand, the real task of macroeconomic planning is how to motivate firms and individuals alike in the absence of all-out warfare. A balancing act between motivation and cooperation, the concept of *managed competition* is a newer invention positing management as a concealed form of delegated authority, of *enlightened authority*. It implies the rule of *benevolent leadership*. There will be more about this later.

* * *

Resistant to any reforming medication, the structural deficiency that induced Hungary's inability to sustain a competitive rate of growth was matched in those years, the 1970s to the 1980s, only by the high decibel moral support it enjoyed in the Western mass media. The country became almost a synonym for uninhibited laboratory testing in the pursuit of ever more clumsy reforming, while hard evidence suggesting its eventual lack of success was totally overlooked. The more Hungary reformed, the more deficient were its reforms' effectiveness. The more deficient its reforms, the louder the cries for more reforms. By then, however, the corporate morass was extending over the Western economies as much as over the disheartened Eastern nations. In the end, this brought out into the open a discussion on the need for revamping the whole concept of large-scale corporate enterprises, and the need to replace them with something else (in the West as well as in the East). In a sense, the Hungarian experience and the high drama surrounding its relentless attempts at corporate streamlining were factors in helping to spread the conviction that a radical overhaul of the whole concept was needed. Old-fashioned interventionist policies were giving ground more and more to calls for decentralization and to a revival of the entrepreneurial spirit in the name of downsizing and debureaucratization. Ineffective beyond repair, the corporate model was to be relegated to the trash bin of history.

But by then, the long cycle of economic organization building had turned the corner once more.

To launch the grand-scale revolution of corporate dismantling throughout the modern industrial states would require preparation, public education, and mass conversion to a new economic mindset. It would also require the jolt that comes from a financial crisis, a stock-market crash, followed by economic shock therapy on a large scale and the proclamation of a new world order. A decade of high-speed/low-speed, on again/off again worldwide economic reinvention was put in motion. The train of *world perestroika* moved on.

As had happened before in the past fifty years, the revolution of corporate dismantling started with a renewed rhetoric on reform. This time it was high drama, high political theater, played on every household TV screen to a global audience. Yet for all of this excitement, the few fundamental questions were the same as those of the early years of central planning experimentation. As the pressure for reform increased, its far-reaching consequences, involving crucial economic, social, domestic and international political issues, were less obvious. The widespread belief that re-forms were attainable without a violent revolution precluded cautious questioning of the scope and the very meaning of reform.

If economic reforms in Eastern Europe were to be the equivalent of a thorough introduction of market mechanisms (price setting, return on capital, and free competition among 'decentralized' enterprises), then, it was assumed, the ultimate measure of the reformers' success would be the attainment of a laissez-faire-oriented economy. Was that possible, at the very time when the United States' own laissez-faire economic style was under fire?

THE AMBIGUITIES OF "DECENTRALIZATION"

Since centrally planned economies were hierarchically structured, the first reaction to any attempted reform always came in terms of its deconstruction through 'decentralization.' Not only was it music to the ears of the unregulated-market enthusiasts, it was almost a spontaneous counterreaction to an existing state of order. It was thinking in alternative terms: from central authority back to local authority. Or, what? From where else was the enterprise's authority to originate?

In the fully hierarchical organization, authority originates from the top executive tier and is transmitted down the chain of command. In all but the most utopian descriptions of a society of individual producers assembled by the market – any modern productive unit is the embodiment of a hierarchical organizational structure. There is the CEO, the head of the organization, and then the lower tiers of departments, group leaders, and rank and file members. In a centrally planned economy, the CEO is the head of state, its officers are the ministries, its group leaders are the heads of enterprises, and so on, down to the last worker at the parking lot.

The system should have worked – it was a sure bet; but it did not. Why not? "If men were angels," we read in the Federalist papers,[21] "no government would be necessary", and "if angels were to govern men, neither external nor internal controls on government would be necessary. . . [However,] in framing a government that is to be administered by men over men, the great difficulty lies in this: You must first enable the government to control the governed; and in the next place oblige it to control itself."

But since angels are not for hire, self-governing is our way of life, and so the question remains: From where does authority emanate? How should authority be enforced? Who guards the guards?

* * *

Let us consider the manager of an enterprise and his overseeing central agency. The central agency supervises the manager, it gives him instructions and it evaluates the enterprise's results. This is a simple top-down structure of authority.

Now the economy is reorganized. Market forces are active while the central agency is withering away. Is the manager the new predominant decision-making authority? Who evaluates his results? ('Manager-as-owner' is not a common formula in the age of corporations even in the American version of capitalism.)

The manager is now answerable to a council of the board of directors – whether a workers' council or a group of stockholders. His function is to implement a production plan, using existing capacities, investment strategies, and marketing objectives. His performance is judged relative to the board of directors' objectives, whether profit maximization, growth targets, market penetration, or market share preservation. Failure in performance attracts dismissal as an exercise of authority by the council's executive powers.

But how does the council reach its own set of norms and targets? Who gives authority to those objectives? Producing an optimum rate of profit for the stockholders is as much an arbitrary criterion for the long-term well-being of the company as is the higher wage arrangements provided for employees through the workers' council. Furthermore, a plan approved by the manager must have been sanctioned indirectly by the council itself when the manager was empowered to carry it out. Now who would be in a position to dismiss the council or the shareholders should they bring the company to bankruptcy through their demands? The shareholders can take their profits to other investments, and the loss incurred by the last buyer on the market does not penalize the authority responsible for the failure.

By themselves, institutions are totalitarian in character. In a corporation, power flows from top down, with the outside public excluded.[22] The system is of 'free enterprise' on the outside, but is a dictatorial system within.

Of course, one can question authority's legitimacy and the extent to which it brings about an efficiently managed enterprise. Yet, any effective decentralizing reform should not only redefine *process* descriptions but also the essential functional *structure*. The real answer to how a centralized and a decentralized flow of information can work together should focus on the macro view of an economy composed of top government policy-makers, enterprise managers, households, and rank and file citizens. Only the economy as a whole is a self-regulating system in which authority constantly moves from one center to another, from one player to another. The electoral process is as much part of the economic process as is the manager's briefing meeting every morning.

But this view turns on their head such market-based concepts as top-down structures and central planning econometrics. In a more relaxed interpretation, central planners are 'experts for hire' rented by the national union of shareholders in the name of international market competition.

Market Competition under Central Planning

Managed competition is already an accepted antinomy in the economic lexicon that stretches both 'market flows' and 'government command' to their semantic limits. It is also the twin brother of the discredited concept of *market socialism*. We therefore follow our examination of the elements of reform of centrally planned economies by scrutinizing three major and intractable questions: *Who should set prices? Who should make investment decisions? What resources are to be used in choosing the allocation mechanisms?*

The market theory of the commodity pricing model is an extreme case. It remains roughly true as long as there are enough firms to compete against each other in such fields as, for example, milk production.[23] But it starts to look like an idealized past, as modern economies move deeper into technological competition. The economies of scale and scope, high-tech monopolies, and national security implications in the development of technology-intensive industries all contribute to the critical reassessment of the notion of perfect markets. *Nationally*, most often the market size is not big enough to promote a practical subdivision of critical industries among several producers. *Internationally*, the notion of spontaneously generated home-grown high-technology industries is belied by the success of nations that relied on industrial policy. *Strategically*, policies designed to take into account national interests serve purely economic goals to the detriment of equal competition: budgetary R&D investments, corporate and national training programs, subsidies and sheltered markets for fledgling industries, infrastructure development and many other forces external to a firm's strength – all these invisible hands play on one's corporate team.

The classical Adam Smith notion of the comparative advantage among nations trading on the basis of free markets is only a cultured expression asserting the supremacy of Nature in the world of productive competition. Nature was perceived as having control over entrepreneurial travails. Random distribution of raw materials, topography, transportation access, technological monopolies, weather, political changes, developments in other countries and so many other variables were the elements of nature's wheel of fortune in the game of free competition.

The lesson of high-tech industrialization, however, attests to a different emerging reality, one in which the natural distribution of favors is neutral to any self-generated advantage. "Nearly everyone now concedes that competitive advantage in high-technology industries is created, not endowed by nature, and that governments the world over have earmarked them for special support. Even the assumption that structural impediments influence competitive outcomes in global oligopolies has becomes commonplace in contemporary discussions of trade policy."[24]

So, when it comes to *managed competition* newly defined as *market socialism*, and its price setting mechanisms, the inevitable question is, what is the underlying theoretical framework? If foreign produced goods were freely sold at free prices, the world market would be, at least partially, the price setter, beyond the enterprise's control. But world-market pricing is no market-pricing at all.

First, since a host of interventionist policies are directed at helping national industries in their own performance and pricing, there is very little information on the foreign competitor's fair price to function as a price becnhmark. Second, having to promote its own brand of industrial policy, a national government sets the grounds for an enterprise's performance by targeting investment, subsidies, import tariffs, and a full assortment of nontariff *structural impediments* to outside competition. The notion of the market as the price setter is, by now, discredited economic purism.

Regardless of the legal status of the enterprise, two elements are essential in the so-called market economy nowadays. One is the monopolistic character of the industrial modern enterprise due to the efficiency of scale and scope. Another is international market competition and the high level of identification between monopolistic enterprises and national security concerns. Ultimately, the chief executive of an enterprise is a member of the governing body of a nation.

International Markets and National Competition

In a neosocialist, international economic order, the answers to questions of price setting, investment decision making, and re-source allocation come, by default, from within. Since world markets are the modern-day arena of competition, defensive trade management requires a strategy in behalf of the state/enterprise joint entity. It can be built around the notion of internal *intrapreneurship* as a form of de-bureaucratization, i.e., business-sizing, of an existing state enterprise, or it can be fashioned through trade associations and trusts under government sponsorship upon the technostructures of private business.

The open markets principle still applies, since national markets are accessible to foreign trade and foreign competition. But, also, the system preserves a considerable measure of government role in brokering the international rules and the agreed-upon common limits to competition. If a non-economic analogy is permitted, the Olympic Games stand as sublimated war among nations, waged on a wide scale and with no ultimate vic-tims on either side. This way, the civilized test of success for nation-al sporting industries is conducted through sports tournaments.

* * *

After a history of trade wars and devastating armed confla-grations, the mercantilist mythology of Say's Law on the natural harmony of supply and demand (on a global dimension) once again looks credible. Yet its net effect would be the polarization of a few rich mammoth multinationals among an oppressed Third World population. It would only help bring about a worldwide Marxist-type class struggle and activate a collapse of the international order.

We see a more benign alternative unfolding: managed trade competition among social market national economies. Instead of yes/no, rather yes/yes. Yes, the international market is the ultimate arbiter of the rational use of resources and efficient production. Yes, the governing bodies set the goals, make the investment decisions, and allocate resources.

Entrepreneurial wealth-creating activity is at its most proficient level when domesticated through social nourishment and civic empowerment. Likewise, the old European Renaissance towns of enlightenment and prosperity, created on the corpus of civic regulations and the rule of law enforceable by the city-state protector, the social market economy is only the larger scale projection of the prosperous commonwealth of townspeople's confederated republics.

Managed Social Markets

Everyone would recognize that the key word in the above expression is *managed* rather than *markets*. Boosted by the social attribute, it becomes almost a converse of the free-market rhetoric. The international framework preordains the national economic blueprint as much as the social framework precedes any group strategy.

Managed trade principles imply, by definition, national economic policy, which in turn requires the mechanism of managed competition. Sophisticated planning mechanisms need to be designed to encourage rationality in both private and public-sector investments around certain national goals, much as capital allocation should serve as an instrument of central control over the direction of enterprise expansion.

The old Stalinist economic school argued for achieving these goals through wholesale command mechanisms: collect detailed technological data from enterprises and demand curves or other preference data from customers, digest the information according to an all-encompassing formula and some external parameters and, finally, issue production instructions to enterprises.

Another approach is through the wholesale use of information tools, since every player in the market is collecting his information from a centralized databank. The minute-by-minute exposure of all 'independent' decision makers to the same *Wall Street Journal*-CNN stockmarket quotations, interest rates, national economic gurus, as well as TV financial advisors, the on-line, real-time computerized monitoring of information commands the 'independent' decision makers in a more subtle way and on a more timely basis.

A Gosplan-run, heavy-handed authority has only a rudimentary, infrequent, and brief central supervisory capacity, while its counterpart, the *information system command*, is democratic and allows for accurate fine-tuning. The marriage of bureaucracy and high-tech information-processing equipment also could be invoked as a brain-child of twentieth-century managing strategy. One would find it an outright enslaving mechanism. Its capacity to overrule from above and the diminishing elbowroom left for initiative from below would seem to deter an entrepreneurial attitude. Yet, in competition with the open-ended, hands-off, winner-take-all, free-wheeling economic anarchy, it looks to be a winning proposition.

From all of the above, it seems abundantly clear that reform, under the auspices of the information technology revolution, is truly revolutionary in itself. *While it decentralizes the sense of authority in decision making, it centralizes its net input.* It disperses the responsibility for risk taking to the periphery, while it maximizes the central coordinating authority over individual enterprises. It liberates both bureaucrats and entrepreneurs from their lock-step waltzing, while strengthening the sense of national teamwork.

* * *

Such innovative redesign of the bureaucratic corporation was actively pursued by the high commands of both the Soviet and the U.S. economic councils of the early 1970s. The academics on both national corporate boards were making plans for the new spirit of détente that was expected to coincide with the liberalized trade legislation in the works in the U.S. Congress. The arms reduction initiative seemed a sure precursor of changes to come.

But by the time this wonderful script was to be acted upon, a more dreaded development threw cold water on the optimism of a post-world war generation.

The increasing specter of a potentially crippling new chapter in cold war history was taking shape. After Nixon's near impeachment, one acute international crisis after another set the stage for a new arms race; devastating spending on weapons and national resource depletion would soon wash away any gains that so painfully were built in the years after the Cuban missile crisis.

The military-industrial complex, which many hopeful observers were inclined to write off in the immediate years of post-Vietnam détente, took control of operations once more. The center of command moved from the corporate board rooms to the strategic planners' headquarters where calculated-risk warmanship was the prevailing style.

For the next twenty years, the topic of enterprise reform was moved into the back burner as the USSR and the United States decidedly took the course toward mutually assured destruction. Enlightened arguments about the best way to increase productivity, to raise standards of living, or about the benefits of international trade were replaced by communiqués on intercontinental ballistic superiority, Star Wars, the cruise missile crisis, first strike survival, the neutron bomb, laser beam weapons, and other nonproductive endeavors.

The world moved into the new warrior interregnum.

Chapter IV

The Life Cycle of the Cold War Industries

If one seeks to identify the foremost goal of the United States' foreign policy throughout the Cold War, one would certainly find support for the opinion that it was the containment of communism. However, if the actions of the United States' tiny inner establishment are a more solid ground for judgment than the mass media-driven campaigns, one would conclude the contrary. The apparent *lack of consensus on a short-term tactical approach* to the European theater was coupled with a complete *long-term understanding of the grand strategic design*, which had at its center China and Asia, and above all the intractable Jewish question. The Jewish challenge to the Western bid for world preeminence had no solution for a long century as it impinged on the West's internal, albeit international, power struggle. In the words of Seth Faison, Beijing correspondent of *The New York Times*: if it seemed obvious to anyone in Washington that the American Administration had no coordinated China policy, "China's military was seeing a clear plan."

Only this can explain actions that were taken by the United States' political leadership, in an often inconsistent pattern, at times even favorable to the Soviet Union's interests and detrimental to United States' immediate national pride and security. In this sense Vietnam, to most Americans, stood as the ultimate symbol of confusion, outrage and betrayal. They were wrong, but the truth could hardly have been revealed or be made, ideologically, culturally, or programmatically, palatable.

On the subject of why and how state chancelleries exercise their leadership over the masses, the most popular intellectual premise has been that leaders, reacting to external events, are driven by subjective considerations and dubious stratagems. Others deeply believed that the ideological and dysfunctional tendency of governments was the ultimate untold story in the book of modern Western history.

* * *

In January 1987, the USSR began to put in place legislation permitting foreign participation in the ownership and operation of joint ventures located in the USSR. By June, the first of these joint ventures with a Western partner acquired the status and rights of a separate legal entity in the USSR. In November of that same year, the first U.S.-USSR joint venture was registered.[1] By November 1990, the cold war was over. In only three years, an unprecedented international realignment of the superpowers was in place.

Indeed, domestic and foreign policies were as closely connected under *perestroika* as they were in any previous stage in Soviet-American development. On the background of the rhetoric of domestic needs, however, it was the weight accorded to strategic goals that bore the greater share in economic planning. There was also an unmistakable parallel between the external/internal pair of priorities that recalled the centuries-old imperial aim and long-term strategy of *stop-and-go* expansion.

Three major international, humiliating defeats in the nineteenth century preceded three major stages in the Russian politics of soul-searching and renewal. *(1)* The unchecked Napoleonic invasion (1812) set the stage for the first major internal civil uprising (1825), which opened up the serfdom question and started the process of its enlightened dissolution. *(2)* The crush suffered in defending Sevastopol from the Turkish-Anglo-French forces in the Crimean War of 1853–56 led to the freeing of the serfs (1861) and unleashed Russia's truly capitalist industrial development. *(3)* The defeat inflicted by Japan (1904–5) and the subsequent uprising (1905–6) was followed by the creation of the Duma (parliament) and by the reforms, under Stolypin, that set the stage for twentieth-century industrialization.

Following a perpetual spiral of increased militarization, from the early nineteenth century onward, the subsequent reconciliation settlements among the European powers of a given day stand as milestones in the process of sanctioning and acknowledging the latest power selection: the Congress of Vienna (1815), the Conference of Paris (1856), the Berlin Conference (1875), the Versailles Treaty (1918), the Yalta Conference (1945), and the Malta Conference (1989). Sometimes they alluded to the notion of being peace conferences – only war inevitably followed peace.

Reversing the old adagio of the von Clausewitz diplomatic school, World War I forced a redefining of the preeminence of internal vs. external factors. It turned *domestic* economic policy into a continuation of *external* strategies. A virtual about-face of historical proportion took place under the pressures of the nascent global economy. Former centers of prosperity and affluence, national economies were becoming bastions of organized warrior tribes. In the new interdependent world, independent state jurisdiction, the last fortress of recognized local sovereignty, became a practical impossibility.

Since the days of the dramatic Treaty of Brest-Litovsk, Russia experienced to the fullest extent the imperatives of the newly emerged type of *war economy*. Its counterpart, Lenin's New Economic Policy (NEP), introduced the notion of *national security* as the preeminent *public sovereign*. Yet, from those ad hoc emergency calls to national economic rationalization that all-out European warfare appeared to demand as a temporary measure, Russia never found a way out. From one emergency to another, from preparations for war to actual war and the aftermath of war, the cycle went on and on.

Responding to this ongoing imperative of a close policy connection between security demands and domestic economic development, the Soviet Union's policy thinking since Lenin has for the most part invoked security demands in order to justify domestic privation. After World War II, an awareness of the need to reduce the military burden emerged for the first time under Khrushchev, who attempted to cut back – ultimately unsuccessfully – on military size and expenditures. Although this policy was reversed in the late 1960s through the 1970s, debates around this issue resurfaced in the late Brezhnev period, which saw a slowdown in military spending. While the Brezhnev leadership undoubtedly regarded the attainment of military parity with the United States as a major achievement, only a few in the military establishment were disposed to recognize the costs of such sustained defense priorities for civilian development in general and consumption in particular.[2]

From the late 1970s onward, it was more and more clear that Soviet technological capabilities could not easily compete with Western weapons development, notably in the area of emerging technologies. The threat of the United States racing ahead in this field was intensified by the appearance of the SDI program. The emphasis on the ABM Treaty, and Soviet willingness to consider deep cuts in strategic arsenals, as well as the unsuccessful effort to bring about a test moratorium through unilateral moves – all underscored the urgency of constraining the technological arms race and of taking the pressure off the Soviet defense industry. "Today what is instrumental to the security of a country," Shevardnadze told a foreign ministry meeting in July 1988, "is not so much its stockpiles as its capacity to develop and produce new things."[3] As Japan's and West Germany's experience showed, world status and influence derive from modern technology rather than from military readiness.

Accordingly, from 1977 through the 1980s, the rate of growth in Soviet defense spending began to drop from about 4 to 5 percent per year to about 2 percent per year. This was a consequence of SALT I, which meant that the USSR needed a respite that would allow the economy and the Soviet military to restructure in order to deal further with the Western threat. From the point of view of the military high command of the Soviet Union, Defense Minister Ustinov and Chief of Staff Ogarkov, SALT I offered not only predictability but also the prospect of an environment of diminished threat, one in which the Soviet military would be able to focus its resources on restructuring the economy so that it might compete in areas that really counted: high technology. But it became more and more obvious that the premises upon which they based their expectations were collapsing very fast. The decision of the political leadership of the Soviet Union to reduce its military spending had been met by three adversarial developments in the West.

First, NATO's decision to adopt the Long-Term Development Program in 1978, which eventually led to the deployment of the Pershing IIs and the ground-launched cruise missiles, meant that the military threat facing the Soviet Union was increasing. Second, by 1979, even before the invasion of Afghanistan, the Soviet high command had begun to suggest that SALT II's ratification by the United States was in trouble. Third, the American military buildup initiated by the Carter administration alarmed the Soviets. Regardless of who would have won the upcoming American election, the military threat facing the Soviet Union in the form of the MX, the Trident II, the B-1, and other programs was perceived as likely to increase. Confronted with the impossibility of obtaining a faster increase in the defense budget, the Soviet high command adopted the only point of view that seemed logical – to reinvigorate the economy as the only key to the country's defense. In 1978, for example, a quote from F. Engels used by Chief of Staff Ogarkov proved the point: "Nothing depends on economic conditions so much as a country's army and navy. Weapons, structure, organization, tactics, and strategy depend above all on the level of production and the means of communication which has been achieved at a given point in time." And, to further illustrate this truth, he followed with examples from World War II: "After the war broke out, the Soviet economy was restructured to meet the demands of the wartime situation; new problems were encountered and new solutions found. All of the USSR's resources were put to work developing new types of weapons. As a result, Moscow, in a short time exceeded fascist Germany in the area of production."[4]

A key article in *Red Star* in 1984, written by the same Ogarkov, goes into even greater detail on the matter of the major changes taking place within the sacrosanct world of nuclear weapons. According to Ogarkov, three major changes had occurred in recent years in military affairs. The first was the decreasing value of nuclear weapons as a result of their quantitative proliferation. The second was the increasing importance of conventional high-technology weapons systems. The third major change, he argued, was "the rapid development of science and technology in recent years [that] creates real preconditions for the emergence in the very near future of even more destructive and previously unknown types of weapons based on new physical principles."[5] Work on such weapons, Ogarkov warned, was already under way; and, he went on, it would be a serious mistake not to consider their implications "right now."[6]

At the beginning of 1981, it was becoming increasingly clear that Ogarkov was emerging as the dominant figure within the Soviet army and the key strategist of Soviet military doctrine. It is even more interesting, therefore, to follow his public position. One of the most riveting aspects of the early 1980s was the degree to which Ogarkov's ideas in the military-technical area seem to foreshadow those later espoused by Gorbachev himself. Finally, although it is impossible to establish a definite link between Ogarkov and the policy of "military sufficiency" introduced under Gorbachev, it is interesting to note that Ogarkov's last article utilized a formulation that could be said to contain the basic principles, at least, of the Gorbachev line. In introducing the concept of military sufficiency in his 1985 Supreme Soviet speech, Gorbachev was largely repeating an idea that Ogarkov (and others) had suggested earlier. Furthermore, Ogarkov's idea of using diplomatic means to prevent the other side from gaining superiority was soon to become party policy.

The self-defeating nature of the arms race was now apprehended through its unaffordable consequences. The inherent conclusion thus was to reverse the military race by resorting to a thorough regimen of superpower détente. It found a receptive audience in the high command of the United States armed forces. The bankruptcy of the American military-industrial complex was another secret well-kept from the world at large.

THE AMERICAN PURSUIT OF A MILITARY ECONOMY

There were numerous dark clouds gathering the skies of the American military establishment at the beginning of the 1980s. The technological pressure that it set on its adversary also threatened to loose the demons of conflict both between the domestic military industrial sector and its counterpart, civilian-commercial information technology, and between the national U.S. civilian economy and the global civilian industry as a whole.

"Because of the peculiarities of cold war outfitting, new atmospheric technologies, such as bombers and satellites, called forth a whole new set of industries that thrived on the continual innovation in weaponry demanded by the Pentagon. We call them Aerospace, Communications, and Electronics industries (ACE). These industries, and the new big firms that led them – Rockwell,

Lockheed, McDonnell-Douglas, General Dynamics, Hughes, Northrop – were marked off from the rest of American commercial business by a 'wall of separation.' Behind the wall they developed a business culture that favored glitz and gimmickry over cost minimization and concentrated marketing efforts on lobbying and negotiating with the Pentagon."[7] The implied choice that was looming would have undermined the political foundation of the system itself: to pursue the total war effort on a totalitarian basis, and enlist all other partners, whether domestic or foreign, to its unconditional support, or strike a deal with the also weakened *evil enemy*.

Geographically located in sparsely populated areas of the country's heartland and the West Coast, the "Gun-belt's" defense industrial bases, the cold war industry functioned on nonmarket principles that favored less capital-intensive plants (unlike the steel, machine tools, or consumer goods industries), but rather highly expensive scientific and engineering industries, unaffected by product cost considerations. The exceptional technical background of the defense industry's management and its contracts with top university scientists and engineers ensured access to the country's brain trust for government-owned production facilities and secretive R&D.

During the interwar period, arms development and much of the production were done in government-owned laboratories and arsenals; only after a weapon proved its merits was it given over to the private sector to produce it in large quantities. This all changed gradually, however, in the postwar period. More and more spending was loaded into selected private sector industries. From 1980 to 1985 alone, during the height of the defense industry buildup, defense manufacturing added 600,000 jobs to the economy (at the cost of 1.6 million jobs lost in the nondefense industry)[8], bringing the total number of people directly working in military-related jobs to at least 6 million out of a total of 27 million manufacturing jobs. By the mid-1980s, the United States' industrial base had undergone a virtual conversion to a state-owned/contracted sector. Close to 80 percent of the aircraft industry, 60 percent of communications, more than a third of the machine tool and optical instruments industries, and about a quarter of the electronic components were *defense-dependent industries* by virtue of the military share of their output. [See **Table 4.1.**] Although less impressive in terms of the overall output share, between 5 and 10 percent, highly specialized industries such as steel, airlines,

Table 4.1

Military and Space Dependency of Major Defense Contractors
1985-1988
DOD and NASA

Company	Primes (millions $)	Sales (millions $)	Primes as % of Sales
Grumman	12,057	13,625	88
General Dynamics	29,015	35,951	81
Martin-Marietta	14,670	20,055	73
McDonnell-Douglas	32,205	52,357	62
Lockheed	22,094	41,719	53
Raytheon	15,301	29,566	52
Rockwell International	22,101	48,209	46
Litton Industries	7,787	18,538	42
Honeywell	7,128	25,830	28
Textron	6,413	23,418	27
Boeing	16,196	62,294	26
Texas Instruments	5,202	21,789	24
United Technologies	14,992	65,831	23
Unisys	7,454	37,821	20
TRW	4,972	25,756	19

Sources: Ann Markusen and Joel Yudken, from Aerospace Industries Association of America, Aerospace Facts and Figures, 1989-1990 (Washington, D.C.: AIA, 1989); Business Week, Special Issues, 1986-89.

computers, industrial chemicals, and semiconductors were dependent on military R&D subsidies, training, low-cost capital, and export promotion with domestic market protection. "The number of industries with more than 10 percent of their output devoted to DOD orders (not including NASA or foreign military sales) rose from twenty-one in 1977 to forty-five in 1985."[19] Shipbuilding went from 45 percent defense-dependent in 1977 to 93 percent, aircraft zoomed from 43 percent to 66 percent, toolmaking dependency rose from just 3 percent in 1977 to 34 percent in 1985, industrial truck production from 2 percent to 22 percent, and radio and television communications equipment from 42 percent to 50 percent in the same period.

The United States' manufacturing base, already uncompetitive on the international markets in a number of critical industries, as illustrated in **Table 4.2,** had to accommodate military orders to an increasing degree. The magnitude of the military demands, and all the noneconomic statutes and regulations that exempted these industries from market uncertainties, were possible only because the military customer remained the single largest underwriter of those industries. At a cost of nearly $10.5 trillion (in 1990 dollars)[10] from 1945 to 1990, the invoice had to be paid by the American citizen and financed through an unorthodox application of market economic principles. To raise the funds to finance bouts of increased expenditures, the government periodically had to jack up interest rates; to maintain control over technology, it introduced a de facto domestic content requirement for military industries ("buy American"); to preserve the source of scarce inventory, it financed outright new plants and equipment (in the 1980s, the chemical feedstock industry); to protect its critical industries, it intervened to cause certain imports to be canceled (e.g., specialty metals); to and to salvage domestic suppliers from foreign competitors, it bailed out whole industries (in 1988, rayon fibers, critical to the production of missiles and rockets).[11]

Given the limited success of commercial business, the vast managerial and engineering input that was channeled through the military-industrial apparatus into the highest national security priorities represented the real story of American industrial policy. Its remarkable technological breakthroughs, from before the start of World War II until the end of the cold war, were only selectively transferred into commercial exploitation through the backdoor of

Table 4.2
Trade Balance in Selected Manufacturing Industries, 1987

Industry	Trade Balance (Billion $)
Total Manufacturing	- $137.7
Aircraft and Other Transportation Equipment	12.5
Chemicals	9.6
Professional, Scientific, and Control Instruments	3.0
Military Arms, Ammunition, Vehicles	2.0
Computing and Office Machinery	1.0
Industrial Machinery	- 6.7
Semiconductors and Other Electrical Equipment	- 7.0
Iron and Steel	- 8.5
Telecommunications and Sound-Reproducing Equipment	- 15.6
Wearing Apparel and Accessories	- 16.9
Motor Vehicles	- 53.3

Source: Ann Markusen and Joel Yudken, from U.S. Department of Commerce, Office of Trade and Investment Analysis, compiled by U.S. Congress, Office of Technology Assessment.

Table 4.3
Growth in Military Sales and Dependency, 1980-85
(in 1977 dollars)

Industry	Military Output (billion $) 1985	Military Output 1980	1985	Share (%)
Shipbuilding	5.8	61		93
Ordnance	0.8	79		86
Missiles	5.3	69		84
Tanks	1.1	68		69
Aircraft	11.7	37		66
Communications Equipment	15.7	42		50
Machine Tools	0.4	8		34
Engineering Instruments	0.7	23		28
Optical Instruments	0.9	13		24
Electronic Components	3.0	16		20
Steel	3.4	6		12
Airlines	3.0	n.a.		10
Oil Refining	5.2	4		6
Computers	2.3	5		5
Industrial Chemicals	2.0	4		5
Semiconductors	1.6	9		5
Automobiles	6.3	3		3

Source: Ann Markusen and Joel Yudken, p. 37.

Hollywood entrepreneurial boutiques. The myth of world-class basement start-ups by college dropouts is only the American business folklore replica of the Rambo movie culture. For each Bill Gates of Microsoft there were the many billions of dollars spent in laboratory research conducted by technocrats and academics hired from around the world by the top agency of the United States' defense trust.

From lavish and secure contracts, access to credit, expertise, critical contacts through the old-boys' network, security clearance, to national attention and advertising, all these invisible hands of defense providence pulled and pushed the marionette of the free-enterprise puppet show. The nineteenth-century Jeffersonian bicycle tinker and the mom-and-pop corner-store genius, national symbols and legends, were now suffering from amateurism, lack of technical expertise, lack of sophisticated laboratories, lack of an institutional support system for cross-fertilizing know-how and specialization. College dropouts might sit in front of personal computer screens and crank out program after program. But it remained beyond their resources, intellectual and managerial, to devise and to build the tools of their craft. Behind every Paganini there has always been a Stradivarius. Nowadays, the old master is the Pentagon's National Laboratories.

> Of 3,400 higher education institutions in the United States, the top 100 spent 83 percent of the total federal funds for research and development. This concentration is especially prevalent in DOD's academic R&D program. Pentagon agencies tend to put most of their money into a few 'centers of excellence.' For example, of the nation's 200 doctorate-granting computer science departments, just *five* received nearly 80 percent of DARPA's academic funding for that field from 1976 to 1989.[12]

The neglected base of commercial industry is best represented by the Ford-type assembly lines mass producing low-tech, low-cost consumer goods for profit. Up to a point, this approach was equally effective in running the large-scale chemical, electronics, home appliances, entertainment appliances, and apparel industries, but it proved to be less and less internationally competitive. These were the industries that were expected to improve the living standards of millions of individuals, to give them a place in the workings of the productive social machine, and to strengthen the national image in competition with other nations. They were important, yet not vitally critical to the national identity. As the Russian example proves, it is possible to be a great power without having a consumer industry. But it is not possible to continue as a great power without a strategic capacity to preempt or inflict a lethal blow to other nations' inimical intentions.

As demonstrated by the Ford Company's experience in trying to unite a civilian business strategy with the rigorous demands of a national security industry, the two are inherently incompatible. The Ford Company went from mass production of automobiles to mass production of airplanes with relative ease. The first successful American cargo airplane, the Trimotor, and later the World War II Liberator bombers, were built by Ford as cheap assembly-line products. By the late 1920s, the Ford Company was the dominant firm in the aircraft industry "selling more than 50 percent of all multi-engine transports in the United States, to both airlines and the military."[13] One can begin to imagine the American worker loading his family members into a mini-plane or helicopter and flying up to his mountain cottage every weekend. Technically, as well as economically, it could have been done. "In those years alone, Ford could fill, in six months of normal manufacture, the entire aircraft industry's need for the next four years." But that would make little sense from the national security standpoint.

While the public argument between the West Coast military airplane manufacturers, such as Consolidated, and the Ford Company, was over the clash of management philosophies and other minor business cultural differences, the heart of the matter had more to do with the unavoidable limits of private business when in collision with security guidelines. In fact, massively available flying machines would have created a *borderless national space*, with all the subsequent vulnerabilities from within as well as from without. Given those hair-raising considerations, mass production and marketing of flying devices in an unregulated environment was undesirable. The airplane industry was to be a special-purpose, military-industrial manufacturing sector.

The commercial transportation business would instead be based on the surface system of highways and small cars. And therefore, in only a few years, by 1933, Ford had to close its airplane business and leave the field to huge holding companies that coordinated their policies with national defense interests. "Even before the Second World War, the aircraft industry was extraordinarily well coordinated, controlled, and dependent upon a military patronage that it cultivated assiduously."[14]

The contrast between the successes of the nurtured defense industries and the orphaned, withering civilian industrial base is significant. In 1967, more than 60 percent of the United States' imports consisted in raw materials and energy (such as petroleum), food products, and industrial supplies; automotive and capital goods accounted for only 18 percent. By 1987, the import of capital goods went up to almost 40 percent while the import of input materials dropped below 40 percent. "In 1987, 21 percent of the cars sold in the United States were made in Japan, another 6 percent were made by Japanese companies in the United States, and another 9 percent were imported from other foreign countries."[15]

In steel production, consumer electronics, computer chips, machine tools, industrial equipment, and so on, the United States' loss of its leading position was making daily headlines. Truly, part of the explanation rests with (1) the "substantial and pernicious oligopoly" in industry after industry and an "ingrown management preoccupied with disciplining labor and managing rather than

Table 4.4
Survey of Scientists and Engineers' Estimates of Occupational
Defense-Dependency, 1986

Occupation	% in Defense Work
Aeronautical and Astronomical Engineers	68.7
Oceanographers	50.0
Physicists and Astronomers	33.9
Electrical and Electronics Engineers	31.6
Metallurgical and Materials Engineers	24.2
Mathematicians	20.3
Physical Scientists	19.9
Mechanical Engineers	17.6
Other Engineers	17.6
Nuclear Engineers	15.8
Industrial Engineers	13.4
Computer Scientists	13.2
Atmospheric Scientists and Meteorologists	9.7
Statisticians	8.9
Civil Engineers	8.2
Chemists	7.1
Chemical Engineers	5.0

Source: Ann Markusen and Joel Yudken, from unpublished data from the National Science Foundation's Survey of Scientists and Engineers.

servicing the market." But it can be attributed as much to (2) the "diversion of top engineering talent" away from the civilian industries and the related absence of a massive, nationally coordinated consumer goods R&D policy. [See **Table 4.4.**] Cannibalized by foreign-equipped steel mini-mills, by foreign-made numerically controlled machine tools, by foreign-made high-tech consumer electronics and so on, the neglect of the American civilian industrial base had also been a result of (3) the conscious decision of the "designers of an 'industrial policy' that orchestrated the decline of America's 'sunset industries.' "[16]

The Aeronautical Industry

In fact, aeronautics was a military industry almost from the day the Wright brothers built their first plane. In 1908, the Army Signal Corps placed the very first order for flying machines. But the First World War had the major effect on the emergence of the industry – the U.S. government ordered 25,000 airplanes. In just ten years, by 1918, $350 million in public money was spent on 14,000 military airplanes, built by a work force of about 175,000 people. At the same time a new government institution was created, the National Advisory Committee for Aeronautics, whose purpose was to further the science and technology of aeronautics and to advise the military and other government agencies on aeronautical research.[17]

Still, after the end of World War I, despite the enormous potential represented by a consolidated industry ready to be converted into a vibrant civilian enterprise, aircraft manufacture did not succeed in securing support from the market. The collapse of military demand meant a collapse of aircraft production from 14,000 units in 1918 to a mere 263 units in 1922. The commercial support system was nonexistent. The government-initiated airplane trade association, the Manufacturers Aircraft Association, alone sought further involvement of government in promoting the establishment of a commercial industry. Its initial plan can best be derived from a 1919 report compiled by the American Aviation Mission to Europe, which included manufacturers, military officers, and War Department personnel, and which was drafted by the general manager of the Manufacturers Aircraft Association. The report concluded that, "For economic reasons, no nation can hope in time of peace to maintain air forces adequate to its defensive need except through the creation of a great reserve in personnel, material and producing industry, through the encouragement of civil aeronautics. Commercial aviation and transportation development must be made to carry the financial load."

The solution was to have governments sponsor the formation of an airmail system, either by granting funds to private enterprises or by direct underwriting of such operations until they became self-sustainable. "It also recommended a complete infrastructure program of airports, weather reporting, flight control, and regulation to be paid for by taxpayers, plus a program to conserve aircraft factories by a 'well defined and continuing program of production for military and naval purposes, over a period of years – long enough for commercial aviation to get a fair start.'"[18]

The subsequent attainment of the recommendations was the Air Mail Act of 1925 that boosted aircraft production from 789 units (342 civilian; 447 military) in 1925 to 1,186 (654 civilian; 532 military) in 1926; to 17,000 units in 1940; and to 96,000 in 1944. At its pre-cold war peak, the aircraft industry accounted for 12.4 percent of all manufacturing employment. At the same time, some big winners such as North American, later Rockwell, managed to invest some $5 million of their own money in order to obtain an additional $79 million in direct governmental subsidies.

Yet, for the second time in its short history, the aeronautics industry went from boom to bust in just a few years. From one million employees in 1944, it fell to a quarter million by 1948. Commercial sales fell from 35,000 in 1946 to 2,500 in 1951 as the civilian demand for the new means of public transportation had been created by neither government nor private industry. As had happened after the First World War, the war economy partners – the private and the public aviation industries – parted again. Ford and General Motors closed their aircraft operations. Hughes, Lockheed, Boeing, Rockwell, General Dynamics, and Martin Marietta closed ranks and shunted away the vagaries of the commercial markets.

At this juncture the emerging cold war created an opportunity to access renewed flows of public funds into the military air industry. By providing fixed capital (land, buildings, and equipment), direct payments, and loan guarantees, the government went so far as to build plants directly or to fund their operation by contractors, all paid with taxpayers' money. Over the years, a country within a country emerged. The Gunbelt was a patchwork of cities and towns strung out along three major centers. Los Angeles was the "undisputed capital of cold war industrial design and production." Washington, D.C., served as the "defense services capital." Boston stood out as the "leading military-educational complex." Based on geographical, economical, and cultural segregation, the military-industrial activity was disconnected from the civilian sector as well as from whole stretches of American society. New England (with three time the national per capita in military aircraft spending, making most of the aircraft engines), the South Atlantic and Pacific regions (26 percent in 1984 of aircraft spending, making most of the aircraft frames) were heavily dependent on defense-related R&D and procurement receipts, higher, respectively about 175 and 157 per cent of the national average per capita, than the east, north and central regions that had only 14 percent. Maryland and Massachusetts universities benefited from 60 percent of all univer- sity-based military R&D funds, principally the Applied Physics Lab at John Hopkins University and MIT's Lincoln Lab and Draper Lab.

The location of military facilities for the missile industry, military electronics and communications software (Route 128 on the outskirts of Boston held 1,800 computer software companies alone, and together with California's Silicon Valley dominated the field), closely followed the pattern of the aircraft industry. If at times military aircraft were not in immediate demand, nevertheless the renewed expansion into as yet unexplored air hardware demanded even more ingenuity. The missile technology, armor and antiarmor technology, propulsion and guidance systems, satellite, surveillance, target recognition, electronic warfare, cryptography and war-game simulation, C³I systems, and extraterrestrial aircraft industries, and all of their support facilities, were just taking off.

The Air Industry's Support Industry

From the very beginning, air power was dependent on the support system offered by the full availability of navigation instrumentation, communication, information processing, and so on. The development of an aviation industry required dramatic and urgent breakthroughs in a series of hitherto exotic physics and other nontraditional science fields. Science became synonymous with advanced engineering as scientists were asked to design the blueprints of the wireless radio, radar, the computer, and all of those wonderful gadgets that made this century the *electronic age*.

The wireless radio made Marconi a household name and gave the U.S. Air Force its first chance to break away from centuries of warfare by long-range delegation. Now, the fighting unit, the pilot, was acting on instant instructions as the arm of the central commander. The fighter pilot was the eyes of his commander as the flow of information connected the action in the air with the calculating strategic mind on the ground. This opened the first chapter of modern war conducted by *remote control*. Nonetheless, the human automaton in the aircraft cabin, serving as the most advanced sensor (of battlefield configuration, enemy moves, weather conditions, airplane performance, its speed, altitude, and technical functioning) and action trigger (where to aim, when to fire) was still the essential factor.

To enhance the fighting capability of the wings, man's own limited reliability needed to be enhanced, his nature-given capabilities expanded, and the machine's and the pilot's performance upgraded. One by one, each task performed by humans was relegated to electronic robots. First, technical innovations were geared to the on-board installation of better aircraft monitoring instrumentation, navigation aids and, not the least, flying superiority. As radar replaced the eye and radio teleprinter links recorded on paper the objects of observation, all of these devices together brought the decision-making process closer to the ground command.

By the time World War II began, most of these basic monitoring features were already working on board fighter planes. The next priority was to have them interconnected and synchronized by a powerful computational machine. The idea of an electronic computer was a most natural outgrowth of the flying war machine combining high speed, precise detection, and accuracy of response under time constraints.

> First, the need to coordinate radar, searchlights, and directions to antiaircraft artillery and pilots required expanded computing ability. Radar-related research also pioneered high-frequency electronics, upon which computers later relied heavily. Second, the need to crack codes, used by all belligerents for long-distance, radio-based communications, enhanced the desire for massive computational capacity especially during the Second World War. Third, new demands from aeronautical research, so much more complicated than landed vehicle or even ship design, fed the pressure for innovation in business machines. Finally, paper work had snowballed, and officers found themselves increasingly unable to cope. The information explosion demanded a shortcut to the computational and storage capacity of the human brain.[19]

The emergence of the computer medium, which made it possible to integrate the multiple elements of combat action in the air with decision making on the ground, revolutionized the nature of war. It soon became feasible to design completely unmanned means of remote warfare action: missiles, satellites, reconnaissance monitors, et cetera. Later on, computer technology also revolutionized the nature of human forces of production in general, and it opened the window of imagination to the possible civilian use of computer automation.

During the cold war rivalry, each high-tech implementation by one side led to an escalation in the efforts of the other side's military research and development department. The increasing complexity of systems of navigation, communication, and control, linking the air, the land, the sea, and the underwater-based weapons and the successive levels of centralized command necessitated by a multitude of immensely destructive weapons, all demanded increasingly more sophisticated engineering. "War planning has mushroomed into a highly complex exercise: thousands of programmers create simulation of missile attacks under a multitude of assumptions about equipment, position, speed, targets, and capabilities. The proliferation of problems in the guidance and communications area has created a new specialization, colloquially known as C^3I, or 'C-cubed-I'-command, control, communications, and intelligence systems."[20]

Once approved, the new systems were implemented in military-dedicated production facilities. Unregulated by such magical economic concepts as demand and supply, and indifferent to cost competition or budget constraints, specialized military manufacturing pursued one single aim: innovative engineering. Separated by walls of secrecy and by geographic dispersion, the American military industry accumulated over the years an increasing percentage of qualified engineering and scientific personnel, the top graduates of academies, the most advanced technological machine-tools from around the allied world, and a qualified scientific approach to its management. Its secretive nature, in permanent fear of inimical intrusion, made its experience unavailable to the nineteenth-century-style civilian commercial establishment.

By 1965, the cold war economy accounted for 20 percent of the nation's manufacturing output,[21] and by 1992, "four out of every ten workers in factory America work[ed] for or in the security department."[22]

Hardly a single management concept or major technological innovation was introduced by American private in the last half of the twentieth century that did not come out of the military's, innovative, *flexible production* techniques. The list of innovations derived from the military is long. At the process level, the new proficiency in product distribution management developed by the so-called "operation research" during the Second World War replaced the *wholesale merchandiser* with the *product distributor* based on palletization, containerization, and warehouse slotting, with exotic statistical quality control methods advocated by Deming and others. This method was first successfully adopted by the Japanese car manufacturers. Crazy-glue and Teflon, fiber optics and sophisticated Internet networking – all came out of the above-mentioned research efforts.

(1) The electronics industry owes much to the academic geniuses of the 1930s, but it owes as much to the military, whose interest encouraged their efforts to support the deployment of on-board radar by developing components to modulate high-speed, high-frequency electrical pulses. The transistor, semiconductor, and integrated circuit were conceived in response to the request for improved performance, miniaturization, and higher capacity. The basic photolithographic techniques used to etch integrated circuits, printed circuit boards and wave-soldering techniques, magnetic amplifiers of various types, magnetic thin films, plate wires, tunnel diodes, superconducting films, and the parametron were all developed in the early 1950s through NBS-administered (National Bureau of Standards) army contracts.[23] As late as 1959, a Senate committee estimated that 85 percent of U.S. electronics research and development was paid for by the federal government.[24] *All* of the early semiconductor production, and integrated circuits, went to military shipments.[25]

The shifting importance from steel and electromechanic components toward the electronic components, in the making of an airplane, brought significant changes not only within the structure of the air defense contracts, but in the cost of components (the electronic gear on a satellite costs more than the launch vehicle itself). It shifted trade from one leading group of manufacturers to a novel industry. The new military contractors were electronics firms rather than airframe manufacturers. Raytheon, Western Electric, Bendix, Hughes, Emerson, Sperry-Rand, and Honeywell started as electronics manufacturers, while others, Rockwell, Martin, Northrop, Lockheed, and General Dynamics converted themselves overnight into high-tech contractors.

(2) Newer among the list of strategic industries, and the fastest growing sector, communications infrastructure and equipment manufacturing, was even more dependent on government leadership due to the complex interplay it required among the standards and methodology of various previously discrete industries. About 50 percent of its output served military contracts (radar warning receivers, surveillance radars, advanced NATO IFF-Identification, Friend/Foe systems); the entire field was dependent on government standards, allocation of airwave bands, frequencies, and regulations on the use of existing avenues.

(3) The computer symbolized, for the whole post–Second World War generation, the incontestable success of the entrepren-

eurial American spirit, but despite military money and a massive effort to build a computer industry, the intervention of the military establishment went *against* the current interests of private businesses such as NCR, the largest electrical manufacturer at the time. "The navy begged NCR, promising considerable subsidies, to capitalize on its wartime lead by continuing to make high-speed analytical machinery after the war. But NCR declined; it was eager to resume its prewar office equipment business, which was high-volume, low-risk, and profitable. IBM was so preoccupied with its role as a maker of electric accounting machines that it saw no commercial market in computers."[26]

Finally, money and the power of persuasion gave military aerospace companies the final push and convinced IBM and Honeywell that there might be some profit to be made by servicing government requests for R&D on computing machines. And they never looked back.

* * *

There are numerous ways to illustrate the decisive role that the military, as an arm of the government, played in the development of an advanced ACE industrial complex in the United States. Ann Markusen and Joel Yudken document this involvement in an exhaustive analysis of the government contribution to R&D, through preferential buying, direct ownership in the industry, its direct and indirect subsidies, training, low-cost capital, management of interfirm cooperation, export promotions, and domestic market protection. It is worth remembering that as of the early 1980s, the Pentagon had invested about $18 billion in plant and equipment, with a replacement value of $100 billion. Its holdings included 146 plants, 60 percent of which were in the hands of contractors. It owned a considerable portion of contractors' facilities, including most of the plant space and equipment in the munitions and strategic missiles industries, and one-third of the plant space and equipment in the aircraft industry.[27]

Over 70 percent of all the sales by the infant electronics and computer industries through the 1950s were accounted for by the U.S. government, just as up to 77 percent of aerospace sales in the 1980s were made to Uncle Sam. *The defense procurement policy assured the virtual socialization of the most vital, dynamic, advanced, and competitive sector of the American economy.*

Contrary to the evidence provided by the underperforming, neglected civilian industry, strategic American know-how has been developed relentlessly under a proven industrial policy approach. As long as it was the platform for the critical technology of future industrial leadership, the United States' military technology had no rival in the Western Alliance. Noncommercial military-industrial operations and high-tech culture had reached nowhere near such a systematic and powerful level of integration – except for the Soviet Union's parallel military-industrial complex.

THE SOVIET UNION'S MILITARIZED ECONOMY

There were many different angles from which one could have been persuaded to view the state of affairs in the Soviet Union. The most prevalent of all took a deprecating position that focused on the Soviet Union's shortcomings in order to argue the Western story of a destitute system of unlawful warmongers, mobilized to take over the democratic consumer society. Needless to say, the reality was far more intricate than that.

By any comparative measurement, the Soviet Union was economically a backward country throughout modern history. But also, by any comparative measurement, the same Soviet Union was the only nation that could engage in an all-out war with the United States, and possibly win. Its overall economic underperformance was compensated for by its exclusive concentration on a first-rate technological base used for its very strategic long-term philosophy.

A good illustration of this paradox, which endured throughout the arms race, against all expectations (according to the Cartesian Western mind), is the state of computer science in the two countries' top laboratories. While still relying on vintage vacuum-tube-based mainframes, Soviet computer programmers in the mid-1980s were producing faster executable program modules than the Americans with their high-powered microchip supercomputers.[28] While less endowed with state-of-the-art manufacturing facilities, high-tech resources and chain stores selling computer components, the Soviets simply took a different approach to the military-economic race.

Since the ultimate goal of the arms race was the *destruction* of the adversary by whatever means, it was always easier, cheaper, and more effective to resort to mutually assured obliteration than to make the effort to be mutually competitive. As the only two nations to emerge, at the end of the twentieth century's carnage, unconditioned by any exercise of superior power over their behavior, the Soviet Union and the United States had to make the rules all by themselves. The exchange of ideological polemics over the heads of their mystified citizens was only meant to mask the real conflict. Two asymmetrical giants squared off: the large and resourceful, but relatively poor Soviet Union, and the technically advanced and rich United States. The Soviet Union's ideology reflected the fact that it could only afford guns or butter. The United States' ideology boasted that it could afford both guns and butter. (Or, at least, so it believed for a long time. Then, following the Yom Kippur War in 1973, out of Machiavellian-like manipulations of oil prices came a dramatic reversal between the two nations. The quadrupling of the United States' energy bill was a cause of the sharp decline in its military buildup. At the same time, the Soviet Union "inherited a large and unearned fortune" as high oil prices coincided with the development of the Tyumen oil and gas fields.[29]) At this juncture the Soviet Union moved up its own military effort to a level that annulled the historical disadvantageous rapport of forces between the two superpowers and ensured virtual parity in nuclear and conventional forces by the late 1970s.

The inequality of the effort invested into the goal of military superiority showed its real dimensions only after the end of the cold war. Information that defied commonly held Western beliefs surfaced in the offices of the Soviet government. The militarization of the Soviet economy during peaceful times was unparalleled by any modern industrial society. Prime Minister Nikolai Ryzhkov, a moderate in the reform movement of Gorbachev's early technocratic elite, gave a first candid account of its extension at the time of its dismantling. "The military-industrial complex does have considerable potential. Conversion requires a certain investment, but this is within our power. Which assembly lines should continue producing weapons and which should be used to produce civilian production is not really a problem. That we have calculated. The ratio between military and civilian production at present is 60-40. Now, as conversion proceeds, by the end of 1990, the ratio will be on the order of 50-50. By the end of 1995, I guess that ratio will be 40% military and 60% civilian output."[30]

For, in the Soviet Union, the military sector of the economy did not have the luxury of rendering a dual service. Civilian spin-offs had, in the short list of priorities, hardly any role to play. Military industrialization was limited only by the social elasticity of the response to calls for sacrifice and belt tightening in the name of war communism. Policy disagreements were only over the extent of additional sacrifices to require, given the natural endurance level of an exceedingly enduring nation.

The arguments and the debates carried on among the Soviet army's high command and its General Staff, during many decades of war economy, can be understood only within the context of this peculiarity of the Soviet economic organization.

* * *

The Red Army was established during the inflamed days of the 1917 revolution, and the Soviet General Staff was the creation of Frunze in 1924, when it was called the Staff of the Workers' and Peasants' Red Army. It changed its name to that of General Staff in 1935. In 1936, the General Staff Academy was set up. During the Second World War, the General Staff functioned as an executive agency for the Supreme High Command, being responsible for "coordinating actions in areas such as operations, intelligence, transportation, logistics, and communications."[31] Its role in the postwar period was increased, as it was charged with strategic planning for all of the military services.

Between the chief of the General Staff and the political leadership of the Soviet Union, the minister of defense played the role of an accommodating interface body. The political establishment and the military establishment mostly converged on the general goals of Soviet society, yet they differed often on tactical and strategic approaches to those goals.

In general terms, the political elite sought a negotiated relationship with Western interests, which would have given the Soviets access to technology, on the one hand, and would ease the burden on their defense efforts, on the other hand. The approach also played well with the Western readers of the Soviet mind. In order to separate propaganda from meaningful *historical* information and to understand the *historical* framework and the *historical* choices facing a nation at war, James McConnell as quoted by Dale R. Herspring offers an excellent insight.

It is a peculiar form of inflated Western self-esteem that turns a literature read for profit in the Soviet Union into a performance for its own benefit. Moscow is, of course, aware of alien eavesdropping; hence, much of the rigid propaganda conventions, the misleading statements, guarded language that borders on the opaque. The substance of the message is not affected, however; the Kremlin cannot afford to deceive its own cadres. If disinformation be defined as communication that the Soviet elite, skilled in reading the literature of its specialty, would declare to be untruth, then there is very little disinformation in the Soviet press.[32]

One could not easily determine the Soviet leadership's unrecorded convolutions and anxieties between accommodating the West and confronting it. While it was expressed mostly in terms of weapons parity, the cold war anxieties reflected rather the military perception of its technological advances and the subsequent level of economic support for furthering the *technological arms race*. In all truth, the arms race during the cold war was indeed the race for new physics-based exotic technology of the next century.

In this high-stakes search for future know-how, there was less and less room for consumer goods markets and old-fashioned business rituals. Thus, while the Soviets and the Americans both lost their edge in the VCR industry to the Japanese, they preserved and further increased their dominant positions in space technology, nuclear power research and technology, communications, supercomputers, and metal technology.

* * *

During the postwar period the Soviet leadership adopted two distinct approaches to military strategy: its technological base, and the nature of preparedness for fighting a future war. This difference in military thinking had a profound impact on the structure, the priorities, and the results of the Soviet system as a whole.

After nine years of tense nuclear cold war engagement between the United States' and the Soviet Union's leaders, a historical reversal came close to a reality in May 10, 1955, at Geneva, the first summit of the two heads of state since 1945. Rescinding their own militant stance, Soviet negotiators "accepted the Western plan for manpower ceilings, reduction of conventional armaments, and the Western timetable and technique for the abolition of nuclear stocks and for the reduction of all armed forces. Most unexpected of all, the Soviets agreed for the first time to Western plans for inspections, including on-site inspections with permanent international control posts behind the Iron Curtain."[33] The Summit opened with the memorable pronouncement made by Eisenhower that "The time has come to end the Cold War."

But it was the irreconcilable split within the American establishment that made the only lasting imprint from this first attempt at closing off the cold war. Factions included *(1)* the partisans of *containment*, often from the traditionalist *farming belt*, midwestern conservatives such as Treasury Secretary George Humphrey ("No business entering into little wars. If a situation comes up where our interests justify intervention, let's intervene decisively with all we have got or stay out"), who later on rallied around Barry Goldwater, the senator from Arizona; *(2)* the *"military-industrial complex*," which instigated for the limited nuclear war doctrine, *peace through strength*.. "Very powerful nuclear weapons can be used in such a manner that they have negligible effects on civilian population," it argued in the name of *total engagement; (3)* the influential oilman Nelson Rockefeller's Council on Foreign Relations and its *Prospect for America* manifesto autographed by Henry Kissinger, Dean of the school of *realpolitik* and undersigned by, among others, Edward Teller, Lewis Strauss, and Gordon Dean of General Dynamics. Finally, there was the Eisenhower administration's more internationalist branch of *(4)* the *old (protestant) Eastern (financial) establishment* that stood behind the concepts of *rapprochement and détente*. Their open-minded efforts to impose budgetary limits on military spending and reverse the ominous emergence of the *"military-industrial complex*," were doomed to failure, then and later, despite the unique political advantage they enjoyed in the 1950s and after.

For the next thirty or forty years, American cold war policy-making was played as a kind of ping-pong among this foursome of jockeying interests. In the first round, powerful opposition from the traditionalists killed the disarmament conference. In the next rounds, the Rockefeller group had control over the rhetorical terms of East-West negotiations as both Richard Nixon and John F. Kennedy ditched Wall Street to formally espouse Rockefeller's Special Studies Project, which became Panel II's foreign policy guidebook. Yet the highest seat of authority resided with the Wall Street group until the last days of the cold war.

For the time being, back in 1956, the first unheeded joint

superpower calls for global peace and disarmament reverberated throughout the world only to be squelched by the Hungarian clamp-down of that same year, and by the Arab-Israeli War.

These events were followed by one attempt after another for the next thirty years, under several U.S. presidents, all derailed by the uncompromising hawkish opposition coalitions (at great loss of prestige for the presidency).

The dramatic second phase of disarmament negotiations, came close to an agreement, again, before the four-power summit scheduled for May 1960 in Paris ended with the ugly U-2 episode. But Khrushchev's platform, spelled out before the Supreme Soviet on January 14, 1960, asserted that "large standing armies, surface navies, and fleets of bomber aircraft were becoming obsolete."[34] From now on, he said, arguing in favor of a new national security course, nuclear weapons were to be the basis of Soviet military strength.

> Given the present development of military technology, military aviation and the navy have lost their former importance. This type of armament is not being reduced but replaced. Military aircraft are being almost entirely replaced by rockets. We have now sharply reduced and probably will further reduce and even halt production of bombers and other obsolete equipment. In the navy the submarine fleet is assuming great importance and surface ships can no longer play the role they played in the past.[35]

Khrushchev undertook the first resolute change of direction from the Stalinist militarization of Soviet society at large. He went from liberalization of the political climate to relaxation of the obsession with internal security matters, to limited economic decen-tralization and freeing of local initiative, to a regime of détente with the United States and to the so-called humanization of Communist regimentation (communism with a human face). Ironically, dismal disappointment accompanied all of those attempted improvements. The economy slowed its growth rate, the expected tech-nological boom did not materialize, military readiness weakened, industrial competitiveness leveled off in comparison to the rest of the industrial world and, even more worrisome, the expected lowering of global tensions was met by an unprecedented belligerence in superpower nuclear posturing.

Given the experience of the Cuban missile crisis, the United

States' abandonment of total reliance on nuclear weapons, and the fact that Russia's own military General Staff opposed it (Marshall Matvei Zakharov was forced into early retirement in 1963 for resisting it), Khrushchev's so-called *one-variant strategy* underwent a full reappraisal in October 1964 at the Plenum of the Central Committee of the CPSU.

Brezhnev's coming to power in 1964 signaled an end to the loose leash on Soviet leadership. The task of the new minister of defense, Marshal Grechko, was now to develop a national capacity for operating on both nuclear and conventional levels and to catch up with the United States in both fields. In his own words:

> In recent years successes in developing the economy, in science and technology have made possible the creation of a powerful and qualitatively new material-technical basis for equipping our army and fleet with new weapons and have led to an all-round reorganization of our armed forced. As a result of this fundamental reorganization in military affairs, the military power of our country has significantly increased.[36]

The military soon found that the new thinking meant a real and fundamental change in the country's allocation of resources, and a decisive pursuit of new technology for the benefit of conventional weapons. The budget allocated to producing new technology increased by 8.2 percent in 1967 alone, and by 15.2 percent in 1968. Shortly, the T-62 main battle tank was introduced along with the Armored Personnel Carrier (BMP), an infantry combat vehicle, mobile antiaircraft weapons and new tactical missile launchers. In addition, a motorized rifle division was now assigned to each tank army and air systems were upgraded. Improvements were made in logistics. For the air powers, airlift capabilities were enhanced by the introduction of new models of MIG-21 and SU-7; for the navy, air and submarine arms were modernized and expanded, helicopter carriers, surface ships, and amphibious capabilities were added.[37]

Not surprisingly, the key to this new approach to military modernization was science and technology. Grechko himself emphasized the simple fact that without exploiting science it would be impossible to build a modern military: "In the course of resolving our army, perfecting military art on the basis of the newest military technology, Lenin's statement that it is not possible to construct a modern army without science is particularly appropriate."[38]

As a result of the high command's new directions, according

to Herspring, Soviet interest in advanced technology during that period centered on four main areas: the effect of technology on all aspects of warfare; a new technology-driven interaction between natural science and military affairs; increased demands on personnel; and pressure for major changes in command and control.

The dominance of army interests over the civilian was argued without restraint. According to Soviet military writings, in the twentieth century "the defense industry is paving the way to scientific-technical progress."[39] And while the military buildup went further ahead under the adamant commitment of its defense minister, Marshal Grechko, the civilian economy became almost an auxiliary sector of the military-industrial complex. Forty-two percent of the entire output of the defense industry was destined for civilian use in service of the military,[40] instead of the other way around.

Truly, the economy was giving signs of weariness and sluggishness, but at the same time the West was also signaling for the first time its readiness to enter into a less confrontational relationship with the Soviets, and so the first round of the arms race ended with the reciprocal acceptance of the principle of strategic parity or equality. When Nixon signed the first SALT I treaty in Vladivostok in 1974, the Soviet Union could celebrate its first postwar superpower success. *For the first time in history, the Soviet leadership, heir to Russian imperial expansionism, negotiated from a position of strategic parity.* Yet, from the perspective of the General Staff, nuclear parity was unsatisfactory as long as conventional forces still lagged behind the United States.

In fact, most Western analysts agree that "during the later half of the 1967 Moscow achieved strategic parity. But despite the impressive gains the Soviet military had made by 1970 in modernizing and expanding its military. . . dual-capable systems were still being developed, and the technological gap vis-a-vis the West remained wide."

The effort to close that remaining gap would consume the willpower and the resources of the USSR for the next twenty years. In Malta, in 1989, the USSR was able to sit the United States down and sign the most comprehensive and radical worldwide system of mutual security arrangements based on the concept of the new world order.

* * *

As early as 1970, the General Staff set up directives for the new generation of high-tech conventional weapons. In Marshal Grechko's words, "great efforts are being directed, as before, toward creation of new – as well as improvement of existing – conventional types of weapons." Such weapons, he argued, would make use of new types of materials and explosives, new sighting and guidance systems, laser electronics and computer technology.[41] References to the importance of science and technological revolution are abundant and unambiguous in the outlines of the Soviet high command. The idea is that the tie between technology and military affairs had become "closer and more diversified," science and technology are "the determining factor in the revolutionary changes in military affairs," that "scientific-technical progress has forced a fundamental transformation in the technical equipping of the armed forces and their organization, and in all systems of political and military education."[42] Technology, Grechko went further, was "the catalyst of all transformations in the means and methods of conducting wars. The nature of war and military preparedness was being driven by developments in "the physical-mathematical sciences, nuclear physics, solid-state physics, electronics, radiophony, cybernetics and metallurgy."[43] Such an acute sense of urgency and of the critical significance of exotic technologies in the early 1970s defined the challenges that the Soviet economy had to face through the 1970s and the 80s. And those options were explicitly military and high-tech; none of them were to include civilian beneficiaries.

By 1971, 45 percent of officer positions were occupied by engineers and technicians as the use of automated systems, operations research, systems analysis, and decision theory methods were appropriated from the general sciences and applied to routine military planning and operations. And while civilian heavy industry's development was still critical to the strengthening of the Soviet army and navy, the same thing could not be said about the consumer goods industries, devoid of technical personnel, material resources, and financial backing.

The Soviet economy was feeling the pinch, as shown by the still-declining rate of industrial growth. Newspaper columnists in the West took it as the early sign of the Soviet system's much prophesied demise. Yet, the Soviet military's achievements during this period were significantly underestimated. Soon after the signing of the SALT I and Anti-Ballistic Missile (ABM) treaties on

strategic arms, the all-out race began between the two superpowers for superiority in conventional and tactical military technological. Indeed, after the death of Grechko in 1976, the appointment
of Ogar- kov as the new chief of the General Staff was an early
indication that the Soviets perceived their efforts to have paid off,
as they came closer to conventional parity with the United States.

* * *

During the wholesale redesign of the United States-Soviet
Union pact during the early 1990s, the events that had taken place
in the mid-1970s within the Soviet high command, immediately
following the signing of SALT I, seemed very remote. Yet it was in
the 1970s that, for the first time in its history of unabashed militancy,
the Soviet leadership selected the executive directorate of its
military-industrial complex on the basis of non-military credentials.
Both the new defense minister, Ustinov, and its new chief of the
General Staff, Ogarkov, were masters of the bureaucratic-
technical apparatus, familiar with the demands of running the
offices of the corporate Red Army, rather than uniformed soldiers.

The Communist party's Political Bureau and its general
secretary, Brezhnev – the board of directors of Russia's largest
single internationally successful enterprise, 'Red Army Inc.' –
undertook a momentous reassessment of the competitive advantage of their holding company in the race with the United
States. They examined the need to redesign its structure, strategy,
and its fluctuating but astutely designated targets, by promoting
well-tested veterans of the proven enterprises' competent
management.

Against the traditionalist free competition approach to the
arms race and scornful of the arms control policy that Grechko and
Kulikov had heartily championed, the political leadership of the
Soviet Union concluded that a sui generis Superpower Antitrust Act
struck with the rival Pentagon would be a better alternative. A
rational regime of superpower-managed competition would more
likely keep the world at peace. It would also restrain the American
military buildup and would allow for a modest flow of technological
information in the Soviet Union's favor. It would permit a better
reallocation of the Soviet Union's limited internal resources and, not
the least, it would reinforce the industrial character and function of
the Soviet army as one of the world's leaders in advanced new age
technology. Both Ustinov and Ogarkov subscribed to this broad

new way of thinking, although they disagreed on minor points.

Ustinov's only brush with military service was a one-year stint in the 1920s as an enlisted man. He spent the rest of his life in civilian clothes. He worked for the Soviet military-industrial complex as a high-ranking manager, responsible for the development and production of an increasingly wider variety of the Soviet weapons systems. "Eventually, he rose to the position of minister of the defense industry. Indeed, if there was a military-industrial complex in the Soviet Union, he was its chief."[44]

For his part, Ogarkov came from the uniformed armed services. Yet his unit's coat of arms had no arms on its blazon: his was that of a technical services officer. He was an army engineer.

A top corporate manager and an elite operations engineer, Ustinov and Ogarkov had little to share with past generations of Soviet military-cum-political appointees. Both outstanding technocrats, one seasoned through a life-long career as chief executive of the vast complex of military-industrial enterprises, the other, both a technician and an exceptional military intellectual and theorist, their primary mission was to integrate the complex technological developments, the strategic security objectives, and the available economic base into a fully effective, Soviet-style, yet modern, committed and utmost competitive corporation.

The Soviet leadership decided early on that the key to its international success would be increased reliance on aggressive technological research and relentless innovation. This would result from developing a home-grown Soviet meritocracy based and continuously nurtured on the latest advances in science and technology. The Soviet long-term strategic goals and its conventional maneuverability, mobility, and sustainability could be attained at once by streamlining the officer corps, removing inefficiencies and duplications, integrating army branches and the military industry, and by reallocating budgetary spending.

Ogarkov set out to modernize the Red Army's operational capabilities. He ended up by setting in motion developments that went far beyond military operational readiness. His comprehensive approach to economic management, technology, and national leadership within the international balance of power, of conflict escalation, its theater of conflagration, arms control, and super-power confidence-building measures – all set the stage for the historical geopolitical redesign that was accomplished later on under the dual leadership of Gorbachev and Bush. Indeed, that was a vast undertaking. The Soviets' bargaining strategy for a future Russian power in the new world order was envisioned by its military establishment, implemented by its military establishment and overseen by its military establishment. (That became the acknowledged political reality of the new, democratic Russia, under the leadership of Boris Yeltsin. He was a veteran of the Soviet military-industrial complex, First Secretary of the Sverdlovsk Oblast – its heart, headquarters and holy seat for the last 25 years of the Soviet arms build-up. The highest ever military technocrat to directly take over the reins of power in Russia, Yeltsin made that move in the guise of the reformed anti-military, anti-bureaucratic, anti-establishment, anti-party populist maverick.) It required an unparalleled effort of integrating all the civilian and noncivilian resources within Soviet society. In essence, it would determine how the available assets were to be utilized and subordinated to the overriding goal of conventional arms parity. Ogarkov made this clear:

> New forms of advancement of scientific research in military training, institutions and the scientific establishments of the USSR Ministry of Defense are developing. There is a strengthening cooperation with the USSR Academy of Sciences, scientific-research institutes, design bureaus, and other scientific centers not only in our country, but in the other socialist states. The comprehensive study of military-political, military-theoretical, military-technical, and military-historical problems is achieved through joint efforts.[45]

As the world of superpower posturing moved further away from a strategic standoff to what is called *theater operations*, it became more apparent that major changes were also underway within the Soviet military organization. Organizational streamlining, occurring under Ogarkov's watchful eye, and more focus on exotic weapons made it possible that in the long run Soviet military efforts would become less costly and therefore more in step with the Western level of resource allocation. And that would not be good news to America.

By the beginning of the 1980s, the net result was that Soviet conventional forces were capable of striking deeper and harder than their earlier forces. The inventory of frontal aviation aircraft increased by about 50 percent. In association with the added assault helicopter force, motorized rifle, heavy artillery, and multiple rocket launcher (all on the order of about 100 percent augmentation), this meant that "targets within 30 kilometers of the forward line of troops can be engaged with these heavy artillery weapons or by hind assault helicopters,"[46] giving the Soviets for the first time the capability of conducting parachute, heliborne, or air and land operations in enemy rear areas.

Contrary to the traditionalist view about the Soviet political establishment, a sea-change took place in the tone of the military calls for revolutionary modernization. "Think new," became the army battle-cry as "past experiences cannot be blindly copied and mechanically introduced into contemporary practice. . . Life urgently demands that we make certain corrections in the theory and practice of military affairs."[47] "The military leader must look ahead."[48] "Every military training establishment must display greater concern not only for military-technical training and the instilling of high personal ideological-political and moral qualities in students, but also for shaping in them the ability and skill of a future personnel educator, instilling a taste for conducting educational work in subunits and units and on ships."[49] "The old control methods can no longer meet such requirements. In this respect, the automation of troop management through computers plays a greater role. In turn, success in the use of automated control systems calls for raising the level of military-technical standards of commanders, the scientific organization of the work of staff, and efficient communications at all levels."[50] "Under new conditions, the work of the staff produces increased demands on the level of theoretical, operational-tactical, and technological preparation of staff officers, who should be distinguished by high qualifications and staff culture, by a deep and detailed knowledge of their subject."[51]

It was recognized by the high command and unremittingly repeated to their fellow staff members that modern warfare was becoming a highly centralized, complex operation based on sophisticated technological and organizational equipment.

> In connection with the equipping of the armed forces with a series of types of nuclear weapons, missile technology, and new means of communications and electronics, the staff has become more multifaceted and responsible, but the conditions of its work have become even more difficult. In the most developed armies the staff masters automated systems of command and control, including computer technology, immediate and secure communications: in the practical work of the staffs, new methods of work are being introduced.[52]

Such statements carried significant weight when measured against the remarkable advances that the Soviets brought to their military's level of technological sophistication at that time. At the peak of 1977-78, the Soviet military could feel confidently superior to any outside threat. Its high watermark was reached in May of 1977, at the time of Ogarkov's last boisterous comments on the fighting potential of the army under his command. He made it clear that "our glorious army and navy now have the most modern combat equipment and possess everything necessary to fulfill the tasks facing them."[53] Two years later, a major change in his public pronouncements, a reversal in the rate of military spending, new rhetoric from the political leadership, and a series of inconsistent international events signaled to the keen observer that the inconceivable had become the actual.

Decisions were made in the year of 1978 at the highest level of the superpowers' political leadership, inexplicable to the general public and unbeknownst even to the uniformed military. (It is a subject of wonder how the Soviet army's chief of staff himself could have been left out of the decision to invade Afghanistan.) The consequences of the grand change of course of the arms race became apparent to the world at large only some twenty years later. Boris Yeltsin's total control of the technocratic, political, economic, military leadership gave a sense of the over-powering influence that the non-uniformed branch of the political-military leadership could command over the civil society even as the uniformed rank and file military personnel was decimated by peaceful means, at once with the party and the adminstrative bureaucracy.

In spite of the evidence of a renewed American military buildup – the controversial green light given by the Carter administration to the costly delivery of the MXs, the Trident IIs and the B-1s, as well as NATO's decision in 1987 to adopt the Long-Term-Development Program that eventually brought Pershing IIs and ground-launched cruise missiles to the European war theater – the the Soviet political leadership reversed its support for an all-out defense buildup. Although the defense establishment's mouthpiece, *Red Star*, continued to call for a tough stand and for coming up with ways to accommodate the civilian industry as part of the country's overall efforts at strengthening its defensive capabilities, the political establishment, in the editorial pages of its *Pravda*, was running emasculated arguments on the merits of improving the living standards of the civilian people as the most critical goal of the Soviet apparatus. Open discontent on the part of the general staff was met by the political establishment with a self-deprecating emphasis on the suddenly discovered food shortages and consumer disaffection.

As if to prove the point, street riots and agitation in Poland called international attention to the Soviet consumer's previously unheard of plight, and honest working-class folk were seen on prime time television arguing for bread and butter against the ruinous obsession with security matters. Propaganda masters in the western fringes of the Soviet empire exploited the mass appeal of promising better housing and consumer satisfaction, and even challenged the foundations of the legitimacy of the poor workers' state. An even more extraordinary event took place on the southern border of Soviet power. Just when average citizens' hopes were being raised by public questioning of the credibility of further defense programs at the expense of the deteriorating overall economic situation – the Brezhnev administration, over the heads of his military advisers, embarked on a mindless military embroglio in Afghanistan.

In combination, the events were to open a debate on the validity of the military option itself. The specter of possible spiraling civil disorders within the Soviet state was matched by the ineffectual use of arms against a minor but strongly national external counter-resistance. What the Americans bitterly experienced in Vietnam was re-enacted now against the Soviets' sense of honor and invincibility. The generals had to cope with unforeseen circumstances. Their plans did not provide that their enemies were to be their leaders, operating from within. (The same thing had happened to the American army ten years earlier. Yet the loss of face in Vietnam was fully compensated by an eminent strategic victory: it stopped Chinese expansionism at the expense of bringing the Soviet advance posts further south, from North Korea, to a virtual encirclement of China. That proved to be the only argument that persuaded the Chinese leaders to enter into the world's balance of power triumvirate as the United States' "China card." With America's traumatized troops evacuating Saigon, American political artists Richard Nixon and his Secretary of State Henry Kissinger were landing at the Beijing People's Airport sporting briefcases filled with new plans to sell against the Soviets.)

To students of Soviet military policy, the unprecedented change in tone of the military establishment's pronouncements stood out as one of those inside stories that Kremlinologists like to digest. Within one year, the tone had gone from unconditional support of the country's political leadership and of its foreign policy, to open opposition to its new orientation in quest of détente, and new moves accommodative to the newborn Western counteroffensive. "Shortly after taking over as chief of the General Staff, Ogarkov published an article in *Sovetskaia Rossiia* that was almost euphoric in its praise of the arms control process. . . Up until the end of 1978 he was supportive, although he had begun openly expressing his concerns over events in East-West relations. After that point he began to move toward increasing opposition until by the end of 1980 he was openly opposing the line advocated by the political leadership."[54]

In fact, for all of the wondering world, twenty years later it became obvious that something more than myopia or simple leadership sclerosis, or, even worse, ideological surrender, was behind the unexpected gamesmanship on the part of the Politburo's highest priests. Cries of betrayal were muffled at first, and a certain confusion set in as the war in Afghanistan bogged down to its unwinnable conclusion. Yet as early as 1980, Ogarkov summed up the situation that was yet to come: "the situation at the start of the 1980s has become noticeably more complicated and is presently characterized by extreme instability, unexpected turnabouts, and a distinct tendency toward intensification of the aggressive aspirations of the imperialist countries and China."[55]

Missing from the all-powerful General Staff's knowledge at that time was the choice that the central executive Politburo already had made in mutual agreement with the American administration. In the same year that decisions were made on the principles of global coexistence, Brezhnev made an unusual visit first to Baku and then, on his way back to Moscow, he stopped in a small train station for a brief encounter. He was accompanied by his constant adjunct Chernenko, and they met in the modest train station hall with two other fellows. One was Andropov, who thus introduced the unknown and relatively young Gorbachev to world history. The conversation apparently took less than half an hour. At that moment, however, the configuration of the future of the cold war, of the new House of Europe, of the principles of the global marketplace, and of the new world order were already, in broad outline, designed and concluded.

Two months later, Gorbachev moved to Moscow.

DÉTENTE

When Gorbachev set out to move the country in a new direction, as was expected, he put forward the doctrine of sufficiency as was advocated by Ogarkov. He called for a stronger, more dynamic arms buildup based on scientific-technological breakthroughs that would remodel the Soviet military on a new spirit of initiative, creativity, and competence and make it the centerpiece of a homogeneous and high-tech, utterly 'sufficient' fighting force. *In fact, he presided over the dismantling of the Soviet armed forces as a bureaucratic state within the state* in order to turn them into advanced technocratic forces.

From 1978 on, Soviet reliance on military-based postwar industrialization was intentionally diminished and finally dismantled. In the rhetoric of economic reform and under the guise of reinforcing its fighting machine, the new Soviet leadership was actually encapsulating the poison pill to be used for its military's euthanasia. Already politically compromised by the Brezhnev administration's well conceived mission to defeat and dishonor in Afghanistan; ideologically obsolete in the minds of a new generation of technological professionals; economically uncompetitive in the emerging world of international civilian markets; financially unsustainable given the size of the Soviet economy; administratively cumbersome; resource-wasteful; a growing gangrene on the body of the civilian society – the armed forces were judged by the year 1978 to have reached the end of their pre-eminent role. This conclusion was obvious to the upper levels of the intelligence community within the Soviet political hierarchy. Only the dangers of Bonapartism, always present, were never more real than at this fork in the road, between the path toward total militarization or toward arms control.

Motivated to escape the costs of a renewed arms race and the limits imposed on both superpowers by their militarized economies (when measured against the successes of the reborn Western Europe, and Japan), the task of disengaging was far more challenging even than a continuation of the status quo. The immense ramifications of a fifty-year buildup will require at least twenty years for both the Soviets and the United States to dismantle.

While the Soviet Union had to face nationality problems,

European competition, and chaos at the very least, the United States' establishment had to prepare its nation for the replacement of its military industrial-backbone with a capitalist, centrally planned economy and government-led industrial policy. A vast and well-coordinated educational process of each one's constituents, allies, foes, and potential opportunists required time, confidence-building measures, proof for the nonbelievers – the vast majority, unversed in the workings of social engineering. The Soviet masses had to be exposed to the creative forces and the individual responsibility that come with market economics. American citizens, fervent believers in the all-healing powers of individualism and unregulated com-petition, had to be reminded of the lessons of the painful depression syndrome of the 'morning after'. And above all, in order to make good use of secret technologies developed in military laboratories, they would have to be brought to fruition publicly as shared social exploits. Yet, before the long-term benefits were to be proven, the inevitable social disruptions brought by the brutal break with a rusted status quo and the induced pain on millions of ordinary people, required having a massive fine-tuning apparatus already in place for the occasion.[56]

In the United States, all through the years of the cold war, there were very few politicians, Republicans or Democrats, conservatives or liberals, who were opposed to the cold war in principle and who supported the end of the arms race. Far greater in number were those who had opposed even the slightest attempt to improve United States-Soviet relations. It was, therefore, a bold move to hire Ronald Reagan in the straw-man role of the Great Crusader, as a cover-up for the enlightened minority elite, working from behind George Bush.

Ronald Reagan waved a magic wand, signaling a return to a fairlyland lost era. The frenzy of the 1980s pumped new blood into the sclerotic American dream. Then came Gorbachev, who outperformed the old actor. He opened the Berlin Wall and made all the crazy geniuses from behind the Iron Curtain pick up their instruments and play the cacophony of freedom on national television.

The world turned upside down for a long, long decade. The blind were leading the foolish. And the mad were given air time and were elected to governmental decision-making positions. An unprecedented scene, the world was left in the hands of the naïve and the state guest house was left open to the incompetent and the corrupt, the spin doctors and the demagogues.

As early as 1983 Paul Nitze, during a visit to the Soviet Union, listened to Gorbachev (who at that time was Secretary of Agriculture in the Brezhnev administration), relating his quest for a thorough investigation of the state of affairs of the Soviet economy and of the reform plans being drawn up upon his soon-to-be made nomination to the top position. "And at that time," says Nitze, "we understood all well that the cold war was over. For us, the negotiators, the war was, by then, over."[57] Testing the boundary between politics and theater, Ronald Reagan's 'evil-empire' oratory took place on March 23, 1983, after the negotiations were already, in principle, concluded.

From 1978 on, the relevance of the Soviet military high command unraveled more and more into the ambiguous chapters of the *politics of reform*. Akhromeyev, Yazov, and Grachev were weak spokesmen for the interests and the autonomy of the General Staff. Obscured by endless political maneuvering between domestic interests and the superpowers' bluffing at the bargaining game, the military leaders lost out to diplomatic considerations. In 1984, less than four months after Ogarkov went to great lengths to hammer home the urgency of improving the "existing strategic as well as operational and tactical means of waging the armed struggle," emphasizing the new physics-based conventional weapons against the reliance mainly on nuclear weapons, he was unceremoniously ousted.

His calls for a new round in the all-out conventional arms race describe best the actual state of affairs in both superpowers' developing arsenals in the mid-1980s. It is characteristic of the Soviets' way of addressing their domestic audience to acknowledge their own security plans and military undertakings through the depiction of the adversary's dangerous arms race escalation. One can read Ogarkov's remarkable monographic chapter on the achievements of the electronic and automated military systems that were actually being assembled by the two superpowers.

> Rapid changes in the development of conventional means of destruction and the emergence in the developed countries of automated reconnaissance-and-strike complexes, long-range, highly accurate, terminally guided combat systems, unmanned flying machines, and qualitatively new electronic control systems make many types of weapons global and make it possible to increase sharply (by at least an order of

magnitude) the destructive potential of conventional weapons,
bringing them closer, so to speak, to weapons of mass
destruction in terms of effectiveness. The sharply increased
range of conventional weapons makes it possible immediately
to extend active combat operations not just to the border
regions, but to the whole country's territory, which was not
possible in past wars. This qualitative leap in the development
of conventional means of destruction will inevitably entail a
change in the nature of the preparation and conduct of
operations, which will in turn predetermine the possibility of
conducting military operations using conventional systems in
qualitatively new, incomparably more destructive forms than
before.[58]

Future events made it more and more plausible that the new round
of the arms race had been temporarily shelved by both armies'
high commands even before the political covenant was worked out.
And after the detailed plans were signed off, that generation-old
arsenal was put on public display in the high-tech Desert-Storm
war, directed for a TV audience world-wide and brought to its
dénouement with the spectacle of the signing of the new treaty on
the future world order.

But before that, the disagreement between Ogarkov and the
Brezhnev leadership was exposed to public view beginning in 1981
and centered on the utility of the arms control process. Both sides
were critical of the West in general and of the renewed Reagan
escalation of military spending. However, the dispute was over
more than minor interpretations of U.S. policies. "Where Ogarkov
argued that the arms control process was bankrupt and that the
key to defending Soviet security interests was therefore a
strengthened Soviet military, Brezhnev, Andropov, Chernenko, and
Ustinov consistently maintained that however bad things might be
for the moment, improved East-West relations remained a viable
alternative [emphasis added]."[59] From the General Staff's
perspective, it made little sense to respond to the U.S. military's all-
time budget increases with a focus on consumer goods, yet,
against all rational expectations, the political leadership engaged
in a campaign of mobilizing consumer demagoguery against the
apparent national security imperatives: "What we are talking
about – foodstuffs, consumer goods, the services sphere – is a
question of the daily life of millions of people. . . It is according to
how these questions are answered that people largely judge our
work. They judge us strictly, exactingly. And, comrades, this must

be borne in mind," (Brezhnev, 1981); "Raising the people's standard of living" (Andropov, 1983); or "Further increases in the well-being of the working people" (Chernenko, 1984).

Where the Soviet high command, for all appearances, saw naked U.S. provocation and unwarranted preparation for aggressive positioning, the Soviet political leadership continued to advocate support for détente and for a slowdown in military spending, according to Brezhnev's line that there was "no rational alternative to détente."

To add insult to injury, the removal of Ogarkov from his position in September 1984 was explained by claiming he had exhibited "unpartylike" tendencies. The truth of the matter was that he stood in the way of the next chapter in the implementation the Soviet-U.S.'s rapprochement policy. As Georgi Arbatov describes the situation: "In the late 1970s. . . our military policy and arms industry had completely escaped political control. The leadership made the decisions, but the military and the military-industrial agencies prompted those decisions and even managed to 'preprogram' the political leadership. Shaped and executed under the cloak of secrecy, military policy ceased being an instrument of our foreign policy and acquired a life of its own. Naturally, détente could not tolerate such a state of affairs for long."[60]

Only one year later, in 1985, entered Gorbachev. His philosophy was *perestroika*: "the truly revolutionary, comprehensive transformation in society." Five years later, the Soviet Union would cease to exist.

* * *

Whether or not hard evidence was readily available to permit an accurate evaluation of the cold war's dark chapters and of its secret agencies, of the innumerable misleading 'leads' poured out of the daily media, or of the distorted – if highly regarded – official statistics, a full report is still owed to generations to come. The historical monograph of the cold war, based on hard facts and not on speculative interpretations of circumstantial evidence, is yet awaiting the great synthesis of a future time.

For the world at large, the victory of democracy over evil dictatorship was accepted as the correct interpretation and celebrated without any fact checking. The Soviets, it was said, just folded up their war tent and closed the military bases and the nuclear complexes.

The numbers were all mixed up on their (and our) charts. Did they have 20,000 nuclear warheads or 30,000, or 50,000? It all depends. In 1989, the Washington-based Nuclear Weapons Databook, in a 443-page volume on the Soviet Nuclear Weapons series, gave the CIA's estimate of some 33,000 along with Defense Secretary Caspar W. Weinberger's estimate of 46,000. But in an update in 1993, Americans found that "The quantity of weapons-grade uranium accumulated [in Russia] is very great' – 1,200 metric tons of uranium highly enriched – enough to make 75,000 of the atomic bombs that destroyed Hiroshima. Moscow's stockpile was 1.5 to 1.7 times larger than the combined stores' totals held by the United States, China, France and Britain."[61]

In fact, compared with the 17,000 warheads in the U.S. arsenal at the time, the Soviet arsenal crested in 1986 at 45,000 warheads, a number that gives a better sense of the Soviet war machine's out-standing performance. Amazingly enough, the actual Soviet stockpile nearly matched the Western estimate at that time of a total of 50,000 nuclear warheads for the U.S., Russia, France, Great Britain, China and Israel combined.

Table 4.5

Warhead stockpiles as revised by the Russian Ministry of Atomic Energy: 1945 to 1993 (The New York Times, Sept. 26, 1993)

According to all the available information, in 1978 for the first time (and only briefly), the United States and the Soviet Union reached a strategic parity level [see **Table 4.5**]. Indeed, the Soviets were said to have been left behind by the Reagan era's effort at "restoring U.S.'s military industrial potential and developing and technically re-equipping its army," as Ogarkov warned. The truth of the matter is that the United States had to prepare its own people for the hour of awakening. And that meant the accepted loss of its previous strategic superiority. It had to prepare its constituencies for the turnabout in its military commitments, which amounted, basically, to yielding to Soviet control over the battleground of the entire stretch of European lands.

* * *

In retrospect, the costs of the Cold War were immense. Agreement is unanimous on the social damage and economic underdevelopment that it brought to large social sections of the engaged parties. But there is a brighter side to it also, which can be assessed only indirectly and in the long run. The value of the top-secret technological breakthroughs to be released to ordinary consumers over time can only be appraised as their compounded ripple effects accumulate.

We already know about some of the new gadgets. The Soviet Institute for Structural Macrokinetics, specialized in high-temperature, created superconducting powders purer than the powders commonly made in the United States. "And the Soviet fabrication process is much faster, taking place in seconds rather than the several days required for conventional processing."[62] Having no resistance to electricity, they are valuable components in electric motors, power transformers, and the like. They were introduced on the American market in 1990. There are entire fields where Soviet research institutes have proven their world-class technology and science. Among them are nuclear fusion-based power generators, high energy lasers, optical equipment, gallium-arsenide solar-power cells, surgical stapling, magnetic casting of aluminum and the synthesis of polycarbonates, metal-coating processes using titanium nitride at relatively low temperatures, and radiation detectors that can measure one-tenth of a millirem of radiation, fifty times as sensitive as the lithium fluoride detector used in the United States.

Yet, far more remarkable, the Soviet space industry stands almost unique in the world. Items on the block include nuclear reactors, satellites, rocket engines, space stations, plutonium for compact power sources and a host of scientific reports on space testing and experiments.[63] Second only to their military hardware, the Soviets' space enterprise was known to be the world's largest, most active, and most advanced. And while they lagged in many aspects of the world's technological revolution, especially those relating to computers and electronic miniaturization, they were well ahead in others. "For instance, its scientists have mastered the manufacture of high-strength, high-temperature alloys that are virtually unknown in the West. These metals can be important in the design of advanced rocket engines and nuclear reactors, which generate tremendous heat."[64]

American behind-the-scenes military hardware successes are no less impressive. Many of the military technologies backed by DARPA, the Pentagon's research agency, have found wide civilian use. The following are some examples. *(1)* Data transmission: In the 1960s DARPA funded development of packed switching, which breaks computer data into tiny bits and routes them over networks in the most efficient fashion. Civilian spin-offs exploded in the 1970s and 1980s, including well-known networks like Telenet, Tymnet, and Internet. *(2)* Lasers: Since their initial demonstration in 1960, DARPA focused on developing laser materials and high-powered devices with the idea in mind of the Star Wars' antimissile defenses. These were later applied to a variety of industrial uses. *(3)* Stealth weapons: DARPA helped create new radar-evading aircraft by developing new materials, shaping strategies, and flight prototypes. A dispersive coating used on the B-2 bomber and the F-117 became the standard material on advanced cookware known as Teflon. *(4)* Computer chips: DARPA fostered the field of computer technology and advanced critical areas of materials science that turned semiconductors into the computer chips at the heart of small weapons and personal computers. *(5)* High-temperature materials: DARPA-financed research pioneered work on advanced crystallography, including titanium-based alloys and nickel aluminide. *(6)* Composites: DARPA's materials-science push was essential in developing the high-strength, light-weight composite materials that are found in everything from tennis rackets to jet aircraft. DARPA has been involved in research on complex weaves as well as random arrays of particles and fibers.[65]

Three consecutive war-led bursts of development in

production techniques and technologies have provided the modern world with big gains in its overall handling of complex, large-scale, integrated problems and have led to unconventional solutions to man's ambition to control his destiny. The First World War gave us the airplane, the radio, the assembly line, the telephone, plastics. The Second World War moved us forward into the electronic age and provided us with computers, social rationalization, the space industry, automation, palletization. On the Third (cold) World War, the jury is still out. The space society, genetic medicine, and universal interconnection, might push the next generation into the age of a genuine Star Wars.

Chapter V

The Global
Economic Scene

THE DRAMATIC DECLINE OF THE SOVIET UNION

Whether or not the arms race would have continued any longer, given a better Soviet economic performance, is an open question. However, arguably more important to the advent of Soviet *perestroika* were the external economic developments. If one argument for *perestroika* was that the Soviet Union's economy had been diverted and handicapped by the excessive military contest with the United States, another was that the USSR had been weakened by insufficient contact and economic competition with the advanced industrial world.

Awareness of the decline of the Soviet Union relative to world economic standards undoubtedly helped to increase the sense of an impending crisis. For, not only had the Soviet Union slipped in its share of world product, it also occupied a lowly (fiftieth to sixtieth) position in world per capita consumption, and compared badly in some respects even with czarist Russia. According to A.S. Zaichenko, for example, meat consumption in urban areas in 1913 exceeded that in the USSR in 1985.[1]

The Soviets' meager four percent share in world trade might not have played an important role in *perestroika* either, had it not been coupled with a conviction that isolation was partly responsible for Soviet Russia's international decline. Furthermore, the composition of its trade was reminiscent more of a Third World country, with energy accounting for over 60 percent of exports. The foreign debt itself was not excessively huge by comparison, 34 billion rubles in 1990. However, the Soviet economy needed far better revenue from the foreign trade. Export earnings could have been far more important for her economic performance including purchases of foodstuff and manufactured consumer goods.

Despite, or perhaps because of, the fact that the obstacles to integration into the world economy appeared quite formidable, economic objectives came to figure increasingly importantly in Soviet foreign policy, starting with Shevardnadze who even called on Soviet diplomats to "economize" Soviet foreign policy.

A new foreign trade system, joint ventures, et cetera, were among the measures intended to help boost export capabilities and educate Soviet managers. But, although neither joint ventures nor other production cooperation schemes were likely to make a major impact on the Soviets' economic integration with the rest of the world, they could act as catalysts of wider domestic economic modernization. Interest in joining international economic organizations such as GATT was another element connecting the domestic and international dimensions of *perestroika*.

The Deteriorating Leadership of the United States

At the end of 1989, the United States' assets abroad totaled $1.412 trillion, while foreigners owned assets in the United States worth $2.076 trillion. That was a historical reversal coming in just one year – in 1988 the United States ran a surplus of $531 billion, as communicated by the Commerce Department on July 2, 1990.

West Germany was the world's biggest exporter for the first three months of 1990. With the dollar low against the mark, the United States redeemed its eroding position for only one year, in 1989, after being surpassed at high speed by West Germany in 1986. Yet the United States remained the world's biggest importer by far, soaking up $125 billion worth of foreign goods for the same period of time compared to only $78 billion for West Germany.

Japan had surpassed the United States in per capita gross domestic product, $22,855 versus $20,766 in 1989, and no matter what system of measurement one might have used, the overall trend was clear.

And all of this was happening at a time when the American rate of productivity was improving at an anemic pace of only 1-2 percent annually as against 4-5 percent productivity increase by its economic rivals.

> If economic growth is a function of high productivity, and if productivity results from investment, and if investment only comes from savings (private or public), then high military 'dissavings' directly impinged on U.S. growth. Nuclear deterrence, more than forty allies to support and spending on conventional weaponry represented high opportunity costs for the continuing progress and prosperity of the American economy. Over the long term it probably represented a recipe for American and Soviet decline relative to other nations.[2]

Definitely, the arms race by itself changed the entire economic power balance on a global scale. By the end of 1980s, it was obvious that a slow but relentless deterioration in their position of world leadership was affecting both of them. The only viable solution was to agree to settle the score the score and work out a mutually beneficial pact.

* * *

In the 1990s, the debate over the depth and the chronic character of America's economic decline (the belief that something was fundamentally wrong with the U.S. system), while an accurate reflection of economic reality, was fueled also by the rapid economic and social changes. The real issue was the competitive decline relative to other advanced industrial nations, coupled with an increased domestic social inequality. From a Star-Wars-style Keynesian economy (massive military buildup), to supply-side market socialism (massive public borrowing), and then back to a capitalist depression (the stock-market crash), all of these sudden course changes were accomplished in the name of the same voodoo rhetoric of the roller-coaster Reagan years – genuinely times of megaconfusion.

Finally, the hour of serious intellectual reckoning marked the end of the twentieth century.

After all, where was all this heading? What was the long-term strategy and what should be the short-term tactical maneuver in response to immediate pressures? Was the world opening up to a genuine global economy, or was it just redrawing its borders, reallocating the spheres of influence into more rational partitions? Were those the days of an information-centered entrepreneurial society, or of some form of entrepreneurial government acting as the unifying force between private versus public interests?

Certainty about the future was hardly sustainable. And the headlines of the day were like the weather bulletin. From moral malaise to boisterous Reaganomics, then to the stock market crash, to the four trillion dollar budget deficit, to socialized health-care reform, the roller-coaster of mass conversion was a grand scale exercise in instant popular manipulation.

In fact, it came as no surprise to anyone who questioned the dire predictions of the 1970s, in the Club of Rome's manifesto *The Limits of Growth*, to find in the 1980s that the pursuit of affluence was in fact unlimited. All of a sudden, it was rediscovered that: (1) economic competition was more important than political, (2) free trade among nations was almost like trade within the nation-states themselves, (3) telecommunications was the new infrastructure of the global village, (4) there were no limits to growth, (5) there was no energy crisis, (6) there was a global trend toward "downsizing" as the road to efficiency, and (7) America's decline was only a myth.

New interpretations of the statistic-juggling were out. Contrary to the mass media's leitmotif of trade deficit, in fact, "In 1986 foreign branches of American companies sold $720 billion worth of goods overseas, seven times the so-called trade deficit for that year. Almost 20 percent of the merchandise imported into the United States is manufactured by foreign branches of American companies."[3] Which only points out the ambiguous nature of the argument. Considering the total sales of U.S.-based firms, regardless of their location, "Commerce Department economists calculated that the U.S. would have posted an overall trade surplus in goods and services of $164 billion in 1991, rather than a $28 billion deficit."[4]

As for the much decried "budget deficit", the subject of decade-long political hysterics, it suffices to mention that: "By 1890, at the top of America's initial economic development, the United

States was a net debtor of $2.9 billion, nearly 4 percent of its total national wealth at the time. . . [In 1990], according to U.S. Commerce Department data, the U.S. net "debt" represents less than 1.4 percent of its total wealth."[5]

One thing seemed certain – as the world was undergoing a profound transmutation in the aftermath of the cold war, so were the forgotten centrally planned economies. Socialism, which at one time looked as if it might take over the world, now faced an implacable challenge: change or perish. A few new socio-economic trends which were widely recognized. (1) A global economy had emerged that would no longer allow any capitalist or communist region to remain isolated and self-sufficient. (2) Technology, especially telecommunications, had effectively made traditional borders obsolete. (3) The new distributive management, based on the computer, made centralization a dinosaur. (4) Changes in demographics required new approaches to welfare spending. (The ratio of working people to pensioners had declined dramatically since the end of World War II, in the United States from 32 to 1, to 3 to 1). (5) The full-scale shift in the work force as a percentage of labor in manufacturing was heading toward zero. (6) The growing importance of the new species of knowledge workers was creating a new social class, the entrepreneurs.[6]

Yet, most significant, a different sort of limitation was afflicting the rate of growth by now. It was the one natural resource that was more limited than any other. And that was human labor.

THE QUESTION OF LABOR SHORTAGES IN THE MODERN ECONOMY

The very idea of a shortage in human labor is something that, ever since Malthus, was fashionable to discount. The focus had been on the plight of the so-called reserve army of proletarians more than happy to sell their, socially in excess, labor-power. Everyone 'knew' that there was a surplus of labor, rarely a shortage. However, since the days of industrialization, the truth is that labor was in deficit.

It started with factory workers, virtually nonexistent in the

agrarian societies of preindustrial Europe. In a population forced to
devote its entire work reserves to the procurement of basic food
necessities, there was little left to be employed in the
nonsubsistence industries such as textiles and foundries.
Moreover, even in very Malthusian terms, the population was in
excess only in relation to the available supplies of foodstuffs and to
agricultural output. This was a cause of human tragedy but not the
source of a stable and productive factory employee. In other words,
if there ever was a reason to contemplate the existence of a surplus
population, it was surplus only in relation to the existing
agricultural productive potential.

'Surplus' population was conceived in Malthusian terms as the
ones excluded from the social banquet for lack of place settings
and destined to a tragic social obliteration. From this landed-class
perspective, these 'surplus' workers were condemned to death by
starvation, due to natural constraints. Now, in a pure gesture of
magnanimity, they were saved by the manufacturing class in
exchange for their industrial labor. The value of their labor was
worth enough to be traded for foodstuffs on the open international
markets with other supposedly less overcrowded nations.

In fact, historical evidence shows a different reality.

To the Egyptians, who used their available human resources
for extravagant purposes, there was little notion of a surplus
population. Actually, there was a shortage of hands relative to the
ongoing large-scale construction needs.

In an exceedingly well documented study, *The Class Struggle
in the Ancient Greek World, From the Archaic Age to the Arab
Conquests*, G.E.M. de Ste. Croix offers a rare instance of a
classical Marxist analysis of the socioeconomic history of that time.
His study helps to reinforce belief in the pre-eminence of the
economic causes that must have brought the Greco-Roman
civilization to its conclusion.

Indeed, both the rise and the fall of that civilization
demonstrably can be attributed to such causes. First, there was
superior Greek production – ceramics, coinage, jewelry, metal
working, silver, textile, wine, pottery, and olive oil. Second, and
eventually more consequential, was the ample supply of cheap
labor appropriated from outside the Greco-Roman economy by the
Roman enslavement of the surrounding continent. But what gave
the great impetus to the Greco-Roman economy was also later to
explain its decline.

Briefly, (1) the economic decline of many Greek cities from the end of the fifth century BC onward was mainly due to the contraction of the foreign market for Greek exports, as local production at the periphery of the Greek trading area began to grow.[7] (2) Faced with this deteriorating economic condition, a consensus emerged among the elite classes of the Greek world, first under Alexander the Great, that a decisive reversal could be achieved only by an oligarchic system of organized domination and enforced slave labor. The history of the Roman slave economy was the history of such a system developed to its extreme limits. The enslavement and dependency on the external supply of slaves extended so vastly that when the supply began to some degree to dry up, the effects on the Roman economy, in the words of Max Weber, "must have been the same as that of exhaustion of the coal-deposits on the blast-furnaces."[8]

From the beginning, the Roman economic philosophy was distinctly different in nature from the earlier Greek economy, which had evolved as an organically expanding local industry within the Mediterranean market. On the contrary, the Roman Empire was a predatory, systematic exploitation of the labor force from the world around.

At the end of an uninterrupted string of conquests over almost two centuries, the year A.D. 106 marked the last major successful looting campaign. The pillage of Dacia brought home vast amounts of gold, large numbers of slaves, and control of the gold and silver mines of Transylvania. But after an exceptionally glorious period of feast and jubilation that followed, until about 168, the natural reservoir of riches accumulated over centuries from those plundered foreign houses dried up.

A new reality emerged and that was basically one of prolonged and agonized defensive redeployment of the Roman conquering machine: externally – for the protection of the usurped or expropriated patrimony from the armies of barbarians; internally – for an increasingly costly suppression of dissent.

The first arms race in European history went from an army of about 300,000 men at the turn of the millennium, under the reign of Augustus, to about 400,000 by A.D. 197 (out of a population of about fifty million),[9] to over 600,000 before the end of the fourth century. (That is about the same untenable percentage of men under arms that the Soviets had – 0.87 Romans versus 1.15 Soviets – in the late 1980s, their most economically devastating years of the Cold War – an army of 3 million uniformed personnel out of a population of 260 million.) Yet, from then on, in the absence of any major war booty to cover its expenses and to provide a positive inflow of wealth, the Roman army's balance sheet remained consistently negative, which amounted to a total net loss for society at large.

2. In addition, a new and parallel administrative bureaucracy, distinct from the venal and corrupt civil administration, had to be set up in order to redirect the grass-roots alienation by channeling it into the Christian mass movement. The original Christian movement was not unlike the modern-day workers' unions and, like them, it was first fought against and then bought and manipulated into a loyal partner. Its leadership, made up of a large network of bishops (by the fifth century, over a thousand) and clerics, was not engaged in any economically productive activity. The number of monks and full-time clerics must have been many hundreds of thousands, their income largely derived from endowments in landed estates as well as from regular contributions from the state or the faithful. The large number of economically 'idle mouths' "had to be supported indeed by the same overloaded Greco-Roman agricultural economy."[10] In the opinion of A.H.M. Jones, endorsed by de Ste. Croix, "if the figures we have for the numbers of lower clergy are at all typical, they must have far outnumbered the civil service. . . The staffing of the Church absorbed far more manpower than did the secular administration and the Church's salary bill was far heavier than that of the empire."[11] By institutionalizing and subsidizing its own brand of subservient social workers, the Church clerics, the Romans only anticipated the modern trade union organizations in their pro-big-business labor management, covert propaganda, and charitable functions at a correspondingly high economic cost.

In other words, the shrinkage of the markets, first, and especially the increased shortage of labor, from the second century A.D. on, explains the decline in the overall economic performance of the Mediterranean eco-system (natural resources and human resources as inputs into the total social output) and explains the transition from democratic polis-based Greek political structures to a labor-camp-state run by a more and more repressive Roman oligarchy. It was the diminishing social rate of labor exploitation, relative to the social body, and, therefore, of the total social surplus value (and not the increase of the individual rate of exploitation), that explains the fatal decline of the Greco-Roman civilization.

It was "as a result of slaves being to a large extent bred within the economy instead of being brought into it under exceptionally favorable conditions," that "the rate of exploitation of the slave population as a whole must have diminished."[12] The subsequent intensified exploitation of the nonslave mass, the majority of the Roman population, was a desperate attempt to arrest the irreversible decline. It was not the cause of the already ongoing decline.

* * *

A thousand years later, the process of industrialization required a concerted effort on the part of the governing class to solve the question of social labor allocation and distribution. This involved a high level approach to social management by the decision-making factors in each nation at the time. The main concern related to industrialization was to ensure an adequate increase in agricultural productivity, high enough to account for the diminishing reserves of available human labor now to be divided between its farming demands and the factory demands.

RUSSIAN-STYLE INDUSTRIALIZATION

The difficulties that had to be overcome in the early years of the industrial age are well illustrated by the case of Russia. As Jerome Blum describes in *Lord and Peasant in Russia* (on whose data this section draws substantially), when large-scale factories began to grow in Russia early in the eighteenth century, the entrepreneurs faced the same problems as did England and France in recruiting labor away from agriculture. The situation was exacerbated by the rapidity of factory expansion and the sparseness of the population. Wages afforded by the nascent industry had stayed low, the work was hard and disagreeable, and there was little incentive for the local population voluntarily to join the plants. Contrary to the conventional belief that factory work was a relief from unemployment and from the *lumpen* condition of the suprapopulation, evidence shows that industrialization, from the earliest times, was an organized effort by the government to reassign peasants from their traditional farming duties to industry.

Government-owned factories collared workers from the state peasantry as *assigned peasants*. "Some of them were required to spend full time on these tasks, while others were called upon periodically. The government also put soldiers, vagabonds, and criminals to work in its factories. In plants owned by nobles the necessary labor was furnished by serfs who belonged to the factory's proprietor."[13]

Tsar Peter I also undertook strong measures to supply labor to factories owned by the merchant class, as "the shortage of available free workers placed these middle class manufacturers at a disadvantage." All through this period, the real competition between industry and agriculture required governmental intervention by decreeing the right of plant owners to keep skilled runaways "if they paid indemnities to the owners of the serfs," an act that transformed the former free hired worker into a perpetual servant to the plant. Merchants also benefited "when state-owned establishments were transferred to private ownership [and] the assigned state peasants went along as integral parts of the plant."[14]

The practice of using forced labor extended through the eighteenth century, such that the Urals' mining and metallurgical industries, the largest and most important branches of Russian large-scale manufacturing, were manned almost entirely at the beginning of nineteenth century by assigned workers. "The total number employed in this sector of production rose from 31,383 male workers in 1719 to 312,218 in 1796."[15] Even by the mid-nineteenth century, on the eve of the emancipation, "there were about 201,00 males assigned to mining and metallurgy."

Before 1724, the pay scale was set by agreements between the assigned peasants and their employers, in a show of equal bargaining power of the two. Then in 1724, a ukase of Tsar Peter established uniform wage scales corresponding to the wages of freely hired labor. This had the paradoxical long term result that a multiple tier pay system developed, such that by the late-eighteenth century freely hired workers received double or even ten times the pay of assigned workers .

Underlying the recruitment difficulties encountered by the industry as a whole was the requirement made upon the peasants assigned to plants in the Urals to journey to their work over onerous distances. Sometimes these trips had to be made several times a year over hundreds of versts, at their own expense. "A report made to Catherine II in 1762 by a specially appointed investigator told of peasants who three times each year had to come to plants that lay 400 versts (about 250 miles) from their homes to work for a total of 120 days. Those who travelled on foot for want of horses averaged 25 versts a day and so spent 96 days a year on these journeys."[16]

However, in England and most of Western Europe, the workers were even worse off. They were forced out of their rural households and left no alternative but to join the ranks of the urban proletariat. Studies made by Frédéric Le Play, who pioneered in family budget studies, show that "an industrial system in which the workers lived on the land and drew part of their incomes from their own independent enterprises was preferable."[17] Despite their smaller monetary incomes, the Russian factory households still had higher consumption levels than their counterparts in England, France, and Slovakia.

In addition to the assigned state peasant/workers, serfs too were compelled to work in the nascent private industry. The use of bondsmen became significant only in the second half of the eighteenth century when members of the landed nobility began to participate more actively in manufacturing. By 1825, government data on the size of the labor force in seven branches of factory production show that plants owned by nobles and manned by serfs had 31.7 percent (66,275) of all the workers in these particular industries.[18] Some counted the serf work as *barshchina*, which was unpaid, some paid wages in cash or a combination of both. Some used to rotate work among members of a village so that only a few were full-time factory workers. Some lords who did not own factories, or who had more serfs than needed to work the land, rented their peasants to manufacturers or to labor contractors. Yet, forced or rented work was not a real bargain. It offered the worst kind of unskilled, undependable, and least industrious labor.

A full third of the factory work was made up of hired workers, originally the few city dwellers and the runaway serfs. They represented the truly idle rural population expendable from the travails of land as the growing productivity of the richest black earth lands covered the needs of the least productive farms. The marginally productive western provinces of White Russia were the first to bail out of subsistence farming. Seigniors there were eager to give consent to their serfs to go off and work elsewhere because it increased the serfs' incomes, and thereby enabled the seigniors

Table 5.1[18]

Annual Per Capita Food Consumption
of Worker Households (in kg)
in the Mid-Nineteeth Century

	Urals Ironsmith	Urals Carpenter	Swedish Ironsmith	English Iron Smelter	Slovak Gold Smelter	French Carpenter
No. of Children	4	4	4	4	2	2
Annual Family Income (in francs)	1,165.77	815.62	1,624.21	2,008.85	975.80	2,103.88
Cereals	289.6	212.7	282.9	107.6	183.9	117.6
Fats	3.14	4.6	14.6	8.4	8.0	3.6
Milk	314.3	263.6	257.1	89.1	165.0	40.0
Cheese	-	-	-	3.4	1.4	1.8
Eggs	6.14	2.9	4.3	0.7	2.9	1.4
Meat & Fish	40.7	37.3	60.0	34.3	27.3	27.6
Vegetables & Fruits	109.1	136.4	105.3	53.3	138.6	59.7
Sweetening & Condiments	8.0	8.3	32.1	24.4	5.0	6.5
Fermented Beverages	2.3	141.4	166.8	150.6	28.9	23.0

Souce: Jerome Blum, *Lord and Peasant in Russia*,

themselves to charge higher *obroks* than they could if their serfs depended upon local agriculture alone. The supply of these hired workers was restricted, however, by the extent to which their masters were willing to give them permission to leave their villages; by the degree to which they could still tend their holdings, and the extent of increased competition on the factory market. The result of these limitations in a 'seller's market' surprised Baron Haxthausen, traveling in Russia in the 1840's, with the high pay scale commanded by the Russian factory worker (relative to the rest of Europe) especially in summer time.[19]

Year	No. of Workers	Hired Workers		Forced Workers	
1767	199,300	18,700	(9%)	180,600	(91%)
1804	224,882	61,600	(27%)	163,282	(73%)
1825	340,568	114,515	(34%)	226,053	(66%)
1860	862,000	479,000	(56%)	383,000	(44%)

Russia's constant shortage of manpower forced it to balance a much tighter demand for both agricultural labor and factory labor than the Western European industrialists. A truly open labor market akin to the Western European model did not develop in Russia, which had to resort to an administrative rationing of the available supply. The table above shows the persistent use of forced labor in Russian factories – in fact peasants only temporarily rented by the factory.

Interestingly, although the *percentage* of hired labor increased through the century, the *volume* of *forced* labor also grew considerably.

THE RUSSIAN AGRICULTURAL REVOLUTION

Industrialization was possible in Europe not outside of but because of the agricultural revolution that preceded it. Agricultural advances furnished the surplus of nutritional resources to sustain a larger population. It was possible, only after almost two thousand years of learning how to cultivate continental inland Europe, to match the productivity rate offered on a limited scale by the once rich valleys of the Middle East.

The history of industrialization in Russia proves the same point.

In 1860, almost 99 percent of Russia's population was still dependent on the land. Russian agriculture, marginal on the European fertility chart, was a major culprit in holding back Russian industry. Although traditionally described by foreigners as the fertile Russian granary, data from all periods of history contradict the claim. Nature has been far from generous with the

soils of the forest zone north of the river Oka, where until the nineteenth century most of Russian people lived. This region stretches
northward from Kiev northeast to Kaluga, then east through Riazan,
Nizhnii Novgorod, Kazan and into Siberia, north of the 55th parallel.
Its predominant soils are light gray earths known as podzols. They
have a sandy, clayish, or stony composite, low in humus content
and deeply leached. They need considerable amounts of fertilizer
in order to yield a relatively modest crop. Going south, the fertility
level increases gradually but not dramatically until the treeless
expanses of the European far south alongside the valley of the Don
River, which is known as the black earth, the land of the
chernozem. Further south it fades into the dry steppe of the lower
Volga. If not infertile, then poor in precipitation, that is the land
inhabited by the Russians.

By the seventeenth century, farming began slowly spreading
northwest up the banks of Dvina, only then turning south and
moving into the Oka-Volga triangle where soil was of medium to
poor quality. The grossly inefficient slash-and-burn and field grass
techniques of cultivation were predominant in the frontier regions
and the three-fields system sporadically followed in the center from
the end of the fifteenth century until the second half of the sixteenth
century.

From the sixteenth century through the mid-nineteenth
century, Russian cereal yields were the lowest in Europe,less than
half the rate of Belgium, Holland, Saxony, Great Britain,
Württemberg, and Baden.[20] Yet despite the low yield per unit, the
total agricultural output of Russia steadily climbed during the eighteenth and nineteenth centuries. And, even more important, it
redirected her agricultural development.

From this time onward, a remarkable revolution of Russia's
agricultural base took place which immoderately improved her
chances at joining the select club of industrialized countries. One
was the shift from the older infertile lands, north of the Oka, into the
black earth zone of the New Russia along the middle and the lower
Volga. "At the outset of the nineteenth century the sowed area in
New Russia was estimated to have been 800,000 desiatins, and in
four Volga provinces 1,000,000 desiatins. In the 1860s these figures
had risen to 6 million and 4.6 million desiatins, respectively."[21] The
other was the steady, although still slow, introduction of more advanced farming techniques.

Not just a fortunate accident, the new course in agricultural development was a deliberate government policy, and it explains the unrelenting eighteenth-century expansionist foreign policy at the expense of Russia's southern and western neighbors, Turkey, Romania, and Georgia. Hand in hand with the military offensive on the international front, an organized effort was made through domestic channels to educate and train the estate managers. Under the guidance of Empress Catherine II, discussion groups made up of selected members of the technocratic aristocracy raised popular awareness of Russian agricultural shortcomings – the unacceptably small yields, soil exhaustion and the inefficient methods of cultivation – and proposed ways to change them. The discussion groups were supplemented by a profusion of new periodicals dealing with agricultural matters.

The results, in the long run, were indeed noticeable. An official Russian commission estimated in 1873 that the average annual harvest for European Russia increased as follows:

Average Annual Harvest
(millions of chetverts)

1800-1813	155.0
1834-1840	179.0
1840-1847	209.7
1857-1863	220.0

This new economic fact meant a substantial change in the balance of power in Europe.

For the first time since the Mongol invasions, the Western powers' nearly absolute economic domination gave way to a new era characterized by economic parity among competing nations, East and West.

Furthermore, what had constituted for centuries a fateful Russian soil quality disadvantage and a real cause of tribulation was now compensated by the vastness of its land resources. Exploiting a huge expanse of arable land, beginning in the early nineteenth century, on a per capita basis Russia surpassed every other European country in cereal production. "A mid-century estimate placed the empire's output at 9 hectoliters per capita, Sweden with 6.6 hectoliters per capita, France with 6.3, Prussia with 6.2, Austria 5.7, Great Britain 4.9, Belgium 4.7, and Italy 4."[22] This single fact in itself accounts for Russia's future role among the great European nations.

In her own way, slowly but relentlessly, from that point on, she gathered the strength to shift the center of gravity among those nations in her favor. From now on, Russia saw that she alone had the internal resources to stand up to all the rest of Europe, and she gave way to the national belief that she deserved a special role in Europe. That national conviction came to be more and more prevalent among people of all social conditions, helping in the end to stir up a century-long national debate that looked for ways to bring that self-fulfilling prophecy to its conclusion. Notwithstanding all the confusion and the soul-searching, the Russian nation finally concluded the debate through a revolution.

In national ideologic expression, the decision was made to pursue industrialization by extreme means, at full speed, and out of reach of the perceived Western imperialist intentions. It consisted in the wholesale removal of labor limitations on the way to industrialization. By deviating from the classical Western market approach to an existing Western labor market, Soviet Russia's centrally planned industrialization built on her centuries-old tradition of forced industrial labor. It reversed the rate of growth for free hired labor down to zero, and increased the rate of forced labor to new heights.

The limitations imposed by the chronic persistence of factory labor shortages were removed with the stroke of a pen. In only seventy years the percentage of industrial labor, loosely defined, increased from from one percent to nearly 75 percent of the total national labor force. The new Russian way of implementing rapid industrialization was through the unrestrained exploitation of its only internal resource, its agriculture, modestly performing by world standards yet still resilient enough to support a minimum standard of living across the nation.

Following a different strategy the United States in the same period was assiduously skimming off the best skilled and professionally brightest and most competitive upper echelons of labor from the European industrial nations, under the terms of the U.S.-dominated international labor marketplace.

Between the two now giants engaged in the contest for the best national team players, the issue was clouded in rhetoric over the arms race, the technology race, and the ideology race. In fact, the only real race was fought over the hearts and souls of the working class, professionals, and skilled technicians.

LEVERAGING LABOR THROUGH SERVICE AUTOMATION

The lesson for modern post-industrial policy makers is rich in patterns parallel with the age of industrialization. The latest stage in the economics of "empowerment" of the individual employee was the tidal wave of privatization of the welfare state, a trend which rolled from one country to another in the 1990s. Advertised as the concept of "popular capitalism" in Great Britain, the so-called stockholder-owned socialism in Eastern Europe, and the self-employment trend in the United States – they all were simply revivals of managerial tricks used in the history of European/Russian peasantry.

While the latecomers to the celebration of industrialization were still struggling with capital constraints and limited labor, the sudden rediscovery of a surplus population was the novelty of the so-called productivity revolution in the more advanced countries in the post-industrial years of the 1990s. All of a sudden, there appeared to be too many people competing for fewer employment opportunities in the "making and moving" of things because, it was explained, productivity increases reduced the number of workers needed, to no more that one-fifth of the work force in those countries.[23]

In fact, the demand for labor was so high in that same period that it urgently necessitated industrialization of the tertiary economy, the next labor frontier to be conquered. That would make it possible to reclaim sources of social labor by squeezing out such traditionally insulated pools as clerks and doctors, research scientists, retail traders, managing agents, lawyers, educators, accountants, and telephone operators.

The changing nature of the business activity that emerged under such circumstances became the single major issue in the concluding years of the twentieth century. Faced with the imminent prospect of full automation, whole industries were slated for extinction. That incurred massive social and economic disruptions that masked the real issue – the unlimited economic expansion and the demand for more and more labor, not less – and that required new approaches to economic and social macromanagement.

The 1950s saw the triumph of *The Organization Man*, as it was epitomized in the writings of William H. Whyte in the apparent success story of big business. Nevertheless, by that time the bureaucratic character of the large corporation and its inability to survive a competitive future was understood by a good number of people. The unacceptable choice between corporate bureaucracy and the under-resourced, undercapitalized entrepreneur was the insurmountable issue of the industrial state. Only with the advent of *electronic technology* has it became possible to claim both the innovative entrepreneur and corporation-like resources in infrastructure support. Technological advances began converting factory assembly floors into home-based miniature appliances. The cheaper, telecommuting, virtual home-office worker, a viable new labor species, is becoming the equivalent of the self-sufficient unit of the historic household-farmer.

This is called the *information technology revolution*, yet the major impact is less on technology and more on people, on the work and the skills of the new class of *portable employees* and the corresponding new breed of *information managers*. It is impelling the dismantling of the factory system, of corporate institutions, of educational boards, of economic and financial macromanagement methods, of the state bureaucratic administration, of the political establishment and of international trade rules, and a reassessment of the world order and of assorted international security arrangements.

From a centralized corporate state system to a *distributive electronic farming system* – the call is for a revolutionary new brand of *entrepreneurial labor*. It reclaims the individual act of master work within the context of *social market interchange*. It replaces the collective mechanics of the assembly line with *subcontracted, individualized service*. It reinvents the depersonalized hierarchical organization as the *virtual work village*. It substitutes the industrial army with the *service community*. It replaces command with *expertise*. It franchises ownership rights and the responsibilities that they incur.

The revolutionary entrepreneurial society thus matches up to a genuine New Economic Policy on a large scale and on a long-term basis. It reverses the industrial social employment blueprint, reverting in a sense to the principles of the advanced feudal system of farming, reviving features analogous to the autonomy and the flexibility of medieval Europe's well-tested forms of *retaining*, the renting of the fields, along with *indenture*, the *contract* system and no less, *hired* labor. Then as now, changes in political and economic life worked simultaneously to the benefit as well as to the disadvantage of the employee.

REINVENTING THE FEUDAL WORK SYSTEM

Many Western medievalists, when speaking of feudalism, define it entirely with reference to those few free men who were each other's lords or vassals, united by bonds of loyalty and the creation of benefices in the form of fiefs. Although that narrow usage was connected with the emergence of the peculiar Western European feudal structure, mostly associated with a political form of organization, there is a larger sense to it that rests on a special form of dependent labor, serf labor. In this second sense, feudalism is associated with serfdom and "can exist and has existed in societies which have little or nothing [else] in them that can be properly called 'feudal.' "[24]

As far back as the eighth and ninth centuries, at the time of the ascent of the ruling elite, of the warrior princes and their retinues, over the inhabitants of the Eastern Slavic lands, the economy of the realm was already orbiting around land colonization and the relatively prosperous, communal, frontier farming. At first a band of robber barons in search of prey, war booty, and easy trade, the future princes and rulers of the land were slow in deciding to turn themselves into economic, active factors, taking on the responsibilities of managing complex agricultural communities.

Finally, by the tenth and eleven centuries, the opportunity for profitable agricultural production became evident. As a consequence of the improvements in the techniques of farming and of a rise in industrial production the population doubled and even tripled by some estimates, to 7-8 million in Kievan Rus alone. Active local and interregional trade, the increased use of money, the growth of cities, and an expanding market for farm products induced the warlords to transform themselves into legitimate rulers and proprietors of the source of riches – the land itself. By the middle of the fourteenth century they were in possession of an affluent country that could pride itself on having the largest cities of Europe. Moscow and Novgorod, with a population of about 100,000 each (before the 1400s) were rivals of Milan and Venice, each with almost the same population, but ahead of Paris, with a population of about 80,000 (1378), and of Florence and Kent, with a population of about 55,000 (mid-1400s).

Yet, with the introduction of large-scale private ownership of land, Kievan Rus followed the history of European subjugation of labor. "The available evidence points to the conclusion that into the eleventh century all free men enjoyed a certain amount of equality. But when land that belonged to peasant communes was converted into the private property of a large landowner, the peasants found themselves changed into renters of fields that had been theirs, and some of them were apparently pushed off their holdings and became hired hands, indentured workers, or contract laborers of the proprietors."[25]

In the ensuing power struggle among the princes, ceaseless feuds among their retinues, and the weakening brought by the outside threat from nomad invaders, the emerging system of the Russian economic-political entity collapsed. The realm was divided into weakened princedoms, the population declined, and the power elite lost its hold.

This prolonged time of troubles, however, benefited the entrepreneurial peasants, improved their lot, and strengthened their bargaining position.

The private landowners, like the industrial princes later on, were confronted with a shortage of manpower with the expertise to settle the new frontiers of innovative production and were forced to hold out many inducements to attract the best and the brightest to their establishments. They no longer could command the work of professionals and so essentially turned over their properties to contractors in return for rental payments. They allowed the renter virtually all the rights of ownership over his holdings, so long as he worked them and met whatever obligations were required of him. "The princes and the landowners made these concessions because their political power and their economic well-being depended upon their having peasants on their lands. Had they held out less favorable terms they would not have been able to attract the renters they needed, and their fields would have yielded them no income."[26]

It was a relatively good time for the average 'professional', yet the unsettled political and economic conditions did not operate in favor of the peasant in the long run. By the latter part of the fifteenth century, the status of the peasant renter had deteriorated. In the struggle between the upper estate of the princely court and the nobles, and between church leaders and the estate managers they hired, the need for support from the middle tier persuaded the rulers to give jurisdiction and administrative privileges to landowners. As the Grand Dukes of Moscow established themselves as the absolute rulers of the land, the retrogression in peasant status continued until finally the renter became the serf of his landlord.[27]

Yet the struggle continued. In order to achieve their goal of absolute supremacy, the Muscovite princes now had to overcome the opposition of the great aristocracy itself, and to do so they had to compensate the lesser nobility. Through confiscations and, ultimately, extermination, they destroyed the power of the great lords. They gained and held the support of the lesser landowners by giving them land and peasants in exchange for their loyal services.

The new, full cooperation between the new landlord-managers and the ruling house enabled additional demands to be put on peasants, as competition among the powerful put an upward pressure on prices, opened a flourishing market and an era of opulence and grandeur. These increased demands reduced the peasants to still greater economic dependence upon their lords. Economic hardship intensified in the last decades of the sixteenth century and into the next, as it became essential to deprive their peasants of their erstwhile basic right of free move- ment, in order to further the economic well-being of the seigniors.

But the story has yet another twist to it. The lords themselves had to pay the due price for their privileges, as they were called upon for duty to the higher order of the state. In the unique service state that the Muscovite rulers created, after 1613 each subject, from the greatest to the least, was assigned a role that was determined by the interests of the state. "To this extent, the story of the relationship between lord and peasant and of the enserfment, is the story of the subjugation of both lord and the peasant to the will of the state."[28] At the same time, the long struggle to create a unified and absolute monarchy was also fought by the rulers of France, Spain, and England; it was a pan-European phenomenon.

In temporary alliance with the gentry and the lesser nobility, (now loyal instruments of the tsars against the great aristocracy and the powers of seigniors), the centralization of authority establ- ished a new kind of political organization in which the tsar was the absolute ruler. A form of *agrarian corporate state* was set up in response to the unbearable costs incurred under the system of rival cartels that previously brought throughout Europe the winds of the Time of Trouble and civil wars among the landed oligarchies.

With the new emphasis on economic revival and law and

order, as well as a means to assert the central leadership, the new state order was installed as a bulwark against the deteriorating effects of the political power struggle among the local warlords and old aristocratic families. A corporate ethic was introduced throughout the modern states of Europe.

The absolutist monarchies ruled the activities and obligations of all subjects as they fell under the jurisdiction of the state, from the "greatest lord to the meanest peasant." For administrative purposes, a state bureaucracy was created in order to regulate the useful functions of each division and department within the corporate entity. By spelling out its mandate in clear terms against the dangers of renewed turbulence, the state authority also was prescribing the limits and the substance of the privileges and freedoms that a subject might enjoy only as a result of the functions he was expected to perform for the benefit of the state.

Of all such social constructs in modern Europe, in France, Germany, Austria, Spain, even in England, the Russian Empire state corporation lasted the longest. Before long, all the other feudal organizations started conflicts within themselves. The Russian state's hold on its absolute rule continues until today.

THE INDUSTRIAL TECHNOCRACY

Two major events occurred during that period in the history of the Russian Service State. One was the apparently unprovoked emancipation of the serfs in 1860 by the absolute will of the feudal state itself. The other was the violent claim to supreme power in the industrial state by the newly emerged *industrial technocracy* in the name of the Bolshevik Revolution. Both of them happened as consequences of changes in the social balance of employment, and both of them originated as deliberate reactions to developments taking place outside of Russia.

In both, the central state power had to reclaim its leadership capacity against a collusion of private interests. The old feudal state, weakened by the events of 1860, held on with a defensive half-baked act of land reform. The new industrial state reasserted itself in full vigor after 1917 as an active industrial agent.

By the middle of the 19th century, it was clear to most socially conscious Europeans that a new way of life was in the works. The demand for industrial development, factory workers, capital, and generally nonfarm labor was vital to the survival of a competitive state economic base.

In a sense, the centuries-long trend in Russia's economy is a true vindication of the free-market philosophy, with the qualification that one has to look at the social labor marketplace as a whole in order to find the real interplay of forces: producers vs. owners, laborers vs. managers, farmers vs. industrial workers, working class, vs. ruling class, artisans vs. communes, manufacturers vs. traders, blue collar vs. white collar, unskilled factory workers vs. technical professionals, and so on.

It was this interplay of scarcity versus abundance of one or the other of the elements of the social productive complex that determined the economic, social, and even political forms of organization. There were shifts in the demand for one social group or another as the variable outcomes of geographic conditions, population growth, internal as well as external wars, progress in the development of the means of production, and shifts in competitiveness with foreign nations, had their impact on the nature of the vital activity for the well-being of the social whole from one historical time to another.

As the nature of the essential social component underwent a transformation, so did the rest of the social organization, from its democratic reliance on farming in the earliest days, to the oligarchy of the armed warlords, to the oppressive structure of a European-style state bureaucracy, to the mass coercion imposed by the factory industry, as well as the *war communism* enforced by the military contest. The search for a hidden national character to explain unique political forms, or for some evil forces, common at times among well-intended observers, was but a short-term myopic view when only the long-term view illuminates the nature of economic and social forces at play and their dynamics over time.

From the long-term perspective, one event still might be seen as an accident of history with far-reaching if in some ways ominous consequences. Tsar Alexander II's deliberate act of emancipating the serfs and his inadequate land reform, which failed to endow the newly independent farmers with the required farm ownership, for example, was at least one of the root causes of the Bolshevik Revolution and of the ensuing seventy years of a totalitarian state. Yet the totalitarian state was not an avoidable anomaly of the industrial society; rather the opposite is true.

* * *

For a very particular set of conditions, the mass coalescence of the proletariat into an assertive social group failed to take place in one specific country of the industrial world, and that was the United States. Here, the proletariat had no voice among the nation's social forces due to its special immigrant status. The American proletariat was and is quasi-external, ethnically fragmented, ideologically either conservative or immature, geographically dispersed, and lured by the real possibility of a uncommon social upward mobility – the perplexing prospect of enhancing, by the next day, one's own social and economic status as a result of the arrival of the next wave of the ever newer, fresher, external proletariat.

It was this exceptional fact of the United States' successful stand against the rest of the world's proletarianization, resisted until the end, that put a different twist on the reputation of the totalitarian movement as a whole. In fact, the organization of nations into supercorporations was predicted well in advance and correctly anticipated by many of the celebrated minds of the nineteenth century. As it turned out, the industrialization of the state, with its corollary set of social rationalizations, was not a consequence of the *militarized factory society*. Wars throughout history do come to conclusion, even among totalitarian states. Furthermore, life under totalitarian incorporation brought affluence, security, social stability, and even a spiritual renaissance to the people.

The first example was Germany under Bismarck, then Russia under the Bolsheviks, followed by Germany, again, under the national socialists and China under the Communists. Scandinavians were enormously successful, the Latin American states conducted a variety of totalitarian experiments, with mixed results. The Arab socialist nations, the developing Asian tigers, Japan under the conservative party, the Korean one-corporation nation, all followed the pattern of concentration and centralization of economic management. Notwithstanding national variations due to historical circumstances, the proletarianization of the state was the underlying tendency of the twentieth century, and not the exception.

Proletarian totalitarianism finally came to its historical, inevitable end. It did not end because of political will or resistance in the war against it, but because factory production became obsolete in the same way that the feudal manor passed away when it lost its economic reason to exist. Under the inevitable pressure of technological advancement, new informational tools were proven to be far superior to the lathe and the hammer. These technological breakthroughs came to be realized for the first time, whether in some utopian free-enterprise garage or not, under the auspices of totalitarian military institutions and sponsored by advanced laboratories of the military-industrial complexes of the world's superpowers.

* * *

Events and human acts in history seemed often to be unique, fateful turning points that usher nations onto an exclusive alternative path. It is the 'Cleopatra's nose' syndrome; the causal model of reasoning versus dialectical logic. Was the Russian revolution a historical accident in a series of countless smaller accidents, or was it the result of a teleological historical necessity brought to life through a sequence of accidental agents? Concepts such as the *necessary evil*, the *law of history*, the *times of trouble*, the *historical contingent* are eloquent and insubstantial. A *necessary accident*? In hindsight, the Russian revolution was rather an *accidental necessity*.

In the world's grand scheme of industrialization, the Russian way was accidental. Within the world as a whole, Russia's moment of violence and Stalinism was her 'kicking and screaming' march toward industrialization. The development of American-style free enterprise was another such accident.

They were local perspectives on industrialization. What was inescapable was global industrialization. The necessity relates to the world as a whole. The accident relates to the nation and the interplay of its social forces. In this sense, an event is necessary, when it refers to the process; accidental, when it refers to the specific ways of its implementation.

THE HISTORICAL CURVE TOWARD GLOBAL MARKET SOCIALISM

As a perfect illustration of the dialectical categories thesis/ antithesis and synthesis, at the end of economic ideology, one finds *market socialism*. Russia went from the earlier Bolshevik no-money economy to complex computer-based algorithms used by *Gosplan* in the process of allocating the national financial resources in the 1980s; at the same time, the United States went from the idyllic farming estates of American liberalism to the crowded inner cities of the bureaucratic state of the late 1980s! They were now convergent realities[29] no longer in sync with the original labels.

The Communist system was far from perfect.

(1) It was thought that specialized management was superfluous and that *the workers* could take care of complex, industrial self-management tasks. – It was learned that specialization is more efficient, from the management level down to the assembly line.

(2) It was thought that equalizing incomes would enhance the initiative and the collective will, and raise productivity. – It was learned that the wage system that makes redistribution dependent on one's productivity is a greater incentive.

(3) It was thought that planning should be done in terms of real things, of physical quantities, and not in terms of abstract money values. – It was learned that only the use of money as a common denominator gives significance to costs and prices.

(4) It was thought that interest was an unnecessary burden on the economy. – It was learned that interest is the measure of the relative value of one investment or another and is indispensable in the process of regulating the money flow.

(5) It was thought that rationing the needs of the people simplifies and eliminates waste from central planning. – It was learned that consumer choice is the engine motive among producers.

(6) It was thought that sophisticated economic modeling methods were a departure from the revolutionary spirit. – It was learned that mathematical methods of planning were essential to macro-economic design.

(7) It was thought that trade and commerce in general were fraudulent practices to be restricted and made unprofitable. – It was learned that the comparative advantage among nations stimulates productive energies rationalizing the prospective commercial profit.

The lessons were opposite for free-market capitalism.

(1) It was thought that the public sector is a heretical idea to be outlawed. – It was learned that in an increasingly complex economy, whole sectors are left out of the private interest: among

them utilities, transportation networks, civil administration, the military, education, telecommunications and postal services, often the banking industry, insurance, health care, wilderness management, and an array of underperforming yet indispensable industries, from coal mines to autos.

(2) It was thought that income was a matter of individual discretion and not to be subjected to a collective and abusive interference. – It was learned that taxation and fee collection are accounting matters needed to provide capital for as much as half of the economy.

(3) It was thought that free competition is a natural right. – It was learned that safety requirements, national security considerations, environmental restrictions, and antimonopolistic regulations, while they are all limiting factors on the exercise of free enterprise, are necessary for the benefit of public well-being.

(4) It was thought that education and access to knowledge was a sign of distinction and a privilege that came with wealth in a class-based society. – It was learned that education is a national as well as a corporate concern and asset. The use of high technology and the emergence of the *knowledge working class* requires that education be made not only generally available but compulsory.

(5) It was thought that market forces are preeminent in the service of the national interest. – It was learned that whole vital sectors of the economy could survive only through massive governmental intervention and subsidies to such sectors as the agrobusiness or aviation, symbols of national prestige.

(6) It was thought that planning itself was an anti-business bureaucratic intervention. – It was learned that long-term thinking and strategic coordination of efforts among leading corporations prevent inefficiency and waste through lack of standardization, overlapping redundancy, and technological obsolescence.

(7) It was thought that international free trade is the only framework for the profitable conduct of business among capitalist nations. – It was learned that free trade is antinational, devastating under raider-nations' competition, is unfit for financial stability, long-term investment, infrastructure building, and the preservation of the national fabric itself. Managed trade is the alternative.

The friction over joining the two one-sided systems into a more harmonious one cut across multiple interests from cultural to military. In the end, the goals of macroeconomic management were to be integrated between the two commonwealths of the Eurasia and Pacific regions.

(1) The size of the public sector would be generally less significant as more was to be leased out to private franchises.

(2) Management decision making would move into the hands of the technocracy in response to the expansion of the number of shareholders and the dilution of their powers.

(3) Prices would be more integrated and stable, less open to individual manipulation, a result of the interdependence of information management, auditing, and government controls through the new methods of taxation and sales taxes.

(4) Decentralization of the hierarchical corporate structure would proceed through professionalization of more jobs and through information dissemination among the knowledge workers.

(5) The increased use of the lease/concession approach would distribute responsibilities and risks to a larger number of participants on a subcontract basis.

(6) A more efficient central coordination of economic activity would be planned, through the use of computer technology, statistical analysis, updated and thorough personal and corporate information databases, and sophisticated use of the mass media.

(7) Growth in the rate of education, both technical and nontechnical, would allow for an increased acceptance of and accommodation with the concepts of market socialism and the spread of civility.

(8) An international integration would proceed through large economic regional blocks and an international division of labor within the new structures.

The process of convergence was analyzed as far back as the 1950s, among a few farsighted economists with a pragmatic attitude. Jan Tinbergen provided an insight. To him, convergence was already real, ". . . particularly," he wrote in 1961, "for the main question about the degree of decentralization in production decisions and planning. It is to some extent also true for the process of price formation. It is less clear with regard to the formal side of property, but a distinction between formal property and the real situation must be made. As already observed, both the income from property and the freedom of decision with regard to its use have been strongly reduced in the west and the process may continue."[30]

In later years the tendency toward the socialization of

production, did indeed continue; socialization through increased industry regulation, through tax code provisions for income redistribution, through professionalization of decision making, and through the spread of shareholder property. These were also the main elements introduced by Russia in its own version of *perestroika*.

If the model holds true, it resembles, in our story, the Russian Service State of the 1600s. The old class of Muscovite boyars elected Mikhail Romanov, one of their own, to take command of the state and to do so in the name of the lesser nobility against the great aristocracy. Today's boyars are the elite group among the efficient and energetic managerial CEOs, and the lesser nobility could be found among the upcoming and ambitious class of entrepreneurs and independent professionals.

Seeking the *optimum*, one rejects the extreme. Yet, the constant endeavor to reach the *extreme optimum* is an ongoing, unbounded historical movement along the evolutionary curve of the making of global market socialism.

Chapter VI

Pitfalls of a Competitive Market

The idea that free-market shock therapy combined with thorough privatization could be the best medicine for the former Comecon economies was widely accepted in the earlier days of *perestroika*. Yet this view failed to encompass the complexity of the issues at stake.

The idea that a well-entrenched economic system could be fixed by a sudden-decreed entrepreneurial life that would provide to newly certified private enterprises, *ex nihilo*, capital, managerial and business skills, technology, and operational know-how, was a faulty conjecture to begin with.

History and life are full of paradoxes. One of them concerns *perestroika* and the Soviet/Western alliance's ambiguous relations. The internal changes within the Soviet Union significantly affected international affairs along the lines of politics, ideology, economics, nationality affairs, military developments, the legal system, historiography itself. It also transformed international political and economic institutions and organizations.

For the first year or so after Gorbachev's assumption of power in March 1985, it seemed that the new Soviet leader was giving top priority to the improvement of relations with Western Europe.

However, it soon became apparent that the restructuring of relations with the United States took precedence over relations with Western Europe. For observers of the Soviet political scene, the preeminence of the *Americantsy* (Soviet specialists in American Affairs) in the central decision-making apparatus was one of the signs. At the international level, it manifested itself in the complete reversal of the anti-American positions and rhetoric to which Brezhnev, Andropov, and Chernenko had tenaciously clung. Now, the main question about the Soviet Union's new overall policy was: Were current Soviet international policies a direct extension of requirements generated by internal *perestroika* or, if not, what were their "driving forces" (*dvizhushchie sily*)?

No single answer suffices.

THE MARKET ECONOMY AND PRIVATIZATION

Privatization was recognized as the key to the transition from state socialism to market capitalism in the countries formerly belonging to Comecon. That this transition would likely be unsuccessful without a large-scale transfer of state property to private ownership was the view held by many economists from all socio-political quarters, both within the region and in the West. President Gorbachev himself, it was said, had come to the conclusion that 'market socialism' as an economic system combining markets and state ownership was not a viable alternative to Western capitalism.[1]

Conversely, by involving market forces in the process of allocating the factors of production, whether capital, raw materials, energy, means of production, or consumption and labor, the system was, in fact, legitimizing a decentralized exercise of property rights. Discarding thus the top-down decision-making process in resource allocation, the new economic framework was expected to guarantee the demise of the old center of power and also to set it on an equal footing with capitalist Western Europe.

Nevertheless, a closer analysis reveals a more complex outcome depending on how privatization was implemented. Because the transfer of state property into private hands was an all-encompassing notion lumping together a multitude of forms and distinct phases, the term 'privatization' could be understood and manipulated in a number of ways.

In addition to outright auctions of state property in which the state was the seller and the individual was the buyer, numerous other forms of property transfer were labeled 'privatization' without any real change of ownership taking place. This includes *(1)* leasing, *(2)* the expansion of the limited, existing private sector, *(3)* simple transfer of cooperative property to private share ownership, or *(4)* the development of new institutions, which would constitute the legal framework for processing transactions previously unavailable under state ownership, such as capital markets, stock markets, and commodity markets. It was obvious that Item (4) offered the most fertile ground for forms of nominal owners as well as for the accompanying obfuscation on the matter.

Above all, there was one fundamental way to enlarge the existing state ownership legislation to include new forms. This was the transformation of state enterprises into so-called joint-stock companies or corporations, the shares of which were still owned by the state (a process that was known alternatively as 'commercialization,' 'corporatization,' 'denationalization,' or 'destatification'). These were new forms of public ownership that came to be traded on the newly created stock exchanges. And herein resided the largely overlooked dual nature of the market under state supervision. *The sale of stock in state-owned, joint-stock companies can involve a minority of buyers that are individual private citizens, while the most sizable share of buyers by far were those themselves owned in whole or in part by the state.*

In addition privatization, in whichever form it took, required a series of support programs that were meant to bring a measure of market internationalization in matters such as: *(1)* price liberalization, *(2)* reduction of control over enterprise management and foreign trade, *(3)* the establishment of a convertible currency, *(4)* macroeconomic stabilization programs that were directed at reducing inflationary pressures, if necessary, *(5)* the creation of a legal and regulatory infrastructure required for a capitalist economy to function correctly (for example, antitrust provisions); *(6)* the overhaul of the traditional Soviet-type credit and banking system, and *(7)* the establishment of a safety net to moderate the costs of the transition for displaced workers and others.

This general juridical-economic framework was the focus of

reformers as well as of their critics, for such ambivalent and far-reaching plans were also under the scrutiny of Western would-be reform experts and, noisily, of paid commentators. International standards were applied in order to test which countries were up to the task of breaking away from the old practices and patronage structures and whether one country or another had truly embarked on independent free-market integration. But the question remained: Integration into what? "The old Soviet economy was highly integrated and functioned after its own special fashion. Though inefficient, efficiency wasn't the point. The task was to produce what was ordered by bureaucrats in Moscow, who set priorities in distribution as they judged the state's interests. In that context, managers of the huge enterprises managed very well."[2]

If one stopped to remember Gorbachev's stated ambition, the challenge was to integrate the former Soviet state economy with the mixed Western European economies. Or, reading the fine print, was it not to rather to integrate the fractious Western European system into a rationalized, Eurasian common house, on a large scale, Russian-style?

"Free Market" without Markets

Russia's natural potential for bursting forth as a great economic power was evidenced by its oil reserves, the vastness of its forests and mineral deposits, its shrewd and talented people, its rich culture and traditions. Were all of those resources turned into consumer goods on a rational basis, Russia might indeed become the twenty-first century's economic powerhouse. All that was missing, it was thought, was the reciprocal gesture of acceptance from the world at large. And that would bring access to the world's technology, capital, and markets. Would that be attainable?

To estimate the needed input from Western economies and the enormous amount of capital that was required for the capital stock of the countries in the East to reach the level of Western nations, it is instructive to compare them with estimates made for the former East Germany. With a population of only 10 million, the capital expected to be invested by the reunited Germany's government were well beyond $50 billion a year ($92 to $110 billion in the first years of the '90s) for several years. To respond in the same fashion to the capital needs of the nearly 400 million people of Eastern Europe and the Commonwealth of Independent States would total, by conservative estimates, some $180 billion a year, but it could be as high as $3 trillion a year.

There were several underlying developments at this historical juncture, as global negotiations were mapping out capital movements and trade flows for the foreseeable future. They might offer a consistent explanation for the apparently conflicting trends.

(1) Growing Transatlantic Trade Disputes

One trend was the growth of trade disputes over transatlantic trade tariffs among the 103 nations belonging to the General Agreement on Tariffs and Trade. According to the *New York Times*, "the dispute threatened to turn into a trade war and disrupt the already stumbling global negotiations aimed at reducing international trade barriers."[3] The talks had already been deadlocked for 16 months and there was little optimism for the success of a general settlement. Trade officials had expressed real misgivings that should the trade talks remain stalemated, trade disputes would grow and more nations would act unilaterally to impose punitive measures. One example was the 1988 Omnibus Trade and Competitiveness Act, otherwise known as Exon-Florio. Its provisions require all mergers and acquisitions by foreign firms in the United States "affecting national security" to be screened by a committee; based on its recommendation, the U.S. president could order a foreign investor to divest its assets.

> The EC believes that the uncertainties created by the law's wide and undefined scope could potentially damage business confidence. Already, these concerns have prompted EC investors to notify voluntarily proposed acquisitions to the Committee on Foreign Investment in the US for screening. In the future, if 'national security' grounds are used for essentially protectionist reasons, the damage to the EC-US economic relationship and to the global economy could be very serious.[4]

(2) European Investment vs. American Investment

The second obvious trend was the move toward an interdependent Europe on multiple levels. The integration of Western Europe that kicked off on January 1, 1993 was only one side of it. There was also the slow integration of the former Eastern bloc nations into the European common market that was to create a totally new Europe.

Statistics in support of the continuous process of intra-European integration were abundant. With few exceptions, the former Comecon countries were more and more dependent on Western Europe.[5] It was highly expected that this would increase even more over the long term.

One may compare the $2 billion in aid that the United States gave to the entire Eastern European bloc from 1989 to 1992[6] with the capital flow from Western Europe into the same region – $50 billion from Germany alone.

As Polish government figures showed, while American companies invested some $62.5 million between 1989 and 1991, German companies outranked them with $153 million invested. The trend held true for Czechoslovakia, Romania, the Baltic States, and the rest.

(3) Similarities in the former Comecon Countries' Reforms

The real dimensions of the privatization process that was taking place in Eastern Europe were, fundamentally, not much different from one country to another despite the widely disseminated images of advancing first, second, or third level reforms on a country-by-country basis.

Let us take the case of Hungary, advertised at the time as the most open free-market economy in the region. By the end of 1991, the mass media noted that some "5,600 joint ventures with foreign firms had been established and the number of partly or wholly privately owned corporations exceeded 45,000."[7] Nevertheless, considerable evidence to the contrary was overlooked.

(a) Through both the First and the Second Privatization Programs, there was only minimal progress in the selling of the large- and medium-size state companies. "More generally, the number of state-owned enterprises, trusts, and subsidiaries remained virtually constant from the end of 1989 until mid-1991, then decreased by only 111 during the next six months."[8]

(b) But even in those cases of privatization that figure in most statistics as a fact of life (since auctions for the right to lease began in April 1991), local councils and other governmental bodies took a long time to establish clear ownership rights. "Consequently, from April 1991 until the end of the year, only 2,120 *leases* or ownership rights were granted out of the 10,240 stores that had been earmarked for conversion."[9] In other words, according to *MTI Econeus*, January 10, 1992, only 21 percent of preliminary privatization up to that time had been carried out and even that percentage is misleading since it actually had lumped together the outright ownership rights with a more vague regime of leasing rights.

(c) A still more significant development, however, was the beginning of a cartelization of state enterprises in their bid to preserve the old order of patronage and power. Under the guise of discouraging the sale of national assets to foreigners, an intercompanies policy of cross-ownership, managed by the state bureaucracy still in power, gave a new twist to the concept of privatization. A largely publicized case was the Hungarian state-owned Ibusz tourist agency that, listed for international bidders, attracted widespread foreign interest. It finally was "privatized" in April 1992 by being "sold to a state-owned bank and a state-owned insurance company."[10] In effect, the state sold to the state under the guise of privatization.

(d) An overview of the results of the same privatization process in Hungary reveals a disappointing participation of domestic investors. A whopping 80 to 90 percent of all privatization proceeds through the end of 1991 came from foreign investors. "Domestic investors using their own resources and nonpreferential credit accounted for only 12.5%, while only 2.5% came from investors taking advantage of preferential credit. Strict collateral requirements and high interest rates (20 to 50 percent interest) have been blamed for this ineffective performance."[11]

In Russia as early as 1995, the eight largest commercial banks were preparing an arrangement with Viktor Chernomyrdin's government. The banks would provide credit to the Russian government, and in exchange the government would give the banks control over state enterprises scheduled for privatization in

1995. Ivan Kivelidi, at the time head of the Russian Business Roundtable, an association of independent private businessmen, saw this as a crooked, sweetheart deal because the banks were not independent but were in fact themselves controlled by the state (through government-owned shares) and the state capitalists. The deal would enrich the old *nomenklatura*, now burrowed into the commercial banks, and was meant to link the state ever more closely to the 'privatized' sector. Although up to 60 percent of the Russian economy was said to be privatized, in fact, 80 percent of those 'privatized' assets were controlled by the banks in the hands of the old *nomenklatura*.

Kivelidi saw the state and the *nomenklatura* in witting or unwitting alliance with organized crime. The state, through confiscatory taxation, forced businessmen to choose between bankruptcy or felony. Those who avoided bankruptcy must have joined corrupt officials or forged links to organized crime, hid their assets or transferred them abroad. In Kivelidi's view, that was the way state capitalism settled its accounts with private business. "The honest businessman had no right to survive or to be let alone."

That was Kivelidi's last public statement. On August 3, 1995, he and his secretary Zara Ismailova were taken to the hospital with signs of acute radiation poisoning. He joined the other 46 independent businessmen murdered in 1994-95.[12]

PLAYING THE MARKET ALONG WITH THE SOCIALIST NOMENKLATURA

The test of validity for a market socialist economy is not whether it is practical or not. As long as the alternative model, the so-called competitive system, is ultimately unstable, that system's latent but inexorable disequilibrium sets forth the rationale for its sociopolitical revision. The destructive undercurrents that pervade any system constructed on the premises of competition sooner or later manifest themselves through antagonistic polarization.

One may think of ownership rights as the crucial difference between a capitalist market and a socialist one; yet elaborate new forms of social ownership can be put forward as we discussed above. The dividing line also could be based on a clever distinction between 'enterprise control' and 'enterprise income,'[13] a participatory ownership through a combined variety of private owners and public shareholders.

Such legalistic hair-splitting notwithstanding, the process of dissolution of the distinction between one type of market and another was unmistakable and inescapable. The economic process is by definition nonentropic, which is to say it is *not unidirectional*, but is a process of continuous, *non-irrevocable* transformation from low entropy into high entropy and vice versa.[14]

In this sense, Marx's controversial notion of an ever more acute contradiction proper to capitalist economic process is one-sided. Beyond such a process, the social *corsi i ricorsi*, in the words of Giambattista Vico, moves the economic system from *domestic egalitarianism* to social enrichment and *stratification* and back to the restoration of equality under the new law, as a new *cycle* begins.

The pendulum of history resets the low entropy clock over and over again. This is what Kevin Philips observes when, reflecting on the encapsulated instant of history in the 1980s, he quotes Will and Ariel Durant and their study *The Lessons of History*: "'Liberty and equality are like buckets in a well. When one goes up, the other goes down.' During the 1980s the bucket of liberty and economic freedom rose, while the bucket of income equality fell."[15]

* * *

The inherently calamitous nature of the free-enterprise system became apparent immediately after it was imported from its Anglo-Saxon book-model orthodoxy – most savage of all varieties – to the highly socialized structures and networks of embedded economic commonwealth of the Eastern European countries.

First, the GNP plunged across the board. On a compound basis over a three-year period (1990 to 1992) it sank by 50 to 55 percent in Romania and Bulgaria, between 35 and 40 percent in Hungary, Czechoslovakia, and Poland, and 39 percent in Russia (50 percent by 1994) – while industrial production declined on average by another 25 percent. Unemployment soared from a base of practically zero to 13-14 percent in Poland, Hungary, and Bulgaria and 8-9 percent in Czechoslovakia and Romania. Within the same three-year period, inflation ran at almost 500 percent in Romania, 250 percent in Poland, and Bulgaria, 170 percent in

Hungary, and about 45 percent in Czechoslovakia.[16]

Unequal in its devastation, the economic collapse had a greater impact on regions dependent on heavy industry, military hardware manufacturing, Comecon-related exports, and steel- and energy-based industries. Whole national industrial parks ground to a halt. Others drastically reduced their production. In such cases unemployment went up far higher. In Slovakia, in February 1995, in 11 districts the unemployment rate was above 20 percent, in 14 it was higher than 15 percent, and only 3 districts had a rate lower than 10 percent. The highest rate (28.9 percent) was in the district of Rimavska Sobota.[17]

The ghost of the nineteenth century robber baron, violent dispossessor of millions, came to life to disintegrate stable communities and enterprises. It left behind a haunted and confused social consciousness plagued by guilt over the questionable morality of the new principles. Fleeing the ideological imperialism of Soviet hegemonic bureaucracy and running straight into the Western gangster's merciless rapacity, the disgruntled Europeans were left in a state of delirious animation. Barely freed from the grasp of command regimentation, they found themselves in the wide open fairground of the world's market, exposed to the come-ons of salesmen, advertising geniuses and hucksters of every stripe.

They found that their wares were worth nothing in the absence of willing purchasers, thus they were in the weakest bidding position in the global market. They had only their skins to offer, and poor quality workmanship. But even on those grounds there was competition from other quarters – the traditional poorest of the world have made an unenviable profession of trading on their lowly position in the hierarchy of the downcast. Those were not only poor but had a claim to a special legacy.

Having been mostly isolated from the pains of the Western nations' nineteenth-century labor history, the Eastern Europeans' rudimentary brush with Marxist-capitalism was worthless. Free-enterprise competition was really not socialism plus affluence. It was rather *upper-class socialism*.

The formerly mandatory weekly hour of ideological instruction on the subject of private capitalism's wicked ropes and levers, although a regular staple for every socialist citizen for about forty years, had the reverse of the intended effect. It sowed a deep skepticism of those critiques of the capitalist exploitation of labor. The massive underclass produced by capitalism, underscoring the real costs of the competitive system, was overlooked in the awe and fascination with the affluence of Western European nations. Memories of their own past tribulations were overlaid with the fresh and steady offerings coming out of the new Disney-like, Western show "Business". In the end, the widespread derision for the slick salesman's conceit took its toll by hastening Eastern Europeans' economic ruin.

In fact, widespread dissatisfaction with their lot and obsession with economic self-righteousness, supported by a minimal exposure to a few showcases of Western excellence, obscured the examination of acute and very converse trends that developed in the United States during the very years when the rhetoric of easy riches was creating massive poverty and enlarging the class of the underemployed working poor.

> The exaggerations of cyclical theorists notwithstanding, these policy shifts and mood swings do seem to have recurred at forty- to fifty-year intervals. There has even been a somewhat predictable sequence of outcomes: economic benefits have come first, as enterprise-oriented policies unleashed latent capitalist energies; then the dislocations have followed, including speculative excesses and even market crashes. After ten to fifteen years of heyday psychology, *some* major economic or market contraction occurs.[18]

By early 1995, the State Statistics Committee in Russia was reporting that those Russians with the highest income had 15 times as much as the lowest. On January 5, 1993, *Vechernyaya Moskva* reported a ratio of 11:1, up from 4.5:1 in 1991. In January through November 1994, 10 percent of the population received 30 percent of the total income, while the poorest 10 percent received only 1.9 percent. About 65 percent of the population had incomes below the average level.[19] This was a reversal of joyless proportion after only three years of unregulated capitalism in Russia.

PLAYING SOCIALISM ON THE STOCK MARKET

The new economic philosophy was the old hymn of capitalism repackaged over and over again from Charles Dickens to Peter Drucker, turning civilization into a natural reservoir of dividends. Money is nowhere else in the world so openly and viscerally pursued as in the highly religious United States. In his unreserved dissection of oligarchic America, Kevin Philips goes beyond nicely tailored economic theories to the belly of street vendors' entrepreneurial philosophy. He brings out a few ironic examples: In the country that proclaims that "all men are equal," W.G. Summers, professor of political science at Yale, had no qualms about proclaiming that "millionaires are a product of natural selection,"[20] while professor Matthew Josephson acknowledges that "the type of the successful baron of industry now presented itself as the high human product of the American climate, the flower of its own order of chivalry, much wondered at, envied or feared in foreign lands whose peers had arrived somewhat earlier at coronets, garlands and garters."[21]

Out of this Anglo-American-Nietzschean protestant cult of individual redemption, the *new individualists* of the 1980s were also to be the last ones. News of the fallacy of the fantasy and the irony contained in the myth of the Lone Ranger no longer escaped the generation that followed the Organization Man. "For the parents of the organization offspring, the pioneer myth offered an imaginary solution to the real contradiction of the individual and the group. Indeed, it performed the same function for the pioneers themselves, for the frontier – that borderline where civilization meets the wilderness – was *not settled by rugged individuals but by federal troops, railroad conglomerates, grain and cattle brokers, cattlemen's associations, the judicial system, and hordes of lawyers.*"[22]

Nevertheless, by 1982 a new symbol of that confusion had stepped on stage. His name was Ronald Reagan and his simple five-point program contained the manifesto for latter-day Communist redemption. First, discard the unhealthy notion of economic egalitarianism by focusing on 'nurturing wealth' and on the pursuit of 'the proliferation of the rich.' Second, replace socially regulated *demand* economics with *supply-side* investment chiefs. Third, remove government as a 'factor of production,' price regulator, and market moderator. Fourth, open up the gates of entrepreneurial individual heroism and renunciation of the collective. Fifth, seal all of the above with a tax reshuffle (this became famous as *tax-Reaganomics*: "to help the poor and the middle classes, one must cut the taxes of the rich."[23]

Ten years later his advice was embedded in the official Soviet 'five hundred days plan' and others to follow in the newly set up reformed cabinets. Was the intention to have economic failure (the old communist system) cured with a *junk-bond*-type of economic medication? We know very well the American variant's outcome. After years of voodoo economics, one can draw the bottom line.

Three different categories of measurements expose the failure of orthodox free-market, supply-side economics.

A) The constant *erosion of the standard of living*, income, and purchasing power of the American worker:

- The weekly real wage per worker, inflation adjusted, went down from $366 in 1980 to $312 in 1987;
- The real average weekly wage for all workers, white collar and blue collar, in constant 1977 dollars, fell from $191.41 in 1972 to $171.07 in 1986;
- The median real earnings in constant 1985 dollars for men of all ages with a high school diploma were $9.90 an hour in 1973, $9.73 in 1980, and $8.62 in 1987;
- The weekly wages for both hourly pay and worked hours in the first quarter of 1988 were 2.4 percent below 1980, falling at a rate of 1 percent a year;[24]
- Over two decades, from 1972 to 1992, nonsupervisory worker average paycheck rose from $136 a week to $359. But when adjusted for inflation it actually declined by 19 percent.[25]

B) Dramatic *social polarization* stemming from the impoverishment of the growing majority of the lower and lower-middle classes for the benefit of a tiny upper-class:

- According to Federal Reserve data, the share of total net worth of American families underwent significant changes. The richest 1 percent increased its share of the country's total net worth from 31 percent in 1983 to 37 percent in 1989. The next 9 percent of richest families showed a deterioration in their position from owning 35 percent in 1983 to 31 percent in 1989. At the same time, the remaining 90 percent of the American families slipped from 33 percent to 32 percent (to 42 percent in 1995). By 1989, the top 1 percent (834,000 households) were worth about $5.7 trillion – more than the bottom 90 percent combined (84 million households).[26]
- The percentage of total family income that went to families in the top fifth increased from 15.6 percent in 1970 to 17.4 percent in 1990, while receipts for the lowest fifth declined from 5.5 percent down to 4.6 percent during the same period.[27]

- In retribution for the eroding performance of American companies in the 1970s through the 1980s, the gap between CEO average base salary and the average manufacturing worker's pay, for the top Fortune 200, went from an after-tax ratio of 24:1 in 1973-75 to 157:1 in 1987-89.[28] But that disproportionate imbalance between company's performance, executive remuneration, and workers' salaries is even larger when we take into account the executive packages of benefits, pensions, insurance, golden parachutes, and especially the company stock option, most often in the range of tens of millions of dollars per year.
- Overcompensation of executives included the cross-company system of a closed inner circle of boards of directors. In absolute disjunction from the performance-pay myth, outside directors' base earnings could adjust executive pay upward considerably, sometimes by as much as another annual salary; as Robert A.G. Monks and Nell Minow document.[29]
- At the other end of the social spectrum, the economics of *benign neglect* induced an increasing number of social ills from homeless working poor and mentally ill, to rampant educational deficiency, collapsing infrastructures, increased crime and violence, and structural unemployment.

(C) *The demise of America's technological leadership* was only a side effect of run-away internal disintegration. Despite the enormous influx of foreign capital, about $1,000 billion in ten years, the economic performance overall showed an unmistakable backslide.

> In the 150 years since the onset of the Industrial Revolution, American productivity growth averaged a little less than 3 percent per year. In the twenty years from 1947 to 1967, productivity growth was slightly better − 3.3 percent per year. With a 3.3 percent growth rate, living standards double every twenty-one years. From 1980 to 1990 American productivity grew at a 1.2 percent pace. With a 1.2 percent productivity growth rate, standards of living double every fifty-eight years.[30]

A direct consequence of poor technological enhancement, the product quality of American companies had experienced a sharp depreciation of its international edge. According to the *World*

Table 6.1
Assessments of US and Japanese Comparative Standings
in Selected Technologies, MITI

| Technology | Level of Technical Development 1983 | | 1988 | |
	Technology	Capability	Technology	Capability
Database systems	U.S.	U.S.	U.S.	U.S.
Semiconductor memory devices	Equal	Equal	Japan	Japan
Computers	US	Equal	Equal	Equal
Videocassette recorders	Japan	Japan	Japan	Japan
D-PBXS	US	US	Equal	Japan
Microprocessors	Equal	Equal	Equal	Japan
Laser printers	US	Equal	Equal	Japan
Copying machines	Equal	Equal	Equal	Japan
Assembly robots	Equal	Japan	Equal	Japan
CAD/CAM	US	Equal	Equal	Japan
Communications satellites	US	Equal	Equal	Equal
Photovoltaics	Japan	Equal	Japan	Japan
Aircraft engines	US	US	US	Equal
Skyscrapers	US	US	Equal	Equal
Advanced composite materials	US	US	Equal	Equal
Fine ceramics	Equal	Japan	Japan	Japan

CAD/CAM = computer-assisted design, computer-assisted manufacturing;
D-PBX = digital private branch exchanges.

Source: Ministry of International Trade and Industry, *Trends and Future Tasks in Industrial Technology, 1988 White Paper.*

Competitiveness Report, published once a year by the World Economic Forum, in 1991 American companies ranked 12 in respect to product quality, 10 in on-time delivery, 10 in after-sales services, and 12 in on-the-job training.

The alarming comparative forfeiture of its technological lead plagued the United States' *invisible hand* approach to economic policy. In only five years it meant the loss of technological supremacy in all but two fields, database systems and aircraft engines, mainly to the concerted Japanese assault. **Tables 6.1** and

Table 6.2
Position of the US Computer Industry
in Selected Critical Computer Technologies

Technology	1990	1995
Database systems	Ahead	Ahead
Processor architecture	Ahead	Diminished lead
Network and communications	Slightly ahead	Parity
Human interface	Ahead	Diminished lead
Visualization	Ahead	Diminished lead
Operating systems	Ahead	Diminished lead
Software engineering	Ahead	Diminished lead
Application technology	Ahead	Diminished lead
Displays	Behind	Further behind
Hard-copy technology	Parity	Behind
Storage	Slightly ahead	Slightly behind
Manufacturing technology	Slightly behind	Further behind
Integrated circuit fabrication equipment	Behind	Behind
Microelectronics	Parity	Behind
Optoelectronics	Slightly ahead	Parity
Electronics packaging	Parity	Behind

Source: Computer Systems Policy Project

6.2 show the dramatic reversal and also the projected trends in the hi-tech industries.[31]

When it comes to measuring the free-market philosophy's success, the result of its American implementation is lamentable. In the biggest economic laboratory of the 1980s, it proved to be the second biggest failure after the centrally planned economies.

The obvious conclusion for any serious observer of the competing twentieth century economic systems is that, by the beginning of the 1990s, the search for new avenues of reinvention was due to begin. The two hitherto extreme economic ideological positions both missed the optimum ingrained degree of complexity and heterogeneity inherently prevalent in a mature economy. The straight economic policies that marked the success of Germany's and Japan's productive expansion in the 1960s through the 1980s were, by contrast, free of ideological exaggerations, and were socially flexible and responsive to a holistic management.

Under the headline *Gap in Wealth in U.S. Called Widest in West*,[32] Keith Bradsher makes the situation clear: "New studies on the growing concentration of American wealth and income challenge a cherished part of the country's self-image. They show that rather than being an egalitarian society, the United States has become the most economically stratified of industrial nations. Even traditional class societies like Britain, which have inherited large differences in income and wealth over centuries, going back to feudal times, now have greater economic equality than the United States." In 1989, according to Federal Reserve figures, the richest 1 percent of American households – each worth at least a net $2.3 million – had nearly 40 percent of the nation's wealth, compared to 18 percent in Britain, down from 59 percent in the early 1920s. But the general poverty of the majority of Americans is best illustrated by the fact that the 20 percent of the nation's households, having an average net worth of $180,000 or more, owned more than 80 percent of the country's wealth and commanded 55 percent of the total annual after-tax income (averaging a mere $55,000 and up), leaving the remaining 80 percent of the country's households to scramble for a living on income ranging from just below $50,000 a year down to the poverty level (where almost 15 percent of the households converge).

And the article concludes: "When you have a child poverty rate that is four times the average of Western European countries that are our principal competitors, and when those children are a significant part of our future work force, you have to worry about the competitive effects as well as the social-fabric effects."

THE CONCEPT OF MANAGED MARKETS

Clearly, if this trend, intrinsic in the unilateral pursuit of the free-enterprise system, were left to follow its own course, the United States' irreversible decline would have been only a matter of time. It would also have been rather short, for the displacement of the United States as the world's leading manufacturer would have occurred within the time span of one technological life cycle.[33] Consequently, the imperative need for a dramatic change of direction became apparent to millions of Americans, and the political will to respond to it arrived with the new Democratic administration in 1992. The abandonment of free-enterprise, laissez-faire orthodoxy seemed inevitable. The free-market line was replaced by managed competition.

The significance of such a change of mind-set however goes well beyond some technical details of economic policy. It calls for the reassessment of all of the conventional wisdom that institutionalized free-market philosophy as the foundation of capitalist conservatism, i.e., of the belief in free-enterprise's potency as the generator of development, of the belief in its Darwinian blood-cleansing function, of the belief in its rationale for the opposition to state intervention in the economy, of the belief in the value of individualist entrepreneurship – all at odds with the notion of managed competition.

But what is managed competition?

Finding the answer should be both revealing and rewarding. When one looks back at Russian *perestroika* and its struggle to articulate a logical transition from the earlier state monopolist capitalism, one also comes across the multiple forms of social-market capitalism that they were faced with. The middle ground between the extremes is, inevitably, a common ground. For one thing, humanity's experience, in all, points to managed competition as the winning formula that mixes together valid economic solutions developed worlds apart.

* * *

By the end of the nineteenth century, hardly any perceptive observer of classical capitalism would have disputed that an unconcealable process of Hobbesian selection, concentration, and monopolization of production along efficiency's path of scale and scope was taking place in the United States as well as in Western Europe, especially in Germany. The ominous pre-disposition toward the inexorable concentration of production, along a feared Marxist- promulgated pattern, demanded the first act of managed competition, which was the Sherman Antitrust Act of 1890. "That act not only reinforced the common law by declaring such combi-nations illegal; it also provided, as the common law did not, an instrument – the executive branch of the government – to bring action in the courts against presumed violators."[34]

Although not exactly ideologically contentious, the antitrust legislation reflected instinctual social acknowledgment of capitalism's terminal – if left untreated – illness. The American political leadership's candid acceptance the limits of capitalism helped reinvigorate capitalism itself and accentuated its separation from class politics. The social cap on its divisive, centrifugal tendencies was the one-time act of enlightened inclusion of the economic within the political, which clearly defined its autonomy within the political supremacy. On a day-to-day basis, the economic sphere would live as an animal spirit of its own. But the political would represent the ultimate interests of society as a whole above it. That Antitrust Legislation was the defining act that made a radical evolutionary step forward by having the political foster and patronize the economic, rather than the other way around. "The legislation, amplified by the Supreme Court's decisions in the 1890s and enforced by the executive branch in the early years of the next century, remained uniquely American; no other nation adopted a comparable law before World War II. That legislation and the values it reflected probably marked the most important noneconomic cultural difference between the United States and Germany, Britain, and indeed the rest of the world insofar as it affected the long-term evolution of the modern industrial enterprise."[35]

The new legislation, in one move, took away pure economic freedom from the economic agents per se and bestowed supreme economic omnipotence upon the head of the political power, while it removed the politicizing of economic enterprise. The process of electing the president by popular vote now had, via subsequent appointments to the Supreme Court, the ultimate say on matters of economic competition, economic policy making, mergers and acquisitions, and monopoly price setting, but not on matters of micromanagement. In utmost irony, the historic antitrust act stood tall above the small world of the free-enterprise system, making it possible. Enterprise continued to be free as much as subordinated to the political machine, functioning more and more under the double dimensions of impassioned profit maximization in subordination to the popular electoral will.

The Act also gave the first sign as to where the limits of economic freedom might be reached – at the political stop sign, which is the electoral process. That was the lesson of another historical legislative act, the Keynesian-type state intervention following the Great Depression. Socially designed redistribution programs helped retard the speed and the depth of a socioeconomic cleavage that could no longer be ignored.

The agony of the 1960s and the 1970s and the subsequent acts meant to create the great American society were no accident, as the socioeconomic/political covenant was due for an update. The unfinished attempts at compromise of those years, born out of the new generational tensions between the economic and the political, brought about a general social dissatisfaction. The malaise of mounting regulations in the business community, and the despair engendered by the cycle of the underclass's moribund dependency on welfare redistribution, explain the reemergence of a national will focusing on radical change in the terms of the social compact. The short-lived regime of orthodox Reaganomics offered a unilateral, lopsided philosophy of economic accountability. Although it could have lived on at any social cost under the free rein of social Darwinism, it, not surprisingly, saw defeat in the inner-city ghettos (the Los Angeles riots in the summer of 1992 were ominous signs) as well as in intercontinental strife with Japan, Taiwan, Korea (the soaring trade deficit said it all).

The limits to economic freedom were reached at the periphery of nationally constituted economic entities. The inner-circle exercise of oligarchic capitalism had an unmerciful test on the collision course with the other international oligarchies.

The American economic enterprise was mounting a defensive war under siege and in isolation from two powerful traditional associates. Squeezed in the middle – between the dejected labor constituency and its rejection of subordination to state economic policy – the American cowboy monopoly stood an easy victim to the loss of competitiveness. The political-economic cartels of foreign interests took the strategic offensive while applying the ancient tactic of teamwork. They stormed the American fortress with coordinated economic force.

One could see this story as a new version of the unwieldy Spanish caravels of the *Invincible Armada* and their defeat by the integrated English fleet of small fishing boats acting in teamwork. Once again the contrast between lone competing giants and the managed co-operation of Lilliputians was illustrated. To contain the incoming tide, the United States was finally forced to undertake a wholesale revamping of its national economic strategy – a long journey, indeed.

The external dimension of managed trade came first. It meant the reintroduction of surreptitious trade barriers. Antidumping laws using imaginative computations (the infamous Special 301), quotas across the board (textiles – 15,000 pieces a year per each Eastern European country), so-called *voluntary export restraints* (VER) – 20 percent limits on Japanese auto imports, the *voluntary import expansion* (VIE) – 20 percent of Japanese superconductors to be imported from the United States), and so on.

In all, the emerging hi-tech international trade demonstrated the nonvalidity of the concept of natural comparative advantage across nations that was the basis for two hundred years of free-trade philosophy. The hi-tech industries were obvious cases where man-made competitive advantage took precedence over the natural distribution of mineral, climate, and skills endowment. A nationally coordinated policy was far more advantage-creating than spontaneous entrepreneurial exploitation of available resources.

The real question came to be not *whether* a national industrial policy should be pursued, but *which*. In terms of national strength and security, the costs of an unrestricted laissez-faire policy were simply too high.

Until recently, the traditional 'cleansing' effect of competition was limited to a particular group of losers, most often the working poor, that were displaced from their jobs temporarily or permanently, always to be followed, sooner or later, by a compensatory economic boom of good times and new industries. Traditionally the suffering, unfair as it was, had been confined within a particular industry, town, or trade. Unequal in its impact, the competitive gamble of short-term profit maximization was accompanied by an ad hoc regrouping of the defeated army of workers, as the fortune seekers moved their tents down the river to start the cycle anew. Pain and sorrow were followed by joy and a sense of adventure. And the wheel of fortune kept turning.

The stakes have changed dramatically. Now, the whimsical wandering of foreign investments could leave an entire nation at the mercy of another, or whole nations at the disposition of one or another rainmaker. Unfair international trade practices were not the equivalent of the wheeler-dealer turn-a-buck philosophy. If once before one could have argued the benefit to consumers in defense of domestic price competition, now the long-term consequences of an international price war would endanger the very existence of domestic productive capability.

Strategic direct foreign investments, as much as predatory free-trade, are different faces of the same grim international pressure when set on a targeted market. One employs plain neo-colonialist tactics, the other is a more subtle use of the *Trojan horse* stratagem.

Supporters of foreign direct investment point to the jobs,

capital, technological know-how, and organizational skills that the imported enterprises contribute to the national cache of assets. But experience has shown at least three converse outcomes of direct foreign investment. First, it actually displaces or deters the entrance of new local contenders in a marketplace dominated by a global player. Second, the newly established foreign firms usurp the market shares controlled by the existing domestic industry, "either by buying them out directly or by squeezing them out gradually."[36] Third, on top of the commercial dimension of national encroachment, we have the modern national security considerations posed by high technology applications. "The growing concentration of the global semiconductor equipment and materials industries by a handful of Japanese companies poses a similar strategic threat to both commercial and defense interests. According to a 1990 study by the Defense Science Board, Nikon, one of only two Japanese suppliers of certain kinds of semiconductor manufacturing equipment, withheld its latest models from foreign customers for up to 24 months after making them available to Japanese customers."[37]

In the end, the open-door economic policy came to be questioned even by its hard-core, die-hard advocates, the United States of America. Its own internal search for new avenues of economic national policy was indeed the world's best laboratory for testing recommendations to be advanced to the new economic big players: the European Union, Russia, Japan, China.

The options were numerous, and one case is not a carbon copy of another, but there were some common dilemmas. (a) Should they all embark on the bankrupt course of free enterprise? (b) Should they look at the largely successful mercantilist policy of Japan with its export-led economy (sometimes legitimate but most often exploitative of foreign weaknesses), just as it was raising widespread resentment and countervailing defensive attitudes? (c) Should they cultivate a more autarchic orientation or a closed/ open economic integration upon the North American or the European models? (d) Should they integrate into a larger Western European-North Atlantic free-trade area? Cheap Mexican labor would be as disruptive to the American social and economic fabric as the Eastern Europeans' fledgling industries were for the most advanced Western European nations. (e) Or, should they concentrate on internal national markets surrounded by trade policies strictly managed against outside competitors, sheltering their industries but cultivating all the ills of noncompetitiveness and economic preservation?

Just a simple listing of the available options, together with the many more combinatory variants, revealed the limited effectiveness of any of the purely economic terms of the international formulas for economic integration. The trade-offs were large and mostly at huge cost to whole nations, regions, and segments of the population deprived of any strong comparative advantages or the shelter of the state-corporate alliances.

Faced with mounting competition, both superpowers were doomed to a process of mummification. The official American separation of political from economic management would have made its economy resemble more and more a Swiss cheese in which the internal holes grow larger and larger. The traditional Russian top-down state corporation would have been left as an Eiffel-Tower skeleton of a deceased economic colossus. The American popular aversion to a national pooling of resources through a coherent economic policy would mean the lonely entrepreneur was left short of cash. On the other hand, there is no much doubt as to the hopeless condition of the ambitious Russian *plunger into the sea*[38] when matching up against the shrewd capitalist. Selling stolen state property on the international free market might be a good bet in the short run only when compared to bureaucratic treading water. The capitalist range of choices was indeed limited: should one gamble against foreign gamblers and risk losing the national inheritance – or sell the silverware piece by piece?

Coming from opposite directions, the runaway economies of the two wounded protagonists faced the same precipice. They both looked by now like the old uncle, a little bit dumb, deaf, and with poor balance, under the attack of throngs of diminutive cheerful devils. The Soviet-American old chumps would scare no one.

But there was a higher order of reality that explains why the entire focus of analysis needed to be redirected toward the political underlinings of the East-West puzzle. The scramble for market share was not the real business. Horse-trading and back-room deals were still executed among the powerful.

Chapter VII

The Invisible Revolution

OWNERSHIP DISTRIBUTION
IN THE UNITED STATES

The favorite politically correct term of the early 1990s undoubtedly was the *collapse of communism*. It implied the triumph of *capitalism* over its destitute rival. But capitalism, as a model for the now defeated challenger, was at its own hour of truth.

With the exception of the anomalous 1980s, the century-long trend in wealth distribution, income disparity, distribution of management functions, all revealed a pattern of moderating from the extreme level of the nineteenth century. *Ipso facto* asset socialization was no longer a program but a fact of everyday life. Notwithstanding temporary deviations from the general trend, wealth distribution in the United States does show an enlargement of social participation in its allocation.

According to Populist Representative Robert L. Henry of Texas, who in 1912 took part in "a sensational investigation conducted by a House banking subcommittee early that year[,] twelve banks in New York, Boston and Chicago held a total of 746 interlocking directorships in 134 corporations – railroads, insurance, manufacturing, public utilities, trading companies, other banks," which meant that they "dominate more than 75 percent of the moneyed interests of America, more than 75 percent of the industrial corporations which are combined in the trusts, and practically all of the great trunk railroads running from ocean to ocean."[1]

By 1929, 200 corporations controlled close to half of American industry and their assets accounted for about 22 percent of all national wealth. By 1932 Adolf A. Berle, in his classic study of corporate concentration undertaken with Gardiner C. Means in *The Modern Corporation and Private Property*, calculated that 600 American corporations owned 65 percent of the nation's industry.

The share of wealth held by the super-rich, the wealthiest half of one percent of U.S. households, at the same historical high mark in wealth concentration in 1929 stood at above 32 percent, while the one percent wealthiest owned over 36 percent of nation's total assets. That is about the same level of wealth concentration that occurred under the Reagan administration's watch.[2] By 1992, the top one percent of U.S. families owned 37 percent of total U.S. assets, up from 31 percent in 1981.

Yet, by the late 1980s, the historical process of wealth concentration took a new twist. This was the socialization of wealth The nineteenth century image of the headquarter-acropolis, up on the hill, employing the toiling masses in the sorrowful valley of poverty seemed to be fading away.

By 1990, pension funds controlled 38.2 percent of the assets of all institutional investors, or $2.5 trillion (up from $891 billion in 1981[3] out of a total of $6.52 trillion holdings, which represented by themselves 20.5 percent of all outstanding assets. That is to say that the pension funds' share alone was of about 7.8 percent of all outstanding assets of this country. But in terms of their share of common stock, pension funds represented in 1990 20.1 percent out of a total of 30.4 percent for financial institutions of all types.

Furthermore, when it comes to the actual productive assets, according to Peter Drucker, by 1992 these funds already owned half of the share capital of the country's large businesses and held almost as much of these companies' fixed debts.[4] The single largest owner of the country's means of production was by now the collective persona of the 'employee.'

An identical result – pension funds' ownership of 20 percent of the total U.S. financial assets for 1991 – was reported by Henry Kaufman who lists the major institutional groups as follows. "Deposit institutions have about $5 trillion in assets. The next largest financial intermediaries, the insurance companies, have assets amounting to nearly $2 trillion, followed by pension and retirement funds with $1.9 trillion. Far behind are finance companies with $600 billion and open-end mutual funds and money market funds with about $500 billion each."[5]

This process of socialization was taking place in synchrony with the even more pervasive process of industrial concentration. Already by 1976, the five largest industrial corporations had just under 13 percent of all assets used in manufacturing. The 50 largest manufacturing corporations had 42 percent of all assets. 162 of the corporations alone owned more than half of all nation's manufacturing assets, 54 percent. The 500 largest had 72 percent of the total assets. 3801 firms, each above the $10 million mark in assets, owned 89 percent of all assets. The 100 great corporations had 69 percent of all prime defense contracts, as the top "126 large firms performed nearly three quarters of all industrial research and development and received 93 percent of all federal support for such work."[6]

All through the following years, a formidable consolidation of production continued into fewer and larger corporations which resulted in a furthering of asset concentration so that by the late 1980s, the 200 largest manufacturing corporations could claim some two-thirds of all manufacturing assets of the country. This is not a surprise but is consistent with Marx's basic nineteenth-century observation on the inevitable historical process of concentration of production concurrent with a socialization of ownership.

This antinomy that typifies the Hobbesian/Marxist process of the concentration of economic wealth together with the socialization of its ownership is best illustrated by the modern-day epic of the growth, domination, and final metamorphosis of the Rockefeller Group's social and ideological alignment.

A thorough investigation made by James C. Knowles[7] of Stanford University and published after minute scrutiny by a large number of academics, in 1973, concludes that "in the U.S. there are 10 or more major financial 'interest groups' consisting of wealthy corporate families allied with other wealthy families, the leading ones owning stocks in major banks or groups of banks and many sitting on their boards. The banks are the core of a credit supplying fount for their respective corporations and are allied with enormous pools of capital in major insurance companies and investment entities. Around this insurance-bank nucleus, usually is 'gathered' a set of law firms, investment banking firms, foundations, universities,

Table 7.1
Main Holdings of the Rockefeller Group as of 1970

A. The financial core as of 1969
1. Chase Manhattan Bank
2. Chemical Bank (Manufacturers Hanover included since 1992)
3. CitiBank
4. First National Bank of Chicago

B. Closely allied 'mutual' life insurance companies ('mutual' because they have no stockholders, are run as personal preserves [under law] by trustees who in turn are named to the posts by well-placed money-market people)[9]
1. Metropolitan
2. Equitable
3. New York Life

C. 1st Tier: Completely controlled family corporations

1. E.I. du Pont de Nemours	8. International Basic Economy Corp.
2. W.R. Grace Inc.	9. Pittsburgh Coke and Chemical
3. Corning Glass Works	10. Commercial Solvents
4. Owens Corning Fiberglass	11. Deering-Milliken
5. Cummings Engine	12. Field Enterprises
6. Hewlett-Packard	13. Mercantile Stores
7. R.R. Donnelly and Sons	

D. 2nd Tier: Industrial corporations over which the group individually or collectively exerted undisputed control (with rank in Fortune 1000 in parenthesis, followed by name of nominal major owner)

1. Standard Oil -NJ	(1)	Rockefeller	13. Global Marine		n.r.	Hillman
2. Mobil Oil	(7)	Rockefeller	14. Marquardt Corp.	(671)		Rockefeller
3. Standard Oil - CA	(13)	Rockefeller	15. GCA		n.r.	Rockefeller
4. Standard Oil - IN	(18)	Rockefeller	16. Shakespeare Corp.		n.r.	Hillman
5. Int'l Harvester	(31)	McCormick	17. Stone & Webster		n.r.	Stone & Webster
6. Inland Steel	(93)	Block	18. Federated Dep't			
7. Marathon Oil	(126)	Rockefeller	Stores		n.r.	Lazarus
8. Quaker Oats	(195)	Stuard	19. Walgreen		n.r.	Walgreen
9. Wheeling-Pitts	(213)	Hillman	20. Marshall Field		n.r.	Field
10. Freep't Sulph	(462)	Rockefeller	21. Transcont'l Gas		n.r.	Stone & Webster
11. Itek	(521)	Rockefeller	22. Texas Gas Trans		n.r.	Hillman
12. Copeland			23. Consolidated Edison			
Refrigeration	(639)	Hillman	24. Anaconda Copper Co.			

E. 3rd Tier: Under coalition control (40% of directors) or joint control (22 to 36% of directors) with other syndicates

Mainly with Morgan:	With others:	
1. AT&T	5. Chrysler	(6)
2. U.S. Steel	6. Olin Corporation	(99)
3. Monsanto Chemical	7. Pan Am	
4. General Foods	8. Colgate-Palmolive	(103)
	9. Berg-Warner	(108)
	10. Home Insurance Co.	

Source: F. Lundberg, *The Rockefeller Syndrome,* based on James C. Knowles' research.

and other institutions of power and influence associated with the group."[8] According to Knowles' study and in agreement with Ferdinand Lundberg's assiduous research in the early 1970s, by then the Rockefeller Group, or Syndicate, was the largest and the most important of all, exceeding the Morgan Group gathered around the Morgan Guaranty Trust Company and Morgan, Stanley and Company. There were similar groups in "Boston, Cleveland, Philadelphia, San Francisco, Connecticut, Chicago, Texas, and Pittsburgh (Mellon)," but these were essentially local or regional as opposed to the national and international scope of the Rockefeller and Morgan Groups.[9] Yet the vast network of the principal holdings of the Rockefeller Group alone, shown as of 1973 in **Table 7.1**, is only a partial measure of the inexorable process of wealth concentration, and so of the socialization of the economic base, in the United States.

In fact, according to the most publicized, thorough accounting of the Rockefeller family's total asset ownership in the same period, 1974, vice-presidential hopeful Nelson Rockefeller pointed out at the time of his congressional confirmation: "The total holdings of all the living descendants of my father, both outright and in trusts, do not amount to more than 2.06 percent of any of these companies."[10] Actually: 1.0 percent of Exxon, 2.06 percent of Cal Standard, 1.75 percent of Mobil, and 0.23 percent of Indiana Standard. Furthermore, "none of these descendants of my father serve on the boards of any of the oil companies and we have no control of any kind over the management or policies of any of them." However, while that was a sizable shrinkage from the level of 8 – 16 percent that the Rockefellers held in the various Standard companies' stocks, as disclosed in the hearings of 1937, another even more remarkable development occurred in between those years. It was a distinct change in the *nature of ownership*.

For John D. Rockefeller, ownership meant *his personal* ownership, for the fourth generation of Rockefellers, personal ownership was already divorced from Rockefeller Syndicate Ownership. In the old days, the Rockefeller name identified an individual in possession of wealth, by the time of the forth generation it denominated an economic affiliation, economic party, economic association, economic bloc, links of almost feudal personal loyalty among public officials, politicians, managers of the corporations, and wealthy shareholders, that allowed those inside the group to make a real profit, almost at the expense of individual Rockefeller descendants' own interests and often at cross-purpose with some of them, now ideological opponents of big capital. In a truly historical countermovement, the monopolistic and protean acquisitive tendencies of the Rockefeller institution turned its newer intellectual and sensitive Rockefeller members into activists of the anti-Rockefeller revolution.

Former Chase Bank Chairman Nelson Rockefeller confronted by his daughter Abby is a typical historical revolutionary paradigm. "We had terrible, violent discussions," she confided with candor in 1975.[11]

> We would have the capitalism versus communism scene quite regularly. I would argue the idea of communism as I had read it in Marx's *Manifesto*. My father would doggedly bring in all this "factual" stuff he knew about Russia in order to defeat me. . . He asked me how it was that I repudiated everything he believed in; how could that have happened? I said that I thought I had learned a lot of what I thought from them; that I thought I had learned, especially from my mother, that there was no order in the fact that we had all this money, that there was no justice to it. And I said that I had learned from him that people should be decent to each other, and that it now seemed to me that the only thing systematic about our wealth was the indecency of it. I think he asked me directly why did I prefer communism, how could I think that it would be appropriate? I answered that it was really a question of two things: one's view of human nature and one's view of which system would bring about decent human conditions the quickest. So we got to talking about human nature, and he said that he believed in the carrot-and-whip theory. That he believed people needed to be prodded and then rewarded to be made to work. That those two stimuli would keep people going. In effect, he absolutely corroborated that capitalism is based on laziness and greed. I said I disagreed with his view of human nature. People were capable of being made like that, but they were also capable of being otherwise. It seemed to me true that people were capable of behaving in a variety of ways, and that the system could elicit either the good or the bad, and that it seemed to me that capitalism elicited the bad. And he just said, well, he disagreed.

In all of the United States' previous history, such assertions seemed extremist and subversive. Now, the economic, social, and intellectual elements of ownership socialization were here as the result of the inner workings of capitalism. The practical implications of such developments are yet open to speculation and analysis. But above all, the story of the Rockefellers is the story of the Morgans, the story of the Rothschilds, the story of the Morozovs and the Mamontovs, the story of the Lenins and Marxs. It is the story of *revolution*.

EMPLOYEE STOCK OWNERSHIP PROGRAMS

In 1974, only 13 public companies were in a position to have profit-sharing employees-stockholders as their largest stockholder, according to a study by Douglas L. Kruse and Joseph R. Blasi, two Rutgers University professors of management and labor relations. Of these companies only one, Sears, Roebuck & Co., could report a 20 percent employee-ownership.[12] The next largest percentage of employee-stockholders was found at Ford, U.S. Steel, Textron, McDonnell-Douglas, and Burlington Industries – all with around 12 percent employee ownership. By 1984, a 20-fold increase in the number of companies with employee stock-holdings of over 20 percent has been documented by the same authors. "If one assumes that a 15-percent holding is typically the dominant holding in a public company, then 41 percent of these public corporations [Employee Ownership 1000] either have 15 percent or have said that their employee plans are the dominant holder."

From a different perspective, by 1990 12.5 percent of the private-sector work force, or about 10.8 million American workers that were surveyed from the companies with more than 4 percent employee-ownership, were actually stockholders of their own company. This is a larger share of the working force than the entire trade union movement, at the time of only 12.2 percent.

Employee stock ownership had emerged under various circumstances, sometimes as labor-management mutual "concession bargaining" in which companies were merely shifting the risks from their own pockets to the employee; sometimes as wage cutting through a percentage payment being dispensed as a profit sharing. Quaker Oats increased its percentage of pay under profit sharing alone to 8.1 percent.[13] Tax advantages allowed the company to have it both ways: while increasing their nominal pay to their employee, their after-tax costs remained relatively unchanged.

Another incentive for companies to promote stock ownership came from large cost-cutting benefits derived from the replacement of so-called defined-benefit retirement plans. It meant the end of an era when employees know how much benefit they are entitled to receive, based on their salaries and years of service.[14] A special provision in the excise tax speeded up the migration particularly from 1986 to 1988.

The concept was designed to lower the costs for the company, pass the long-term risks to the most vulnerable, and stimulate employee participation in productivity increase. But the new philosophy had its up-side for the employees as well. The hard won nineteenth century system of compensation based on a fixed wage system and fixed benefits system was no longer an advantage to the employees themselves.

As long as the alternatives were, on the one hand, unregulated income varying by individual skills, age, and personal misfortune, or, on the other hand, a minimum guaranteed uniform price for all labor across the board, the better choice for employees was, obviously, a predetermined income expectancy throughout one's life. But things have changed with the vast potential for income enhancement through higher productivity in an open, affluent society. International competition as much as the aggressive *lean and mean* approach induced by the new technology-based work all made the security of the wage contract less advantageous.

The collective rights of industrial laborers were won at the bargaining table of the class struggle. However, in matters of innovation, creativity, experiment, or invention, such a rigid framework for labor was no longer, individually, right. The alternative to the collective employee contract is vertical subcontracting. Flexible units of work, as large as a company or as small as an independent consultant, based on performance and level of productivity, allows for every form of participation in the division of labor and for a fair measure of labor input and income. In Joseph R. Blasi's words: "Employees are being transformed from receivers-serfs-tenants to members-investors-owners."[15]

While employee stock ownership can be only a tool for passing business failure on to the employees, as Blasi documents more than once, it must be seen in the larger historical context.

The employee-ownership trend took on a life of its own, mainly as a defensive device against the takeover mania of the 1980s. The trend was presaged by the battle over the takeover of Hi-Shear Corporation in April 1973 by one of its individual shareholders named Klaus; and in 1978 national attention was focused on court wranglings over the takeover bid on Calumet Industries, under attack by one of its shareholders, Podesta. This in turn was followed by a number of disputed takeover actions, such as the purchase of Continental Airlines, Inc. by Texas International Airlines in 1980; the Grumman Aerospace Corp. offer made by LTV Corporation in 1981-82; and the full-scale war waged on Martin-Marietta by the Bendix Corporation in 1982. But takeover mania set a record for conversion to employee-ownership in the Macmillan Inc. defense carried in 1987-88 against the combined assault by Harcourt Brace Jovanovich, Robert M. Bass Group and Maxwell Communications.

By 1988, it became apparent that a new form of corporate entity had emerged through spontaneous generation. In that year, the first company, J.C. Penney, under no threat of a takeover action, began associated share repurchases aimed mostly at reducing the dilution in earnings per share. Under the scrutiny of an interested raider, Polaroid Inc. resorted to the same tactic of share-repurchase in 1988. They were followed by Cabot Corporation and Texaco Inc. The simple prospect of improved earnings per share persuaded the shareholders' to stick with the company they were holding.

In order to uphold the new consolidated earnings figures, Polaroid's management demanded a wholesale restructuring and rethinking of the company's philosophy. It was the comprehensive approach taken by Polaroid Inc. on three interdependent axes that set the stage for a full-scale corporate revolution: *(1)* wage and benefit restructuring, *(2)* associated share repurchases, and *(3)* a change of corporate culture. It was the first purposeful and systematic offensive on the issue of productivity and shared interests. In the words of I.M. Booth, president and CEO of Polaroid Corp.:

> Here is my bottom line, simply stated: just as Quality was the watchword of the 80s in American business, so Ownership, I predict, will be the most significant issue of the 90s. As pressure for improved performance and increased shareholder value mounts, the question of who is going to participate in making the really important decisions in corporate America will move to the front burner. In a climate

of perceived corporate inefficiency and wastefulness, of increased pressure on institutional investors for quick growth,
and increased demand from employees wanting a stronger
voice in determining how their present and future security is
going to be handled, the answer to the question of who is
going to participate has the potential for dramatically
reshaping the landscape of the American corporate
enterprise in the closing decade of the 20th century.[16]

Only a few years old, employee stock ownership plans were
already an assortment of visionary management revolution and
managerial gimmickry. But whatever the merits or the
shortcomings of the new "marriage of democracy and capitalism,"
the growth in employee stock ownership has been sharp. By the
spring of 1995, the National Center for Employee Ownership in
Oakland estimated that "the proportion of the equity of American
corporations in the hands of their own employees has almost
tripled, to about 6 percent, or $350 billion, today from just 2 percent
a decade ago."[17]

Blasi captures the spirit of the times when he cuts through the
amalgam of all these arrangements and sifts them into five
divisions.

(1) The feudal culture: Employee ownership is only another
code word for rigid management control. It covers a considerable
segment, 20 to 30 percent of the ESOP 1000 as both. The amount of
employee holdings is adjusted up or down, and the size of
employee ownership is changed (from as low as 4 percent to as
high as 40 percent) by the management to suit the company's overall policy. No institutionalized organ is provided for employee
monitoring of financial information. No independent trustee is set
up to protect employees' interests.

(2) The investor culture: The largest portion of the total, some
estimated 60 to 75 percent, this is rather a replacement of the
defined-benefits pension plans with a performance-based plan,
akin to a mutual fund shared by the management and the
employees. The deferred payment of a pension benefit is traded for
paid-benefit where a philosophy of "pay-at-risk" stresses the overall
collective performance and the employee reward. A few old-
fashioned attitudes still permeate the system: The 'management
knows best' mentality, although questionable in running the
business, turns out to be a bonus for the employees when it means
that portfolio management is done professionally and at no cost to
the dilettante employees. As tax-free income, it is viewed as a no

nonsense employee hands-off benefit.

It is also a free ride on the part of the corporation, which enjoys a secured pool of investment capital insulated from the vicissitudes of the stock market and the competition with other firms for stock valuation. Ultimately, it allows for management unaccountability and entrenched addiction to the status quo.

(3) The participatory culture: According to Blasi's estimates only about 5 percent of the Employee Ownership 1000 actually gave a measure of substance to the concept of employee inclusion and had more than 60 percent of workers involved in decision-making on matters of productivity, profitability, and quality. That is more than just an experimental phalanstery, but it is less than would constitute a mainstream corporate culture. This is a rather Don Quixote/Sancho Panza relationship in which the management is the senior partner while the employees are promised a place in the future glory. By devising real, palpable proof of entitlement in the promised land, the employer gives the workforce reason to believe that its involvement in the day-to-day problem-solving effort will pay off. Some of the companies listed under this policy, Weirton Steel Corporation, Avis Inc., Northwestern Steel & Wire, Standard Brands, Hermann Miller, and EDO were on the forefront of including employees in the ranks of the corporate boards and giving their elected representatives a voice. In the early 1990s, Polaroid Corp. remained the most innovative in slashing management bureaucracy and in coming up with a real model of corporate republicanism. It had an elected Employees' Committee that replaced, in a business-like approach, the bureaucratic union structures.

Yet, as an enlightened management philosophy, participatory business democracy requires above all charismatic leadership, something not in excess under normal circumstances.

(4) The shareholder culture goes as far as a business enterprise can in order to identify itself with the human factors of production. It is basically the recognition of a triumvirate of interests and inputs that allow a successful enterprise to expand. They are: the investor-stakeholder, the management-stakeholder and the employee-stakeholder. In the United States of the early 1990s, this model was still only a subject of daring academic conjecture and a signpost of future management's real task.

This is also only a minuscule step away from the highest form of ESOP, which is: *(5) The entrepreneurial culture:* According to the same Blasi, this is to be found in none of the real world enterprises.

There is an undeniable impulse for speculation in attempting to project the future of employee stock ownership. Left and right, both ideological schools of management can claim a pattern of evolution derived from their special vantage point. Yet, the prevailing dual nature of the development of ESOPs is the least celebrated notion. One side of the equation expresses the underlying basis of any business entity, namely, that no amount of principled fairness and idealistic discourse can stand against the imperatives of profit-seeking. Still, the other side is as much proven by history. After all, fairness, productivity, and competitive advantage are one.

THE PURSUIT OF AN INDUSTRIAL POLICY WITH A CAPITALIST FACE

A commercially oriented industrial policy, as defined by the U. S. International Trade Commission, is "coordinated government actions to direct productive resources to help domestic producers in selected industries become more competitive."[18]

Most often the academic approach to the industrial policy theme is whether or not industrial policy is acceptable, beneficial, or feasible. In fact, various industrial policies have been pursued successfully in one country and another and from one period to another.

The real debate on the matter of economic policy cannot be over its desirability, which is unquestionable; it is only over its fine print.

A Historic Framework

Primarily, the first-time mover that sets out to develop a new industry comes across as the only true creator – as such he is not reproducible.

According to Alfred D. Chandler, Henry Ford was the quintessential first mover as the creator of the modern moving assembly line and the father of the American automotive industry. The American electrical equipment industry owes its leading position to the commercialization of inventions made by Thomas Edison, Elihu Thomson, and George Westinghouse. McCormick's harvesting machine set the advantageous position for American industries in two sectors: machine building and agriculture. Gebruder Stollwerck devoted his energies to making Germany the home country of chocolate. Adolph Miller's obsession with electrical batteries established German worldwide manufacturing supremacy in battery making.

> The distinction between first movers and challengers is of major importance to this history. First in the development of a new set of improved products or processes came *inventors*, usually individuals who obtained the patent. Then came the *pioneers*, the entrepreneurs who made the investments in facilities needed to commercialize a product or process – to bring it into general use. The *first movers* were pioneers or other entrepreneurs who made the three interrelated sets of investments in production, distribution, and management required to achieve the competitive advantages of scale, scope, or both. The challengers were the latecomers who took on the first movers by making a comparable set of investments and by developing comparable skills needed to obtain comparable competitive capabilities.[19]

This view, on the merits of the individual entrepreneur, is characteristic of the American school of economic thought. Yet, even if adjusted for the national economic environment that made such first-moves possible, the fact of the matter is that, for a variety of reasons, at the beginning of the twentieth century individuals and companies from one major country, the Unites States, were the first movers in a series of industrial inventions and processes. The rest of the world, with the peculiar exception of England, were challengers. Hence the dual nature of the rhetoric and of the practical approaches to the industrial policy philosophy between industrial haves and have-nots. Germany's systematic embrace of the industrial policy philosophy from the earliest years of the nineteenth century demonstrated the historical longevity of the dynamics between the option of free-market liberalism and governmental industrial management.

Coming from a long tradition of philosophical and practical political thinking that emphasized a statist orientation,[20] the concept of a nationally defined interest was the essence of the German thought system. In terms of economic principles, France theorized more over the merits of mercantilism and on the priority of the state's rights over the individual's self-interests. But Germany, with its decentralized system and a constellation of mini-states, had it both ways: interstate trade within the one-nation framework. It comprised within itself, in a nutshell, the wider, international dimensions of economic interdependence.

The self-interests of provinces and the enlightened action emanating from the establishment of the central Reich turned the public and government officialdom into the driving forces of industrialization, often mediating between the theory of free trade and the need for local economy protectionism and nurturing regulations. The big landowners to the east of the Elbe, the Prussian Junkers, and the western industrial and commercial establishment worked out a compromise solution during the famous reactionary years of the 1850s following the failed revolution of 1848.

Protectionist customs duties and direct economic leadership by the government were the two pillars of the German economic philosophy. Railroads and transportation, water, gas and power supply, mining, industry, and social policy were all outright state functions. Founder, sponsor, and godfather of big industrial cartels, German capitalism "showed a generous admixture of state and association control of business."[21] The most successful capitalist economy on the European continent was in those days "an economic system of mixed private and public ownership."[22] For all practical purposes, Germany's nineteenth-century contribution to the non-Anglo-Saxon species of capitalism remains the cornerstone of every single experiment with industrial policy undertaken, one after another, by all nations.

Although Marx had always stood as the symbol of sinister subversion of the free-enterprise system, the real discreditation of the Anglo-Saxon model can be traced back to the writings of two authentic German economics professors: Adam Müller (1779-1829) and Friedrich List (1789-1846). Here, in their writings, the idea of a supreme national economic interest that supersedes individual egotism is completely devoid of class struggle rhetoric, of prophetic overtones, of ideological evangelism. It is an honest view of social being from a common-sense perspective. From the classical Aristotelian Oeconomic of Germany's provincial rural communities, the German idea of the household as the locus of business activity took the name of state economics. Later on, Russia developed its own version derived from its rural obscie; the Chinese associated

the name of Mao with their version of primitive *peasant economics*;
for the Japanese, the ethics of the rural *samurai* came to represent
the quintessential Asian *Zen economics.*

Yet the German experience alone expressed the market and
the state forces together in the same theoretical breath.

Whether Adam Müller or Friedrich List were accomplished
theoreticians within the accepted academic community is beside
the point. They expressed out loud what proved to be the central
thought of the German collective belief, in the same way that Adam
Smith gave shape to the individualist economic and political
thinking of the Anglo-Saxon national mind. England's *economic
parliamentarism* sought to preserve the aristocratic ritual passage
in gentlemanly tournaments-*cum*-industrial competition. The
Germans sought to reinforce their nation's strength through loyal
workmanship and the pride of industry.

English noblemen, turned industrial barons, saw in Adam
Smith's writings a convenient class-agitprop blueprint – in the
name of the "intérêt des tous." The middle-class German businessman looked on the state as the protective institution in the name of
the "intérêt général."[23] Müller's state was definitely authoritarian; the
citizen was not only to obey the official laws, he was also expected
to acknowledge their absolute authority in all spheres of life in
everyday customs and behavior and within the family as well as in
the areas of religion and science.[24]

It started with private property itself, a cornerstone of the
capitalist enterprise. Private property was defined by Müller in the
traditional vein of the prevailing communal rights and of the
socially circumscribed commonwealth: "a kind of deposit taken out
of the eternal common property, to be utilized and employed by its
owners on a temporary basis for the benefit of the people."[25] Hence
the state economist is in a hierarchically superior position vis-a-vis
the private enterprises; he defends the common interest against
the inherent misappropriation of the common good by the private
interests. More to the point, Müller describes the state economist's
functions within society as necessary "in order to detect the
antinational; to learn how to resist and reject the heartlessness and
depravity of these clerical, aristocratic, or bourgeois individuals; to
learn how little consideration and respect is due to such a bunch of
egotists when the goal is to forge a people; to reinforce the
courage necessary to conceive the eternal nature of the state, to
reestablish it, and to sacrifice without compunction whatever

unworthiness tries to resist it."[26]

Müller filters all of his practical recommendations through the interests of the national state. Money is not simply the means of treasury accumulation, in need of a hedge against inflation, under constant assault from devaluation or unruly speculators. Money is principally a symbol in the market exchange of values and, therefore, the only "real and eternal money" is paper money since it is simply a bank note. It is thus up to the national bank to issue money according "to the needs of the market and the business cycle. We need money that is created when required and disappears in accordance with the reduction of demand."[27]

As a rational housekeeper, the state regulates the division of labor, the guilds and corporations. It oversees the imports and manages the effectiveness of a nation's exports. The ultimate aim of the economic state is not the maximization of profits on a short-term basis or for individual satisfaction, but for the preservation of the 'harmony,' 'equilibrium' and the conserved strength of the people 'in any imaginable crisis.'

Müller's piecemeal solutions are still valid and strikingly modern. His *economic Weltanschauung* is more revealing and more influential than Adam Smith's economic liberalism, in connection with the remarkable success stories of Germany and Japan.

This axiomatic distinction between the two schools of economic thought, free-market capitalism and social market socialism, points to their distinct sources of inception from the earlier days of industrialization, as they were the stepchildren of two opposing economic orders.

Uncoupled from the ideological overtones that inadvertently associated social market *socialism* with Nazism, a more fruitful experimentation with *social market capitalism* was undertaken in bits and pieces by ruined post-World War II social-democratic nations as diverse as Japan, France, Singapore, Malaysia, and Germany. They all brought new insights into the workings and the strengths of economic policy making emanating from a concerted action of a national governing body.

This new economic thinking helped them bolster their devastated industries into first-class economic powerhouses and to replace Anglo-Saxon world leadership as measured by the main industrial indicators – productivity growth rate, per capita income growth, industrial rate of growth – for the first time in modern history. Thus the new economic thinking finally arrived at the door of the superpower war-strategy cabinets.

The overall rate of production increases in the 1970s and 1980s were consistently in the range of 4 - 5 percent for Germany and Japan, as against 1 - 2 percent for the United States. In a 1993 survey on manufacturing productivity, the most ambitious, conservative, and comprehensive at the time, McKinsey Global Institute reported that already "in five of the case studies – autos, auto parts, metalworking, steel, and consumer electronics – labor productivity in Japan is significantly higher than in the U.S. (by 45 percent in steel in 1990). In the other four industries–computers, soap, and detergent, beer, and food processing–Japan is behind."[28] Actually it was 24 percent higher in automotive parts, 19 percent higher in metal-working, 16 percent higher in car manufacturing, and 15 percent higher in consumer electronics. The report concludes that "in metalworking and steel production, labor productivity in Germany has caught up with labor productivity in the U.S."

Ironically, the report is rich in detailed observations, industry by industry, but when it comes to explain the differences in productivity between Germany and the United States, it finds that 95 percent of it is "not explained," while for Japan and the United States, about half of the gap is also "not explained." It admits, disarmingly, that it "is troubling that the economics literature has not provided fully satisfactory explanations of why productivity grows over time within countries, or the related question of why productivity varies across countries at a point in time. Numerous economic studies have investigated the contributions to productivity that derive from capital, education, technology and other factors. Nevertheless, there is no consensus explanation of productivity differences in the literature and many economists regard both the source of productivity growth over time and the reasons for different productivity levels as being, in large part, mysterious."[29]

So much for the science of economics!

In fact, in the final analysis, it all comes down to a rewriting of the national rhetoric and a change in the national economic chain of command. As a matter of restructuring the inner workings of national policy making, the United States had to embark on a comprehensive approach to state economics by avoiding "a one-sided answer concerning the relation between state power and the economic activity of individuals."[30] Its task is to further reform its central institutions of economic policy-making by upgrading their functions and statutes to the standards of a modern commonwealth state in accordance with the experience of the other modern states.

As the past record showed and as other nations' more recent successes attested, clearly stated national goals, explicitly designed institutions, and publicly sanctioned shared responsibilities were the conditions for a successful, national economic policy together with an equitable distribution of costs and rewards. A few such examples are listed below.

The French Auto Industry

The French auto industry had a history of self-reliance, with a successful increase of output from 1,850 cars in 1898 to 45,000 in 1914.[31] However, like many other European industries, after World War I it lost its competitive edge to American mass production. By 1919, the American giant auto firms had cornered Renault, Citroën, and Peugeot into a mere 48 percent of the French domestic market. Although they recovered some of that, up to 63 percent by 1926, in 1927 the French auto industry's productivity lost further ground: "to build one vehicle required seventy man-days in the United States, two hundred in France."[32]

The real story starts well after World War II when the French auto industry, partly nationalized in the 1930s (Renault), partly still private (Peugeot, Citroën), found itself under relentless attack from American and European competitors.

- First, the French government excluded foreign competitors from domestic production, with minor exceptions. It rejected Ford's and GM's plans to build plants in Strasbourg, 1964. It squeezed out the attempt made by Fiat to acquire Citroën, 1973. It blocked the German firm Bosch from entering the French auto components market, and it outbid the British firm Lucas in the same attempt, 1978.
- Second, it took over the task of coordinating joint ventures and pooling research among the French auto firms. Renault and Peugeot agreed to share patents, 1966, then to standardize components, and to cooperate in a components plant, 1979.
- Third, it outright saved Citroën from bankruptcy by a concentrated infusion of government loans and the underwriting of its takeover by Peugeot, 1974.

- Fourth, it thrust governmental resources into subsidized R&D projects, 1979. It supported the design and construction of prototypes of fuel-efficient vehicles, 1981, and further subsidized the research into advanced automation techniques.
- Fifth, it sponsored further expansion of the French auto industry by acquiring foreign competitors. While Peugeot paid for the acquisition of Chrysler-Europe with its own cash, the state stood behind the ensuing success of the operation by easing the rationalization of the new extended company. Painful layoffs and plant closings were possible without social confrontations or major disruptions for business and labor as the government negotiated a series of compromises. Financially overextended and under pressure from the competition, Peugeot was still laying off thousands of workers by 1984, while unable to match the productivity of other European car makers such as Fiat. Fiat produced 26 cars per worker per year, while Peugeot produced only ten. The difference in labor productivity had an obvious effect on profitability and competitiveness. To reduce the gap in productivity, Peugeot had to make large and continuous investments in its plants. Peugeot was able to make these additional investments only with the backing of the French state.[33] Due to a sustained combination of skillful management and the state's unwavering backing, Peugeot returned to profitability by 1985.

The Japanese Semiconductor Industry

Can government foster innovation and purposefully originate and develop new technologies? Can government rationalize the systematic and successful pursuit of technological R&D? The Japanese strategy on semiconductors convinced everybody, whether incurable economic liberals or skeptical CEOs, that indeed it can.

The Japanese administration's first acquaintance with computer technology came in 1955 when MITI (Japan's Ministry of International Trade and Industry) decided to take an organized look into the promises of the emerging computer manufacturing, by and large an American game. The committee drew the only expected conclusion, namely, to put under official restrictive monitoring any foreign imports of such technology, while setting up the institutional framework for a home-based Japanese computer industry.

> The Electronics Industry Provisional Development Act, made law in 1957, authorized research cartels exempted from the Antimonopoly Law, direct subsidies, low-interest loans, tax incentives, and R&D tax credits. Between 1957 and 1961, the industry received only $1 million in direct subsidies and approximately $25 million in indirect subsidies (mostly from the Japan Development Bank). A new electronics division was established within MITI's Heavy Industry Bureau, and an Electronics Industry Deliberation Council was formed as a government-industry forum.[34]

The strategy that the Japanese administration relentlessly pursued for the next three decades, while resembling very closely the French approach to the auto industry, focused more on creating new institutions and new organizations with well-defined functions and purposes. Rather than restructuring and remodeling existing productive capacities, as in the French experience, the Japanese administration had to create a new industry and a new management class for that industry. Simple financial backing or trade policies would not suffice. The governmental decision-making body had to exercise a business function rather than an administrative one, and that set apart the Japanese case from most other state-led economic policies. It combined its administrative prerogatives against foreign competition, as it nurtured its own home-grown baby enterprises, but it also developed, in an imaginative way, new avenues for industrial progeny. Here are the major steps that were pursued in Japan's state entrepreneurial managerial policy:

- First, Japan imposed a resolute set of restrictions on imports of electronic products in general, and computers in particular, by a combination of (1) high tariffs, raised in 1960 from 15 to 25 percent, and (2) a demand of import licensing that would later exclude from import whole segments of the industry, such as small- and medium-sized computers.

- Second, it brought about a gradual limitation and then exclusion of foreign, wholly owned subsidiaries in Japan, such as IBM-Japan, and replaced them with joint ventures under Japanese control: Hitachi-RCA (1961), Mitsubishi-TRW (1962), NEC-Honeywell (1962), Oki-Sperry (1963), and Toshiba-GE (1964).

- Third, it engaged in a strategy of underwriting state-sponsored green-field joint-ventures: *(1)* 1961 – A supercompany, the Japan Electronics Computer Corporation, was established under the leadership of a former MITI vice-president. It was created and financed through low-interest government loans, and it reunited the six best Japanese computer companies. *(2)* 1964 – MITI's Electronic Industry Deliberative Council set up the Information Processing Developing Center, a private information clearinghouse subsidized to develop supercomputers, rationalize the production of computer peripherals and supply the industry with computer technical personnel. *(3)* 1966 – MITI sponsored a 10-billion-yen project, the Electro-Technical Laboratory, dedicated to special research tasks, led by Hitachi and subdivided into mainframe hardware (Hitachi, Oki, NEC), optical-character-recognition hardware (Toshiba, Oki, Mitsubishi), disk drives (Hitachi Fujitsu), software, et cetera. *(4)* 1971 – The Pattern Information Processing System was designated by MITI to produce hardware and software for high-speed computers.

- Fourth, Japan committed its national resources to gaining competitive advantage in the production of the critical elements of the emerging electronics-computer industry, namely, semiconductor chips. Initially, this task was assigned to Nippon Telegraph and Telephone (NTT), already founded in 1952 as a state enterprise under the supervision of the Ministry of Posts and Telecommunications, having virtual monopoly over domestic public telephony and telegraph and privatized only in 1985. Its article of faith was "preferential procurement of Japanese chips. . . consistent with NTT's 'Japan-only' procurement strategies."[35] That was to be the cornerstone principle in awarding contracts to Japanese suppliers of superconductors, NEC, Fujitsu, Hitachi, and Oki. In 1971, the Law for Provision Measures to Promote Specific Electronic and Machinery Industries further strengthened the state's responsibility in the superconductor industry. "MITI was to finance R&D and rationalize production, NTT to handle product and process development."[36] The actions bore fruits very soon: by the late 1970s, only 20 to 25 percent of the large Japanese superconductor market was supplied by American firms. From that point on, the fate of the head-to-head competition on superconductors, and the computer industry at large, was fair game for the Japanese cartel. By the early 1990s, it virtually surpassed all of the industrialized countries' production of computer chips, and if not for the American late-found "managed trade" stratagem, as discussed further, the eminently successful Japan-style industrial policy might have bred a Japan-style world information industry by the turn of the twenty-first century. From the early 1970s, Japanese dominance in large-scale integrated (LSI) circuitry, and (1975) in metal oxide silicon (MOS) memories, the battle for very large scale integrated (VLSI) circuits (1978-79) was followed by the 16K DRAM success story in 1979. "By 1982, Japanese firms controlled 70 percent of the market for 64K DRAMs";[37] in 1986, they controlled 90 percent of the market for 256K DRAMs; in 1988, they controlled over 90 percent of the market for 1-megabit DRAMs. At that point there were only two American firms left to hand over the flag, before DARPA (Defense Advanced Research Projects Agency) led an American counter-offensive that regained all lost ground.

The German Steel Industry

A *cause célèbre* in the tumultuous history of the twentieth century, Germany is also a special case in industrial policy-making. Industrial policy, as *the systematic pursuit of social development*, is a German product. In its basic form, it demanded the wholesale involvement of the state as an instrument for public policy. In its less subtle forms, before World War II it involved state coordination through specialized agencies and institutions, of ambiguous character, such as banking institutions, the military establishment, the educational system, and the corporate monopoly.

After World War II, the defeated German nation was never allowed by the allied coalition to recover to its full functional capability. However, the ensuing cold war and superpower geopolitics helped Germany recapture a relatively high degree of economic self-determination. This alone was enough in aiding Germany to work its way out of post-war destitution. It also forced its reemerged establishment to look for nonpolitical, nonmilitary, and nonadministrative channels of economic command. It soon found them in the enduring institutions, national in character and scope, that were the Deutsche Bank, labor unions, academia, and the mass media, especially television.

German postwar reconstruction and its regained global competitive advantage was built on the new-found social instruments of management that proved one important lesson, that timeless macroeconomic principles supersede particular forms of institutions or policy-making instruments. Here is one example:

The steel industry has been the showpiece of German industrial success. Yet low demand and high competition in the years after World War II required an ongoing process of adjustment, reinvention, downsizing and enhanced productivity in order to let Germany merely maintain its competitive edge.

- First, after a few years of uncertainty and the forced breakup of the large steel cartels – Krupps and Vereinigte Stahlwerke were the leading ones before the war – the reconcentration of the industry was undertaken in the years after 1947. The parallel reconcentration of the banking industry, on the one hand, and the implementation of the *codetermination* principles (union representation on the boards of directors) on the other hand, were other steps in the national reconstruction effort. In addition, special tax credits, with accelerated depreciation provisions, the establishment of the Investment Aid Law in 1952, which required all German firms to participate in a private investment fund, *Kreditanstalt für Wiederaufbau*, government funds provided by the Marshall Plan, et cetera, all helped accomplish the reconstruction of the devastated steel industry by the late 1950s.

- Second, the worldwide crisis in the steel industry, which developed after 1962-63, marked the beginning of the new German-style cooperative industrial policy that reunited management, labor, credit institutions, and local administration. From cartelization – in the name of *Walzstahlkontore*, in the 1950s, to rationalization – in the name of *Rationalisierungsgruppen*, a real turnabout was accomplished on short notice. Starting in 1967, new methods of making steel, such as by direct reduction in electric furnaces and a focus on the specialty steel market, were used to raise productivity, create flexible work units, reduce overcapacity, concentrate control, and reduce labor costs.

- Third, a sense of social co-responsibility on the part of all economic players was essential. *(1)* Banks were willing to make sacrifices if necessary – allowing for a so-called Krupp discount in interest rates that was the equivalent of a veritable private subsidy (1977), or agreeing to write off some 60 million marks in outstanding loans to a number of Saar Valley firms (1978). *(2)* Labor was willing to accept heavy reductions in exchange for orderly relocation and social aid during the transition period. Negotiations conceded to six waves of ongoing job losses, 6,000 employees between 1974-77, another 9,000 employees between 1978 and 1983 in the Saar Valley alone; and some 35,000 employees in the Ruhr Valley, from September 1987 to June 1988 with the closing of Krupp's Rheinhausen plant. *(3)* The Federal government was willing to step up to the plate and provide bridge loans (2.2 billion marks to Arbed in 1982), subsidies, and social programs to the disaffected (half a billion marks in the closing of Krupp's Rheinhausen plant). *(4)* Management was willing to merge their ranks and concentrate the steel industry into fewer and fewer entities. The rationalization of the Saar Valley steel industry, and of the Ruhr Valley group, took painful cost-cutting steps, but was eventually reached without any real resistance. The Arbed group came out on top in the Saar Valley, while the Thyssen group came to dominate the Ruhr Valley. By the mid-1980s, together, they were able to control well over 50 percent of the German steel industry, up from a mere 23 percent in 1960.

Explanations are many as to why Germany outperformed its European and American counterparts. Many such explanations extract one factor or another out of context and advertise it as the central catalyst for economic development: the banks were overseeing company management performance, they replaced the short-term profit-focused shareholder with a long-term view of the business cycles; labor was always skilled and highly productive; there was decentralization among the private, small-size specialized firms; a comprehensive social contract was observed between labor and management, and between companies themselves; the political situation was stable, and so on. But Germany performed outstandingly under national-socialist centralization, it performed under the modern social market welfare state, and it performed under its own nineteenth century brand of liberalism.[38] *Industrial* policy is something more than industrial *policy*, it is *industrial nationalism*.

The United States' Experience

Liberal economists' rhetoric notwithstanding, nationalist industrial policies practiced by the United States on a worldwide scale raised economic macromanagement proficiency to as yet unrivaled heights. While eminently effective, its centralized and coherent character escaped the attention of many astute students of the American system. Furthermore, the politics of the *liberal industrial policy* hadn't been desecrated in ordinary minds as long as its priestly practice assured the mystique of the results.

To the faithful liberal voter the Sherman Act of 1890, the Clayton Antitrust Act of 1914, the Federal Trade Commission (FTC) Act of 1914, and the Celler Antimerger Statute of 1950 all aimed at the strengthening the free-enterprise system. The net result was, paradoxically indeed, the limitation of the free-enterprise system by bestowing upon the state the authority to decide when, how, how much, and how long, a company *is* and *is not* a private enterprise.

Apart from strictly national defense matters, the entire body of political debate and decision-making activity in the United States is, ultimately, consumed by the burning issues of economic policy. *(1)* Crafting the government budget itself is perhaps the major instrument of national economic management. *(2)* Nationally designed financial policies, through money supply instruments, interest rates, banking regulations, and investments incentives, are another set of tools for guiding the national economy. *(3)* Heavy weight lifting is accomplished by exercising the levers and pulleys of taxation and fiscal policy: fees, tariffs, fares, charges, contributions, and deductions. *(4)* Direct business oversight and monitoring, far reaching and pervasive, is made possible by the use of credit allocation policies and trade regulations, the enforcement of antitrust laws, and the endorsement/interdiction of industry cartelization or protectionism. *(5)* Government's outright partnership with the business community at the high end – research and development – is ensured through direct subsidies or shelter from competition, through public subcontracting and bailouts. *(6)* The politicized use of the mass media with its array of opinion-leading outlets, analysts, advertisers, forecasters and spin doctors, through their impact on the larger masses of consumers and by their focusing on the narrow but active business leadership, shapes business and consumer behavior.

In order to understand the peculiarities of the American system, one has to go as far back as the origins of the Anglo-Saxon nation and of its pragmatic spirit. The peculiarities of American industrial policy were due to its imperial scope and scale, but mostly to the use of that English-devised ghostly market, the *invisible hand* approach which was applied consistently to international relations, to state affairs, and to its own government. In practice it meant, (1) Always side with the weak party; (2) Turn your act of assistance into a profitable transaction by selling it, competitively, to both sides; (3) Use the ruin of the stronger as an opportunity, since their reconstruction effort creates new businesses.

The popular culture of the late twentieth century had a brief but intense fling with the laissez-faire myths advertised by the *Hollywood school of economics*, demonstrating the success of that industrial policy when dressed up as a liberal fairy tale.

But it was about time to make a more rational, open and accountable, that is, a socially framed, economic policy.

Chapter VIII

The Making of Eurasia

CONVERGENCE WITHIN EUROPE

The reform process in the Soviet Union/Russia had now become comprehensive, embracing the spheres of politics, ideology, society, the economy, and law. Part and parcel of this process was the search for workable models to help transform the orthodox Marxist-Leninist, centralized, one-party state into a modern, prag-matically oriented economic machine. The transformation, in the nineteenth and early twentieth centuries, of the ideologically radical West European Marxist workers' parties into mass-based, social democratic organizations did provide a model relevant to Gorbachev's efforts at reforming the CPSU. Similarly, the mixture of elements of state planning, market economy and social welfare, so characteristic of many West European countries, had much to recommend as an example to Soviet reforms.

In this context, one school of international thought saw in *perestroika* the condition for an improvement in the European security climate as well. This observation was warranted because of the "new thinking" ordained by Gorbachev and new concepts of Soviet/Russian security that were being advanced. The new concept included the pre-eminence of political rather than military factors of security; "reasonable sufficiency" (*razumnaya dostatochnost*) of armed forces; the achievement of security at "lower levels of armaments"; and the removal of imbalances through reductions rather than increases in the level of armament. Such changes in Moscow's European policy gave high hopes of an unprecedented European unity and the opening of an era of security and cooperation.

By contrast, another view saw in the removal of tactical nuclear forces from the European theater the first real possibility of European conventional warfare in the post-World War II epoch.

The adulteration of the power structure in Europe, the threat of the emergence of an all-dominating German nation, and the increase of interethnic strife to unprecedented levels, all pointed to the need for a radical re-thinking of the European theater. To the question of whether or not all these developments were leading to a new security and cooperation concordat in Europe, the answer should be an unequivocal "yes". Such a concordat, however, was to be delivered through the unavoidable circumstance of social hardship.

In that movement toward a new Europe, the economic and technical high ground enjoyed by Germany initially signaled a German revival and domination from within a Western European-based community. But Germany lacked everything else. From natural resources to military and intelligence institutions, all the elements of a powerful Eurasian arbitrator, an unchallengeable military as well as political hegemon, rested with Russia.

German technical expertise could reinvigorate the dilapidated Russian civilian industry, and could assist in the massive military conversion, but it had no means to ingest the Russian colossus.[1] The newly emerged, vast economic commonwealth from the Atlantic to the Pacific has Moscow, as much politically as geographically, not at its periphery but at its very center. The merging of state economies with social-market capitalism was meant to create the middle ground for a Eurasian commonwealth of mixed economies encompassing diverse nations and ideologies.

In the long run, the economic colossus born out of the new economic giants from across the Atlantic – the Eurasian vs. the North/South-American Commonwealth – was as much exciting as unsettling. A world unto itself, the new bicephalous economic animal would also serve as the strategic redeployment of a new economic tribe against the emerging challenge arising out of Asia.

* * *

The end of the Cold War era marked also the dawning days of real-time social management and the debut of television soap-opera world politics. It was the dismantling of the Soviet war machine that engendered a persistent bewilderment despite the apparently real events staged on screen. What was really happening? How did it come about? What was the significance of such large-scale social engineering and what would be the final impact of the larger movement for world *perestroika* as it was unfolding on a global scale?

The world's business community went through dramatic soul-searching as it struggled between the once in a lifetime temptations of the *new frontier of the wild East* and the vagaries of an unassessed, as yet, political risk environment. Political scientists themselves revised old schemes and theories to fit the curves and intersections of time series of past events, without risking commitment to any *politically incorrect* judgments. At the same time, the ever ambitious entrepreneurs enthusiastically offered unsubstantiated *feel-good* assurances. After all, weren't idealism and hope, in and of themselves, proper components in any successful decision in the making of a great leap forward?

Nevertheless, the general public was at first left rather undecided on how to integrate the last years of the twentieth century within the collective memory of continuity and coherence. To understand that would have required an intellectual guidebook reinforcing a sense of inner logic and consistency of the *multitude* in a *historical* perspective. In seeking the answer, the inherent human predisposition and beliefs held that *change* must be identified through *permanence*, as *existence* that is *becoming*. So the prevailing question was not so much 'what is happening'? as 'what does it all mean?' Were they witnessing the genuine impact of personality on history, that is, the consequences of the enigmatic ascent of a young provincial party *aparatchik* to the center of Soviet power? Was that action somehow derived from the innerworkings of the providential hand or from the dark corners of the Machiavellian handlers of history?

After all, what was the crux of the inside story of Eastern Europe? Many honest scholars of history were enchanted to bring a sense of Hegelian logic to the Brownian world of political passions, in itself an ambition as candid as inspiring when dealing with the raw exercise of power.

* * *

From one viewpoint, Immanuel Kant's *Critique of Pure Reason* and von Clausewitz's *Critique of Pure War* started it all, around the turn of the eighteenth century. Their cultural order reveled in emphasizing the nature of human existence as prescribed by the imperatives of a supraordinate level of intent. Their conclusion: as is the act of reasoning, so is the act of waging war, since both reasoning and war are purpose-oriented human acts of will.

Following in the footsteps of such a voluntaristic blueprint, nineteenth-century Europe witnessed the triumph of the full-scale application of that speculative thinking. History reinforced the validity of this philosophy on two counts. (1) On the theoretical level, Max Weber's celebration of bureaucracy legitimized administrative capitalism. *"The decisive reason for the advance of bureaucratic organization has always been its purely technical superiority over any other form of organization. . . Precision, speed, unambiguity, . . . reduction of friction and of material and personal costs – these are raised to the optimum point in the strictly bureaucratic organization.*[2] (2) On a practical level, the unrivaled success of the corporate-state model engineered through the authority of Chancellor Bismarck's guiding concept of the social state administration.

Enriched by its experimentation and critique, in the end, bureaucratic modern society acquired respect and acceptance in its many forms and shapes in country after country. But it happened that while it was still developing in Germany, its consequences reverberated throughout the world, as much awfully as rewardingly.

* * *

Centered on the continental plateau, unprotected by either natural or man-made barriers, the quintessential challenge for the German nation was to ensure national security. Germany's (and for that matter, Russia's) march on the offensive was a typical effort to counterbalance external adversities. The subsequent power selection process, in a series of European wars, was only the inevitable last act of the Hobbesian assertion of sovereignty over Europe. The ensuing defeat of Germany ended the ongoing battle for dominance in the European theater. It also called for the recycling of her economic and social ideas on new grounds. In Europe, it was now the USSR's finest hour.

The USSR and the United States were left to sort out who

would be the global leader this time. As the scale of the conflict took on remarkable proportions, the nature of the contentious states as military entities remained unchanged. And that was more apparent as both states went further and broader in their push to subordinate their civilian bases to the all-encompassing goal of military superiority.

The end result of such a demanding internal process was the development of highly interlocked and militarized bureaucratic national organizations. Fully 60 percent of the Soviet Union's industrial output was allocated to the production of military and military-related paraphernalia,[3] while 40 percent of the total American industrial output was reported to be serving the military machine. "That means that 4 out of every 10 workers in factory America work for or in the security department!"[4]

Yet there was an unmistakable difference in the two countries' approach to militarization. One was the *war economy* system of the USSR, which regimented civil and military systems into one integrated totalitarian system. The American version of economic militarization was accomplished through a skillful segregation of the civilian and the military.

The American approach to the military-industrial complex was to relegate it to little known federal agencies that virtually monopolized and insulated its pursuits from the rest of the population. On one side there was the capitalist market jungle. On the other side, there was strategic planning and research, industrial policy. It was DARPA, it was Sematech, that enabled the American economy to sustain the war effort. Engine of inventions during the years of the cold war, DARPA originated lasers in the 1960s; and the transmission of data through the development of packet switching that made possible the explosion of the Telnet, later, Internet; in the 1970s, computer chips that turned semiconductors into the hearts of small weapons and personal computers; high-temperature metals, composite materials, modern television, passenger jets, weather satellites, microwave ovens, all the nuts and bolts of our informational technology from Teflon to crazy glue came to life in defense industry laboratories. "Since 1955, the U.S. Government has spent more than $1 trillion on research and development of nuclear arms and other weaponry. According to the National Science Foundation, that represented 62 percent of all Federal research expenditures. In addition, untold dollars went into related efforts, like the civilian space program's $90 billion race with the Soviet Union to land men on the Moon."[5]

The classified character of most of the scientific research, the non-civilian destination of most of the technological breakthroughs, the social insulation of the factors of progress from the mainstream society and the inevitable development of two-tiered nations were evident more and more within each of the two competing superpowers. Unlimited security considerations on the part of an elite group created the largest mass phenomenon of social alienation ever. It allowed for a de facto comfortable socialism for the top ranks in each of the two societies, while leaving the rank and file to scramble for a living in a merciless capitalist fashion.

THE THAW, FINALLY

In January 1987, the USSR began to put in place legislation permitting foreign participation in the ownership and operation of joint ventures. By June 1987, the first of these joint ventures with a Western partner (involving the Finnish firm Kati Mynti) was registered with the USSR's Ministry of Finance and then acquired the status and the rights of a separate legal entity. In November of the same year, the first US/USSR joint venture (involving Combustion Engineering, Inc.) was registered.[6]

By November 1990, the President of the United States was in a position to declare at a formal European Conference that the cold war was finally over. An unprecedented realignment took place over the span of three years.

A close policy connection between security demands and domestic economic development had always figured preeminently in the strategic thinking of both superpowers. The call for more domestic privations was always justified by security imperatives, while the call for military restraints in the name of domestic reconstruction rarely lasted. True, Lenin's short-lived but famous NEP of the 1920s and Khrushchev's experimentation with reduced military budgets were the equivalent of the 'guns and butter' slogans of the 1960s in the United States, but nothing came anywhere close to the large-scale military dismantling that followed the détente of the late 1980s and early 1990s.

As early as the 1970s the Soviet high command concluded that their technological capabilities would not easily be able to compete with its American rival, notably in the area of emerging technologies. The SDI program, especially, sounded very ominous with its implicit threat of a new round of arms race. In 1978, Soviet Chief of Staff Ogarkov drove the point home by bringing up a quote from Engels: "Nothing depends on economic conditions so much as a country's army and navy. Weapons, structure, organization, tactics, and strategy depend above all on the level of production and the means of communication which has been achieved at a given time."[7] The political entourage of Brezhnev was unmistakably signaling, through all of the late 1970s, its willingness to proceed with deep cuts in strategic arsenals, was promoting thorough moratoriums, even unilateral moves to stop new nuclear experiments in order to constrain the arms race.

On the other hand, three American presidents failed to convince their political entourages of the necessity of a similar response. Eisenhower had been stopped by the U-2 spy plane surprise. Kennedy was unceremoniously removed from the political scene for planning a policy of rapprochement, and so was Nixon for his brand of *realpolitik* détente.

Indeed, the near deadlock of the 1970s had to be broken by some unconventional thinking. And the 1980s were unconventional. The imperative conclusion that security and economic development were inextricably linked had to be revealed in a more dramatic fashion by the bankrupting arms race of the Reagan administration.

* * *

At the time of its signing in 1979, SALT II was hailed by its sponsors as the avenue for predictability and the prospect of an environment of diminished threat. Nevertheless, it became more and more obvious that the premises upon which such expectations were built were collapsing very fast.

The United States was moving to deploy its Pershing IIs, ground-launched cruise missiles, MXs, Trident II, and the B-1, and embarked on the SDI program. That and the USSR's unpopular war in Afghanistan were eroding the position of Ogarkov, Chief of the General Staff. His subsequent public disassociation from the

Soviet political leadership's preoccupation with social consumption and social welfare marked the opening of a new era. The ensuing demise of Ogarkov sealed off the future of the military solution as early as 1983. The subsequent events made more obvious that something radical was in the works in the Kremlin.

In fact, it was becoming increasingly clear as early as 1980 that within the Soviet Union's decision-making circles, a conclusion had been reached in response to the changes taking place within the sacrosanct world of the weapons industry. According to Ogarkov himself, three major changes were occurring in those years in the field of military development: (1) The decreasing value of nuclear weapons as a result of their proliferation; (2) The increasing importance of conventional high-technology weapons systems; (3) The expected emergence in the very near future of even more destructive and previously unknown types of weapons based on new physical principles.[8] As Ogarkov noted, "work on such weapons is already under way, it would be a serious mistake not to consider their implications 'right now.' "

And indeed, no mistakes were made. For, at the time that such warnings were heard in the Soviet mass media, decisive steps had already been taken toward the next political gambit. With five years under the guidance of Brezhnev himself, then of Andropov, and then of Chernenko, Gorbachev created the momentum to proceed with the first move in breaking the world's political stalemate. Under the global reign of MAD (Mutual Assured Destruction) strategy, war, in the classical sense of diplomacy pursued through different means, was no longer a real option. In a Hegelian sense, war came to be perceived in its historical circumscribed existence. Nuclear war was no longer just the antipode of peace, but its own invalidation.

War ceased to be winnable. Both powers decided that it was time to settle the score and draw new border lines accordingly.

Signs of an unusual course of events were apparent all through the 1980s. They prompted many observers of history to seek parallels with other series of events in the distant and the recent past. First, there were the speculative excesses of the 1980s that ended with the stock-market crash of 1987, recalling the 1929 crash and the specter of dramatic events to come. But the feared conflagrations of other times were now replaced by even more awesome events in the following years: the domino-effect fall of governments in Eastern Europe, in the fall of 1989, recalled the chain reaction in revolutionary 1848; and the bombardment of Russia's parliament, the White House, in 1991 evoked the storming of the Bastille, celebrating the beginning of another new era. Europe was once again crossed by the recurring specter of revolution.

Yet the unmistakable feelings of *dejà vu* underscored the need for a revised historical hermeneutics. Within the life span of a generation, phases of development were recognized as repeated patterns in the book of political management.

From the 1960s, a time of revolutionary mania, to the 1990s, a time of revolutionary political circus, the notion of revolution as social renewal was an ever-recurring cycle, having lost its daring mystique.

Under open challenge from below, secretly encouraged by the intelligentsia, the entrenched *nomenklatura* of the two systems were shown to be mere travesties of themselves. As was discovered in those days, bureaucracy could easily be flouted by a paper-based counterbureaucracy. Ultimately, the new revolution in the name of the counterrevolution was coming back from the future.

* * *

History books often point to peace-loving democratic societies pursuing urban trades and professions, symbols of civilizations' moments of refinement: the Athenians, emblem of democracy, commerce and sophistry; the Cartagenians, cosmopolitan traders on the Mediterranean; the Venetians, urban residents engaged in trade and the arts. Yet, as a matter of fact, they had also traded other peoples' property and bodies: the Athenians made their bid for supremacy in the Peloponnesian takeover, the Cartagenians in invading the plains of Italy, the Venetians by sacking and looting the riches of Constantinople.

The idea of peace-loving democracies was the ultimate mystification of history. The next round of power politics was to be opened among the two vast and rich commonwealths: the Eurasian vs. the American. Their love/hate relationship was also related to having the Asian nations ambiguously consigned to the sidelines.

EVENTS WITHIN REGULARITIES —
CYCLICAL HISTORY

The classical Aristotelian account on the matter of political cycles distinguishes five forms of public government: monarchy, aristocracy, oligarchy, democracy, and tyranny.

In the beginning there were what Giambattista Vico called *(1) domestic monarchies*[9] – the rule of the supreme sovereign over all of a nation's life. His absolute power and the general equality of all his subjects are, however, only of relative endurance. Slowly, an invisible process of stratification takes place. This process consolidates itself into *(2)* the *constitutional monarchy*. The absolute rule of the autocracy is, at first, diminished by an emerging *power-sharing* compact made with the growing class of the *(3) oligarchic aristocracy*. This is meant to consolidate a common defense against the growing ranks of the poor, but classical class warfare is the sorrowful consequence of the new compromise. Soon, the new order explodes into violence and the *(4)* reign of the *popular government* begins.

Unstable from the beginning, the self-empowered legislature of the *many* soon extends to *all* in an inexorable evolution toward social dissolution, from *democratic participation* to generalized *anarchy*. Yet this unbearable result and the obvious collapse of former social structures call for the reinstallment of the rule of order and unity through the *(5) civil* (presidential) *tyrant*. For Aristotle, tyrants arose "from among the common people and the masses, in opposition to the notables, so that the demos should not suffer injustice at their hands. . . The great majority of the tyrants began as demagogues, so to speak, and won confidence by calumniating the notables.[10]

This way, the popular brings back to absolute power the new guarantor and protector of the collective/many.[11]

> Until the necessary institutions had been devised there was no real alternative to aristocracy but the dictatorship of a single individual and his family. Then, as the tyrant and his successors (from his own family) brought new men into positions of responsibility, and political *aret* (competence and 'know-how') gradually seeped down into at least the upper layers of the social strata below the nobility, a time came when

the propertied class (or even the whole body of citizens) found that they could dispense with the tyrant and govern by themselves.[12]

Indeed, in the old days the tyrant was not so much an evil dictator as a popular antihero, in the words of Glotz:

> The people regarded tyranny only as an expedient. They used it as a battering-ram with which to demolish the citadel of the oligarchs, and when their end had been achieved they hastily abandoned the weapon which wounded their hands.[13]

According to this ageless political routine, on the heels of the dismantling of the bureaucratic-military-political structures of the modern superpower state, an inherent populist, antiestablishment reaction follows. The rebellious sentiment thus incurred is inherently directed against state-administration's mandate and demands a piece of the national assets. The new republicanism displays the hitherto covert polarization between the few timeservers and the opportunists, and the larger mass of the disgruntled, turned overt.

The Aristotelianism of Global Politics

The argument on the national pattern of evolution is also a valid international manifestation of the same cycle, whether one country resorts to *national mercantilism* for its own interests or favors *nationalist protectionism*. The small states' security needs, as clients, are, by definition, protectionist, under the assault of the (1) hegemonic state's open border policy.

Yet, as the hegemonic power integrates within the (2) international system of dependency, it becomes, progressively, protectionist, at the same time that the former marginal nations act more and more like self-determined entities. This is the time of a broad-based optimism and balance of power participation in the world order. It is a time when national interest and self-determination principles expand to more nations on the open arena of international cooperation.

But the unrestricted demand for democratic international participation soon broadens to all states. The open international security space is up for grabs along the lines of (3) power self-determination. It soon reverts to the exercise of violent anarchy.

The state of competition among nations is the only result of the international regime of the *(4)* democratic balance of power.

The proliferating break-ups of state entities along national, ethnic, religious, or just regional divisions creates new tectonic waves shattering the foundations of the hitherto international concert of nations. The collective guarantee for a balance of power among states is now impractical.

Indeed, this paradigm of political dialectic played among the small city-states of ancient Greece is as much a valid model for large nation-states of Europe themselves, as for the global politics among nations. According to its logic, the inevitable conflict among state interests is a recurring event that only creates a newer climate for the imposition of *(5)* the new hegemonic order, until the next cycle of conflict begins.

In times of stability between the world's extreme conditions, it is the imperial power that plays the role of the domestic monarch. The *Pax Hegemonica* sets international rules, international borders, international labor divisions, and economic and trade norms. The empire itself, now, has to rule either through direct appointed viceroys or by a power-sharing arrangement with its allies. It is the latter choice that is more common in recent history: the senior protector nation concentrates its resources on greasing its military machine while the junior partner reserves the 'marginally-desirable' role of administering order throughout the periphery.

The power-sharing international system is certainly the most well perpetrated regime of hierarchical hegemony in the history of the twentieth century. "One might make a good case that the world-economy as an economy would function every bit as well without a semi-periphery [a junior partner – n.a.]. But it would be far less *politically* stable, for it would mean a polarized world-system. The existence of the third category means precisely that the upper stratum is not faced with the *unified* opposition of all the others because the *middle* stratum is both exploited and exploiter."[14]

Soft vs. Hard Style Management

In the new configuration of the *political pyramid*, which is always the first and the final phase in the Aristotelian/Vico cycle of social becoming, the means of exercising leadership is to continuously reposition oneself within the ever-evolving cycles and to stay on top of the particular form of technological advances of one time. In the late twentieth century, the new political management team reaches out for the sophisticated use of advanced technological politics.

Direct leadership through the charismatic use of television and of interactive communication ensures direct access to the hearts and the minds of the masses. It implicitly calls for the elimination of the bureaucratic chain of command.

That means that in the age of the electronic masses, old-style party politics are obsolete. Regimentation through top-down organizational networks is as antiquated as the system of satrapy set up by Alexander the Great. And while the party system was as good as the horse and buggy and the telegraph – its technological support system – it was good only for its time. Transmission belts of power, the party organizations' utility rate is outweighed by the friction and background noise that often overshadow the message itself, not unlike an old Marconi radio.

The party system of governance can be replaced now with a virtual *sovereign presidency*, a Rousseauian television reenactment of *virtual rule*. This technology enables to act upon the virtues of *gentle leadership*, which implies mass persuasion rather than coercion. The War Ministry as patron and instrument of administrative governance gives way to the subtle workings of intelligence management, which is done through initiation and professionalization. The former all-powerful Chief of Staff is being replaced with the almighty Director of the Intelligence Services.

The system of *soft management*, quintessence of the modern concept of *entrepreneurial administration*, is governance through a parliamentary representation that bears the accountability of the genuine *public servant*, as it becomes the dischargeable government. Governance is now just another of the service industries with unlimited access to advanced technology. The government as we knew it is transformed into the *enterprise-government*.

Its end product is the newly engineered masses, while its all-demanding customers are the dominant, old and powerful, "those who own and manage the society."[15]

HYPOTHESIZING ON THE FUTURE

Optimism aside, one obvious condition for a nation's long-term social prosperity is the chance at predictability and at a habit-creating pattern of stability. Existential precipitation out of the physical disorder of the universe, life builds on a paradigm which demands a continuum of repetitive interactions with its own medium in order to affix to itself a nature that is consistent in the face of varying stimuli, so that it takes on both a dynamic character and a methodical quality. That is one of the intrinsic features of the human condition and the premise for a sustained civilization.

That also explains why the geographically sheltered Western Europe was able to thrive and prosper behind secure, natural borders throughout its modern history – due as much to the safe sea-barriers around it as to the more recent safeguards offered by NATO's security umbrella. It was always left to the Eastern Europeans to cope with the whimsical pattern of endless invasions and aggressions pouring in from the deep steppes of Central Asia for thousand of years, along with their legacy of erratic and tyrannizing political mores, open markets or Marshall Plans notwithstanding.

It is important to establish this plain element of historical insight in order to speculate on the direction of the changes taking place in Europe's geopolitics. Within the continental common house, ancient borders were drawn in the traditional way of power politics. Some borders followed lines of relief, but most of them were designed in the late-nineteenth-century, early twentieth-century hegemonic chancelleries. Contrary to the history of the United States, where the melting-pot philosophy suited the convenience of an uprooted proletarian population forced to obey the dispassionate commands of the marketplace, the Europeans rather moved artificial state borders back and forth among settled populations. For, when it came to the ancestral land and the ancestral language, the concept of individual rights bore no substance. More than anything else, the issue of who lives where created havoc and perennial unpredictability.

Who owned a strip of land throughout some two thousand years of collective memory, who speaks a language at home that is or is not the same as that spoken on public television, whose ancestors are the publicly observed heros – these are all at once ethnic rights and ruling privileges.

Raw nationalism derived from the two questions related to land and language. These were the last two most conservative and intractable issues acting against the large-scale urban, capitalist society and were the rearmost defense lines against total social engineering.

Both the collective real estate inheritance and the collective symbolism of shared culture and language brought together a community as a nation. Over time, from one generation to another, and within the space of a common estate, the national states stood as geoeconomic beings unto themselves. Their hybrid intermingling and their unstable interactions within the continental urb were the source of the unsolved balkanization.

Intelligentsia in Power

Throughout the 1970s and 1980s, in all of the former centrally planned economies, it was almost an article of faith for the popular dissenting spirit to expand the scale of social disorder, by testing the limits of the state system on a daily basis. In other words, one would fight the ineffective leadership by creating, supporting, amplifying, and refining the level of social disorder in every possible way, in every possible field.

A state-owned company's chief accountant would, delightedly, send up a report with unsupported statistics. In return, a middle-level official would happily forward down the hierarchy a hazardous decision that would expose its high-ranking planner. The logic would always be supported with a most candid argument. In order to sensitize the upper echelons on the proportions of the mismanagement, utter malfunctioning, and full-scale culpability of the chain of social command, a very strong signal was required. This signal must be an ultimate national calamity of some sort, a disaster of such proportion that it would give an absolute sense of the unconditional social gridlock. The crash landing of the entire state would bring inescapable and irrevocable accountability to its servants and sycophants, and that would deliver the hour of truth. This was the wide-spread conviction and hope as well as the spontaneous popular conspiracy.

It is ironic to discover that the same means were employed for the same purpose by the high level decision factors of the United States; only theirs was a reverse action. The very top factors of the political elite were acting to help quicken the process of disintegration in order to alert the insensitive masses, to confront the self-serving individualistic interests, and to awaken the narcoleptic and secluded upper-middle classes.

This was achieved by shortening the time that society could live on borrowed money, by leading the borrowing frenzy and freeing speculative vice on such a scale that it would grow out of proportion; by encouraging corruption, depravity, inequality, public indecency, and deficiency to unprecedented levels; by bringing the victims, the poor, and the homeless from hidden institutions onto the streets, and by letting crime run rampant and drug use increase and diversify – all while the state powerbrokers, Congress included, went free.

The cumulative effect was a low, overall national performance and an inevitable economic crisis at a time when ever more limited policy options were available. The overburdened credit lines, the financial squeeze, a spreading sense of collective guilt, moral debasement, and ethical drifting were ultimately bringing down the once-unshakable, if intangible, sense of superiority.

Joining ranks, the two superpowers' leading intelligence elites moved away from the discreet minuet of the earlier years, to exercising a direct top-down leadership. Their new joint world directorate allowed for the first time ever to dispense with the services of the broker, proxy, third party, intermediaries, nonaligned individuals or nations for hire. Whether the old Vatican network, the Mafia affiliation, or the newer Jewish connection, they all fell out of favor as times turned in preference for the technological red lines of direct coordination. The historical role of power brokers, agents of influence and small-time arbitrators among the big powers was now over. For the new technocracy in power it would be only a matter of the proper use of specific mass media tools in the two distinctive systems. Reform-minded and innovative, such bold actions were, in retrospect, concocted by the same professional spirit set against the established order – originating from within the common agent of revival in both societies – the *intelligence's intelligentsia*.

By no coincidence a protégé of Andropov's Soviet intelligence community, Gorbachev was, all along his meteoric rise through the ranks of an otherwise monolithic apparatus, mentored and backed up by the top triumvirate of Brezhnev, Andropov, and Chernenko. Alone within the late party Politburo, Gorbachev happened to be the protégé of every one of the top old guard comrades of the Soviet inner circle in each of the key moments of power transition.

The same was true of the American leadership. An elite member of the top intelligence community, George Bush took on the executive responsibilities under the sponsorship of an array of strange fellow travelers: right-wing conservatives, liberal,s financial power centers, the entertainment industry, the Pentagon establish-ment, the consummate Washington bureaucracy, even blue-collar Republicans and ethnic Democrats.

In the end we find out that the very ambitious cold war American military buildup under the escalating Reagan rhetoric about the Strategic Defense Initiative, which was said to have been "at the heart of American military policy," was in fact all along squandering billions that built no weapons, as the regulations and programs' priorities assured that the missile shield would not be implemented. In plain language,"the missile shield was sabotaged."[16] Rules adopted from the start by the Reagan administration stated that "no device could be built until the capacity existed to build the most technically challenging of hundreds of devices." In a behind the scene compromise with the Soviets, the goal was to spend money and make a lot of noisy propaganda but make sure the results were negligible.

Angelo M. Codevilla lists a number of such deceptive devices used to ensure that no missile defense system would be designed. "S.D.I. allocated $1 billion for simulations matching nonexistent offenses against nonexistent defenses and churned out unrealistic standards of performance. Other funds went into supercomputers, in a nutty bid to centralize the management of thousands of nonexistent elements of a hypothetical defensive system." Even the few defensive weapons that "have managed to get close to production have been technically crippled, reducing the chances that they might be able to protect us against any missile, especially Russia's."

Examples of direct defense impairing regulations are numerous. Software in the Navy's Aegis radar was not allowed to track objects higher than 20 miles, nor was it allowed to receive data directly from satellites. "The Army's potentially excellent new defensive interceptor, called Thaad, is not allowed to get satellite data even by phone." Development of shorter-range interceptors was limited to warheads coming at speeds no faster than "about two miles a second." The Patriot surface-to-air missile system was not allowed to receive direct satellite information during the Persian Gulf War in compliance with the Antiballistic Missile Treaty that prohibits space-based sensors from directing defensive weapons. Fabulously expensive schemes "like Defense Secretary William J. Perry's idea of putting defensive weapons on offensive missiles, at half a billion dollars per shot," were meant to bring public ridicule on such proposals and question the intent of those who were in position to decide on spending tens of billions of dollars in order to weaken, delay, or veto any such future weapons.

Aiming to cause an insurrection through democratic coalition-building skills, the elite ultimately succeeded in deploying a vast arsenal, of epic proportions, of political management techniques to implement global social engineering. A top-down command structure heated the social pot from the bottom up, in order to increase the self-perpetuating process of social chain reactions.

The Birth of Euroslavia

While everyone's eyes were captured by the live broadcasts of show-history, a glimpse at the *riddle of history* through the prescient Sphinx's serene obscurity revealed esoteric marvels as the voice of the Oracle whispered: The cold war is over, long live the cold peace.

If classical economic science cannot deal with the international challenge and the competitive advantage of nations, the alternative is classical conflict management. Here is a new version of the age-old scenario. Vintage friends of previously hard times pull together once again to save the Spirit of History.

Weren't the Russians the ones that thwarted Napoleon's foul ambitions for a greater France? And who then dealt with another stubborn generation of Europeans? The Germans' obsession with 'vital space' had to be kept in check by the only standing army that could both be paid in sterling pounds and never leave their compounds in the plains of Eurasia. They pressed their harpoons into the Teutonic back defense and served them a deadly blow from time to time to keep things under control and thus to manage the European balance of power.

It was a masterful act of global thinking, worth the fame of the *perfidious Albion*, that brought Peter the Great into the Western camp before Russia meant anything in Western Europe. And ever since, Russia received second-hand discarded Western technology in exchange for the inconveniences.

For Russians themselves it was also a bargain: they got free technological expertise as well as to rule over their own vast house with an iron fist. Their perpetual state of war also gave them a valid justification to confront their people with the permanence of a war economy. *Gendarmes of Europe*, throughout the nineteenth century, they took the blame for the powder keg resentment of aspiring nationalists, playing the bad guys' characters for the nineteenth-century mass media. They also were good at understanding the balance between costs and benefits as long as the good guys were paying their order's maintenance dues.

As before, the time for a new reengineering of the reemerging Western European challenge was called upon. Here is how it was to work.

First, through coordinated actions in the late 1970s, engineer the largest international debt money can buy, through exorbitant energy price hikes and extravagant interest rate increases, from 6 to 20 percent on loans already disbursed. (By the early 1980s Romania accumulated overnight a paper debt of $12 billion, Hungary, $18 billion, Poland, $38 billion, Argentina, $60 billion, Brazil, $60 billion, Mexico, $80 billion.)

Compromise the superpowers' armies in Vietnam and Afghanistan.

Set up covert-*cum*-dissident *Solidarity*-type mass movements throughout the Eastern European nations. Then, when the social pressure in those countries reached a boiling point, proclaim communism a misunderstanding of modern economics.

Next, at the right time, create joyful revolutions on TV screens, at dinner time, for everybody to see. Fabricate live bloody insurrections and show them on a Christmas holiday, for the last skeptics, with pictures of the Ceausescus' liquidation. Put on the screen free elections with second echelon *neo-partnichiks*, presidents-to-be, and prime ministers arrived just in time from their privileged prison cells (Vaclav Havel, Lech Walesa, etc.) to take command of their battered nations. Promise instant free-market economies – the code word for Western welfare – to those pauper comrades and force German unification just before the European Economic Integration is to take place, but keep the old communists in shadow positions. Purge from public life true Communist believers and let opportunists embezzle the national patrimony – just as in Umberto Eco's best-seller of the 1980s, *In the Name of the Rose*, an inside initiation of the times. Promise economic help and deliver it always too late and in trivial portions. Free prices to world levels and simultaneously void all old contracts. Teach the pauperized labor force to demand new incentives by organizing strikes and work stoppages, and reward them with the benefits of mass unemployment. Give loans that the new governments can never pay back and then ask them to buy their basic needs with hard currency. Set fire to the oil fields and then demand that the brave new free-marketeers pay for their fuel oil at world prices, in dollars that they do not have. Encourage the free expression of all ethnic grievances, and revive those that had been successfully buried, and support their rights against each other. Boil, slowly and hotly, the tempers of some 300 million people and raise the uncertainty level in the minds of the rest.

When waves of unrestricted emigration start to flood peaceful, order-loving Western towns with former criminals, smugglers, Gypsies and desperados, the implications of 'one European common house' start to become clear to the more alert minds. Meanwhile, as much as possible bail out of the exhausted Communist industry, mostly paid for with good but overly proliferated deutsche marks. That will give the Russians some needed economic muscle for the time to come.

Wisely and rapidly, remove all risk of a nuclear war from the scene and keep Europe safe for a limited and self-contained implosion.

The first act is done. Some half a billion people are by now trigger happy, fighting against the invisible enemy from nowhere. A self-made patchwork of divided nations and antagonistic ethnics on the larger continent is now spinning out of control. Upon the approval, by the community's electoral body, of the legislation for integration, there is integration but no constitutional body to carry it out and implement the needed regimen of international security. The principles of self-determination are applied by each group of local interests and results in the breakdown of any coherent system of government and trade.

A generalization of the lowest common denominator, which is

in the end the inevitable rule of anarchy, makes the vast Eurasian continent from Lisbon to Vladivostok resemble a single interdependent entity in need of a supreme leadership body. It will come soon in response to the "grass-roots demand" for order and strong command. The European common home is now a feasible reality in accordance with the superpowers' visionary documents and public statements.

Simultaneously, (1) by weakening the once strong Western countries' economies, having them bail out the former Communist economies and then suffer the consequences of world economic depression; (2) by keeping the Eastern nations under pressure to bring their economic reforms up to some fictitious set of standards, (3) by a campaign of political, economic, and financial Westernization of the Russian empire – an unmistakable process of de facto assimilation of two (formerly) vastly incompatible systems prepares the common ground for de jure integration.

America's own economic deterioration can now be reversed. The time of reconstruction also reinstates order over Eurasia and gives new goals to those hard-working nations, which in turn opens a new era of opportunity to international business. The dangerous game of balance-of-power politics comes to its senses under the sign of the new world order.

Formulating the Eurasian Commonwealth of Independent States is the next act of the European Conference on Security and Cooperation. It must decide on the next steps of integration as well as on practical ways to draw the new border line. . . across the vast plateau of China.

Notes

Introduction

[1] Carroll Quigley, *The Anglo-American Establishment* (New York: Books in Focus, 1981), p. x.

Chapter I

[1] Karl Marx, *Capital*, in *The Marx-Engels Reader*, ed. Robert Tucker (New York: W.W. Norton & Co., 1978), Vol. 1, pp. 302-303.

[2] *Ibid.*, p. 308.

[3] *Ibid.*, p. 309.

[4] *Ibid.*, p. 309.

[5] *Ibid.*, p. 308.

[6] *Ibid.*, p. 329.

[7] Immanuel Wallerstein, "The World Capitalist System," in *Perspectives on World Politics*, ed. Richard Little and Michael Smith (New York: Routledge, 1991), p. 316.

[8] A. O. Hirschman, *Essay in Trespassing: Economics to Politics and Beyond* (New York: Cambridge University Press, 1981).

[9] Robert Gilpin, "Three Ideologies of Political Economy," *Perspectives on World Politics*, ed. by Richard Little and Michael Smith (New York: Routledge, 1991), p. 433.

[10] *Ibid.*, p. 433.

[11] *Ibid.*, p. 433.

[12] Lester Thurow, *Head to Head, The Coming Economic Battle Among Japan, Europe, and America* (New York: William Morrow and Co., 1992), pp. 28-29.

[13] *Ibid.*, p. 31.

[14] *Ibid.*, p. 32.

[15] *Capital Choices, Changing the Way America Invests in Industry*, a research report presented to the Council on Competitiveness and Co-sponsored by the Harvard Business School (Washington, D.C.: 1992), p. 20.

[16] Among them: Harvard Business School, Hewlett-Packard, AETNA, Motorola, California Institute of Technology, Cummings Engine, IBM, Xerox, Rockwell Int'l, BellSouth Corp., National Association of Manufacturers, American Stock Exchange, Texas Instruments, Stanford University, Johnson & Johnson, Dupont, General Dynamics, Ford Motor Co., Dow Chemical, John's Hopkins University, General Electric, American Express, Cray Research, Apple Computer, University of California, George Washington University, *Business Week*, Goldman Sachs, et cetera.

[17] *Capital Choices*, p. 15.

[18] *Ibid.*, p. 73.

[19] *Ibid.*, p. 63.

[20] *Ibid.*, p. 63.

[21] World Bank Atlas, 27th ed., 1994, *New York Times*, Dec. 30, 1994, p. D2.

[22] Peter Drucker, *The Unseen Revolution, How Pension Fund Socialism Came to America* (New York: Harper & Row, 1976), pp. 33-34.

[23] All data is supported by a number of independent researches as well as by the Joint Economic Committee of Congress compilations based on the Federal Reserve Board's results. See also Jeffrey G. Williamson and Peter H. Lindert, *American Inequality; A Macroeconomic History* (New York: Academic Press, 1980), James D. Smith, "Recent Trends in the Distribution of Wealth in the U.S.: Data, Research Problems, and Prospects," in *International Comparison of Household Wealth*, ed. Edward N. Wolff, (Oxford: Claredon Press, 1987), Lester Thurow and Robert E.B.Lucas, *The American Distribution of Income: a Structural Problem* (A Study prepared for the use of the Joint Economic Committee Congress of the U.S., March

1972), James D. Smith, Stephen D.F. Franklin, Douglas A. Wion, *Financial Concentration in the United States* (Washington, D.C.: Urban Institute, 1975), Kevin Philips, *The Politics of Rich and Poor* (New York: Random House, 1990).

[24] Federal Reserve and Internal Revenue Service Report, *New York Times*, April 21, 1991.

[25] Peter Drucker, *The Unseen Revolution*, p. 34.

[26] Severyn T. Bruyn, *The Social Market, A Future for the American Economy* (Stanford: Stanford University Press, 1991), p. 95.

[27] Joseph Blasi, in Nell Minow, *Employee Plans, Employer Boons*, New York Times, Feb. 5, 1995.

[28] Severyn T. Bruyn, *The Social Market*, p. 134.

[29] *Ibid.*, p. 151.

[30] *Ibid.*, p. 151.

[31] *Ibid.*, p. 74.

[32] "This is a collective and imperfectly defined entity; in the large corporation it embraces chairman, president, those vice presidents with important staff positions and, perhaps, division or department heads not included above. It includes, however, only a small proportion of those who, as participants, contribute information to group decisions. This latter group is very large;... It embraces all who bring specialized knowledge, talent or experience to group decision-making." John Kenneth Galbraith, *The New Industrial State* (New York: Penguin Books, 1985), p. 65.

[33] "In which the executives in the administrative hierarchy have no connection with the founders or their families and have little or no equity in the company." Alfred D. Chandler, Jr., *Scale and Scope: The Dynamics of Industrial Capitalism* (Cambridge: Harvard University Press, 1990), p. 240.

[34] *Fortune*, May 1977; Quarterly Financial Report for Manufacturing, Mining and Trade Corporations, Fourth Quarter, 1976, p. 66. In John Kenneth Galbraith, p. 68.

[35] John Kenneth Galbraith, p. 68.

[36] Alfred D. Chandler, Jr., p. 604.

[37] James Bovard, *The Fair Trade Fraud* (New York: St. Martin's Press, 1991), p. 7.

[38] Robert Kuttner, *The End of Laissez-Faire* (New York: Alfred A. Knopf, 1991), p. 28.

[39] Karl Marx, p. 334.

[40] *Ibid.,* p. 211.

[41] *Ibid.,* p. 216.

[42] *Ibid.,* p. 217.

[43] Michael Steward, *Keynes and After* (London: Penguin Books, 1986), pp. 184-85.

[44] Robert F. Kuttner, p. 129.

[45] Peter Drucker, *Management* (New York: Harper & Row, 1985), p. 60.

[46] John Kenneth Galbraith, p. 157.

[47] Peter Drucker, *Management,* p. 60.

[48] Here is the classical Marxist line of class definition: "The first question to be answered is this: What constitutes a class? – and the reply to this follows naturally from the reply to another question, namely: What makes wage laborers, capitalists and landlords constitute the three great social classes? At first glance – the identity of revenues and sources of revenue. There are three great social groups whose members, the individuals forming them, live on wages, profit and ground-rent respectively, on the realization of their labor-power, their capital, and their landed property." Karl Marx, *Capital,* pp. 441-42.

[49] Karl Marx, *The German Ideology,* in The Marx-Engels Reader, p. 173.

[50] *Ibid.,* p. 174.

[51] Nathan Rosenberg and L.E.Birdzell, Jr., *How the West Grew Rich* (New York: Basic Books, 1986), p. 184.

[52] Alfred D Chandler, Jr., p. 8.

[53] John Kenneth Galbraith, p. 69.

[54] Noam Chomsky, *World Orders Old and New* (New York: Columbia University Press, 1994), p. 181.

[55] Russell Baker, "Bestrides Like a Colossus," *New York Times,* January 21, 1995.

[56] Peter Drucker, *The Frontiers of Management* (New York: Harper & Row, 1986), p. 31.

[57] Lester Thurow, *Head to Head,* p. 18.

[58] Severyn T. Bruyn, p. 4.

Chapter II

[1] T. Skocpol, *States & Social Revolutions*, (Cambridge, 1984), p. 234.

[2] John H. Kautsky, "Revolutionary and Managerial Elites in Modernizing Regimes," in *Comparative Politics*, (July 1969), 1: 441.

[3] Robert Putnam, *The Comparative Study of Political Elites* (Prentice-Hall 1976), p. 195.

[4] Andrei Kozyrev, "Russia: A Chance for Survival," *Foreign Affairs* (Spring 1992).

[5] Sandra Halperin, "Cycles of Social Progress and Retrogress, Economic Advance and Regress, in the Rise of the Eurocentric World System," (Paper delivered at the 1994 Annual Meeting of ISA, Washington, D.C.), p. 2.

[6] All data refer to the alluvial area only.

[7] "A wagon-load of wheat, costing 6,000 dinarii, would be doubled in price by a journey [by land] of 300 miles. It was cheaper to ship a grain from one end of the Mediterranean to the other than to cart it 75 miles." in A.H. M. Jones, *The Later Roman Empire 284-602*, (1964), 2: 841-42.

[8] *The Atlas of World History* (Maplewood: Hammond, 1993), p. 74.

[9] G.E.M. de Ste. Croix, *The Class Struggle in the Ancient Greek World* (Ithaca, N.Y.: Cornell University Press, 1981), p. 294.

[10] M. Rostovtzeff, "Social and Economic History of the Hellenistic World," in G.E.M. de Ste. Croix, p. 294.

[11] G. E. M. de Ste. Croix, p. 298.

[12] *Ibid.*, p. 232.

[13] *Ibid.*, p. 227 and also footnote.

[14] "After defeating Decebal, the leader of the Dacians, the powerful Roman Emperor Trajan brought the Roman people five million pounds of gold, twice as much silver, besides vessels and various expensive things, almost impossible to evaluate, as well as cattle and weapons...," Crito, *Getae*, in Vasile Parvan, *Dacia. Civilizatiile Antice din Tarile Carpato-Dunarene* (Bucharest: Editura Scientifica, 1972), p. 267; also: "According to the writer Joanes Lydos, the Romans took out of Dacia huge riches, including 165,000 kilos of gold and 331,000 kilos of silver." Andrew Mackenzie, *Archeology in Romania. The Mystery of the Roman Occupation* (London: Robert Hale, 1986), p. 49.

[15] G.E.M. de Ste. Croix, p. 231.

[16] George Ostrovsky, *History of the Byzantine State* (New Brunswick: Rutgers University Press, 1969), in Sandra Halperin, p. 20.

[17] J.M. Roberts, *History of the World* (London: Penguin Books, 1987), p. 479.

[18] *Ibid.*, p. 483.

[19] *Ibid.*, p. 649.

[20] Albert Allen Bartlett, "A Forecast for 2050: Scarcities Will Force a Leaner U.S. Diet," *New York Times*, Feb. 18, 1995, p. 8.

[21] B.H. Slicher van Bath, *Le Climat et les recoltes au haut Moyen Age*, in Fernand Braudel, *Civilization and Capitalism* (Berkeley and Los Angeles: University of California Press, 1992), 1: 123.

[22] *Ibid.*, p. 123.

[23] *Ibid.*, p. 652.

[24] Interestingly enough, Turgenev described the Russian national character in his *Certophanov*, a nineteenth-century precursor of the future Bolshevik hero, long before it became legendary. One of Certophanov's dreams was to assemble the largest carriage ever built, which he does at the price of having it break to pieces at the first attempt to haul it by a team of sixteen horses.

[25] A good history on the subject is to be found in Jerome Blum, *Lord and Peasant in Russia From the Ninth to the Nineteenth Century* (Princeton: Princeton University Press, 1972).

[26] Maureen Dowd, "Capital's Virtual Reality: Gingrich Rides a 3rd Wave," *New York Times*, Jan.11, 1995.

[27] Carroll Quigley, p. 235.

[28] U.S. Bureau of the Census, *Historical Statistics of the United States* (Washington, D.C., 1966) Z1-19.

[29] Most of the raw cotton used by the English mills came from the southern U.S. plantations.

[30] Ferdinand Lundberg, *The Myth of Democracy* (New York: Carol Publishing Group, 1989), p. 9.

[31] J.M. Roberts, p. 555.

[32] *Ibid.*, p. 625.

[33] Carroll Quigley, p. 114.

[34] *Ibid.*

[35] *Ibid.*

[36] *Ibid.* p. 116.

[37] J.M. Roberts, p. 809.

[38] *Ibid.*, p. 809.

[39] *Ibid.*, p. 810.

[40] *Ibid.*, p. 821.

[41] *Ibid.*, p. 828.

[42] Christopher Simpson, *The Splendid Blond Beast*, chap. 5 (Grove, 1993), in Noam Chomsky, *World Orders Old and New*, p. 41.

[43] Noam Chomsky, *Deterring Democracy* (New York: Verso, 1991), and chaps. 1, 11, in Noam Chomsky, *World Orders Old and New*, p. 41.

[44] Carroll Quigley, p. 191.

[45] Stephen Kinzer, "O, Niederkirchnerstrasse, Be Some Other Name," *New York Times*, December 1, 1994.

[46] J.M. Roberts, p. 835.

Chapter III

[1] Aristotle, *Politics* (Grolier), p. 34.

[2] K. Marx, *Critique of the Gotha Program*, in *The Marx-Engels Reader*, p. 531.

[3] *Ibid.*

[4] E.K.Trinberger, "*Feminism, Men and Modern Love. Greenwich Village 1900-1925,*" in Joan Roelofs, "Fourier and the Computer Dating," no. 65, *Telos*, (Fall 1985), p. 131.

[5] *Ibid.*

[6] Jude Wanniski, "The Future of Russian Capitalism," *Foreign Affairs*, (Spring 1992).

[7] K. Marx, *Capital*, p. 432.

[8] Jerzy F. Karcz, "Agricultural Reform in Eastern Europe," in *Plan and Market*, ed. Morris Bornstein (New Haven: Yale University Press, 1973), p. 211.

[9] Alan A. Brown and Egon Neuberger, eds., *International Trade and Central Planning* (Berkeley: University of California Press, 1968).

[10] Alan A. Brown and Paul Marer, "Foreign Trade in the East European Reform," in *Plan and Market*, ed. Morris Bornstein (New Haven: Yale University Press, 1973), p. 158.

[11] "Measured on any scale–as portion of total national income going to shareholders and other business owners or as the rate of return on investment–profits declined or stagnated from the mid-1960s onward. From a peak of nearly 10 percent in 1965, the average net after-tax profit rate of America's nonfinancial corporations dropped to less than 7 percent in 1980, a decline of more than one-third." Robert B. Reich, *The Work of*

Nations (New York:Vintage Books, 1991), p. 76. See also *Tangible Assets, Profits, and Profit Rate of Nonfinancial Corporate Business in the United States, 1945–94* in Federal Reserve Flow of Funds Accounts, diskette version, March 1995.

[12] Alan A. Brown and Paul Marer, p. 159.

[13] Ellen Commisso and Laura D'Andrea Tyson, eds., *Power, Purpose, and Collective Choice. Economic Strategy in Socialist States* (Ithaca, N.Y.: Cornell University Press, 1986), p. 25.

[14] Michael Keren, "Concentration Amid Devolution in East Germany's Reforms," in *Plan and Market*, p. 138.

[15] *Ibid.*, p. 138.

[16] *Ibid.*, p. 139.

[17] Bela Balassa, "The Firm in the New Economic Mechanism in Hungary," in *Plan and Market*, p. 347.

[18] *Ibid.*, p. 357.

[19] *Ibid.*, p. 353.

[20] "On the Description and Comparison of Economic Systems," in *Comparisons of Economic Systems: Theoretical and Methodological Approaches*, ed. Alexander Eckstein, (Berkeley: University of California Press, 1972),p p. 42-48.

[21] Attributed to Alexander Hamilton or James Madison; in *Federalist No. 51.*

[22] Noam Chomsky, *World Orders Old and New*, p. 185.

[23] John Kenneth Galbraith, *The Industrial State*, p.

[24] Laura D'Andrea Tyson, *Who's Bashing Whom? Trade Conflict in High-Technology Industries* (Washington, D.C.: Institute for International Economics, 1992), p. 9.

Chapter IV

[1] D. Nigh and K.D. Smith, "The New U.S. Joint Ventures in the USSR: Assessment and Management of the Political Risk, *Columbia Journal of World Business* (Summer, 1989).

[2] M. McCain, "Allocation Politics and the Arms Race: a Soviet Constituency for Arms Control," in *Essays in Honor of F.C. Barghoon* (New York: Macmillan), pp. 125-30.

[3] Eduard Shevardnadze, "Report on 25 July 1988 to the Ministry of Foreign Affairs," *International Affairs* 10 (1988).

[4] Ogarkov, *Military Science and the Defense of the Socialist Fatherland*, p. 145.

[5] *Ibid.*, p.112.

[6] *Ibid.*

[7] Ann Markusen and Joel Yudken, *Dismantling the Cold War Economy* (New York: Basic Books, 1992), p. XV.

[8] *Ibid.*, p. 6.

[9] *Ibid.*, p. 38.

[10] Greg Bischak, *Building the Peace Economy* (Mansing: Economic Research Associates, 1990), p. 10, in Ann Markusen and Joel Yudken, p. 3.

[11] Ann Markusen and Joel Yudken, ibid. p.36.

[12] *Ibid.*, p. 115.

[13] *Ibid.*, p. 45.

[14] *Ibid.*, p. 42.

[15] *Ibid.*, p. 60.

[16] Adam Smith, *The Roaring '80s, A Roller-coaster Ride through the Greed Decade* (New York: Penguin Books, 1988), p. 58.

[17] Ann Markusen and Joel Yudken, p. 40.

[18] Howard Mingos, *The Rise of the American Industry*, in Ann Markusen & Joel Yudken, p. 41.

[19] Ann Markusen and Joel Yudken, p. 21.

[20] *Ibid.*, p. 22.

[21] *Ibid.*, p. 44.

[22] *New York Times*, March 4, 1992.

[23] Kenneth Flamm, *Creating the Computer* (Washington, D.C.: The Brookings Institution, 1988), p. 17.

[24] *Ibid.*, p. 16.

[25] Ann Markusen and Joel Yudken, p. 48.

[26] *Ibid.*, p. 50.

[27] *Ibid.*, p. 52.

[28] *New York Times*, April 1992.

[29] Georgi Arbatov, *The System* (New York: Random House, 1993), p. 209.

[30] "A Talk with Nicolai Ryzhkov, Economic Czar," *Business Week*, June 5, 1989, p. 63.

[31] Dale R. Herspring, *The Soviet High Command 1967-1989* (Princeton: Princeton University Press, 1990), p. 8.

[32] James M. McConnell, "Shifts in Soviet Views on the Proper Focus of Military Development," *World Politics* 37, No. 3 (April 1985), p. 319, in Dale R. Herspring, p. 29.

[33] Peter Collier and David Horowitz, *The Rockefellers* (New York: Signet, 1977), p. 272.

[34] Dale R. Herspring, p. 32.

[35] N.S. Khrushchev, *Disarmament for Durable Peace and Friendship* (Moscow: Foreign Languages Publishing House, 1960), pp. 38-39, in Dale R. Herspring, p. 33.

[36] A. Grechko, "A Celebration of the Leninist Idea of the Defense of the Socialist Fatherland," *Kommunist vooruzhennykh sil*, No. 20, 1967, p. 34, in Dale R. Herspring, Ibid., p. 34.

[37] Dale R. Herspring, Ibid., p. 65.

[38] A. Grechko, "V.I.Lenin and the Development of the Soviet Armed Forces," *Kommunist*, no. 3, February (1969), p. 23, in Dale R. Herspring, p. 67.

[39] M. I. Cherednichenko, "Modern War and Economics," *Kommunist vooruzhennykh sil*, No. 18, September 1971, in *U.S. Air Force, Selected Soviet Military Writings*, 1970-1975 (Washington: Government Printing Office, 1977), p. 53.

[40] V. Sokolovskii and M. Cherednichenko, "Military Strategy and Its Problems," *Voennaia mysl*, no. 10 (October 1968), in Douglas and Hoeber, *Selected Readings*, vol. 5, pt. 2, p. 12.

[41] Dale R. Herspring, p. 81.

[42] A. Grechko, "*Vooruznhennye sily Soiuza Soverskikh Sotsialisticheskikh Respublik*" ("The Armed Forces of the Union of Soviet Socialist Republics"), *Kommunist*, No. 3, (Feb.1972), in Dale R. Herspring, p. 95.

[43] A. Grechko, "Armed Forces of the Soviet State," pp. 138, 148, in Dale R. Herspring, p. 96.

[44] Dale R. Herspring, p.125.

[45] N. Ogarkov, "*Voennaia nauka i zashchita sotsialisticheskogo otechestva*" ("Military Science and the Defense of the Socialist Fatherland"), *Kommunist*, No. 7, (1978), p. 142-43, in Dale R. Herspring, pp. 149-50.

[46] "Soviets Refurbish Artillery for Deeper Attack Missions," *Defense Week*, (Dec. 5, 1983).

[47] N. Ogarkov, "*Sovetskaia Voennaia nauka*" ("Soviet Military Science"), *Pravda*, (Feb.19, 1978).

[48] N. V. Ogarkov, "*Teoreticheskii arsenal voennogo rukovoditelia*," ("The Theoretical Arsenal of the Military Leader") *Krasnaia zvezda*,Sept.3, 1971; FBIS, *The Soviet Union*, Sept.10, 1971.

[49] N. Ogarkov, *"Povyshat' vospitatel'nuiu rol' sovetskikh vooruzhennykh sil,"* ("Raising the Educational Role of the Soviet Armed Forces"), *Krasnaia zvezda*, June 5, 1980, in Dale R. Herspring, p. 150.

[50] N. Ogarkov, *"Voennaia nauka,"* p. 117.

[51] N. Ogarkov, *Shtab* ("Staff"), *Sovetskaia Voennaia Entsiklopediia*, vol. 8, p. 535, in Dale R. Herspring, p. 153.

[52] *Ibid.*

[53] N. Ogarkov, "The Great Feat of the People," *Izvestiia*, May 9, 1977; FBIS, *Soviet Union*, May 12, 1977.

[54] Dale R Herspring, p. 160.

[55] N. Ogarkov, "Raising the Educational Role of the Soviet Armed Forces."

[56] In a study published in 1979, the International Labor Organization projected the curve of manufacturing jobs to decline from 31 percent in Western Europe in 1980 to 26 percent by 1985, to 21 percent by 1990, and to 16 percent by 1995, as the U. S. manufacturing work force would diminish from 26 percent in 1980 to 21 percent by 1985, 16 percent by 1990, and around 5 percent by the year 2000.

[57] "Round-table with the participants in the cold war negotiations for arms reductions between the Soviet Union and the United States," CNN, May 14, 1993.

[58] N. Ogarkov, *"Zashchita sotsializma: opyt istorii i sovremennost',"* ("The Defense of Socialism: The Experience of History and the Present"), *Krasnaia zvezda*, May 9, 1984 in Dale R Herspring, p. 175.

[59] Dale R. Herspring, p, 202.

[60] Georgi Arbatov, *The System*, p. 183.

[61] William J. Broad, "Russian Says Soviet Atom Arsenal Was Larger Than West Estimated," *New York Times*, Sept. 26, 1993.

[62] John Holusha, "Growing Soviet Export: Military Technology, *New York Times*, May 3, 1990.

[63] William J. Broad, "U.S. Is Shopping as Soviets Offer To Sell Once-Secret Technology," *New York Times*, November 4, 1991.

[64] William J. Broad, "U.S. Is Shopping."

[65] William J. Broad, "Pentagon Wizards of Technology Eye Wider Civilian Role," *New York Times*, October 1991.

[66] Books written by high ranking State Department employees posing as Hegelian philosophers were making official waves in the mass media by using catchy headlines. See Francis Fukuyama, *The End of History and the Last Man* (New York: The Free Press, 1992).

Chapter V

[1] M.S. Gorbachev, "Perestroika: New Thinking for our Country and the World" (New York: HarperCollins, 1991), p. 219.

[2] Richard Rosecrance, "Concert of Powers," Foreign Affairs (Spring, 1992).

[3] "World-Trade Statistics Tell Conflicting Stories," Wall Street Journal, March 28, 1994.

[4] John Naisbitt and Patricia Aburdene, MEGATRENDS 2000 (New York: William Morrow and Co., 1990), p. 35.

[5] Ibid., p. 38.

[6] Ibid., p. 220.

[7] M. Rostovtzeff, Social and Economic History of the Hellenistic World, 1957.

[8] Max Weber, "Social Causes of the Decline of Ancient Civilizations," in The Agrarain Sociology of the Ancient Civilizations, (1976), pp. 389-411.

[9] A.R. Birley, "The Third Century Crisis in the Roman Empire," in Bull. of the John Rylands Univ. Library of Manchester 58: 1976, p. 253-281, in G.E.M. de Ste. Croix, p. 656.

[10] G.E.M. de Ste. Croix, pp. 496-97.

[11] A.H.M. Jones, The Later Roman Empire 284-602, pp. 933-34, in G.E.M. de Ste. Croix, p. 496.

[12] G.E.M. de Ste. Croix, p. 237.

[13] Jerome Blum, Lord and Peasant in Russia from the Ninth to the Nineteenth Century (Princeton: Princeton University Press, 1971), p. 308.

[14] Ibid., p. 309.

[15] V.I.Semevskii, Krest'iane v tsarstvovanie imperatritsy Ekateriny II, 2 vols. (St. Petersburg, 1881-1901), 2: p. 304-305, in Jerome Blum, p. 311.

[16] Le Play, Les ouvriers européens, II 120-121, 160-161; III 18-19, 416-417; IV 20-21; V 448-449. Cf. Baster, "Some Early Family Budget Studies," pp. 468-480, in Jerome Blum, p.316-317.

[17] Le Play, Les ouvriers européens, in Jerome Blum, p. 317.

[18] Jerome Blum, p. 318.

[19] Ibid., p. 322.

[20] Ibid., p. 332.

[21] P. I. Liashchenko, Istoriia narodnogo khoziaistva SSSR, 2 vols. (Moscow, 1947-48), p. 519, in Jerome Blum, p. 331.

[22] Jerome Blum, ibid. p.333.

[23] Peter Drucker, "The New Productivity Challenge," in *Harvard Business Review*, Dec. 1991.

[24] G.E.M. de Ste. Croix, p. 268.

[25] Jerome Blum, p. 602.

[26] *Ibid.*, p. 604.

[27] *Ibid.*, p. 604.

[28] *Ibid.*, p.606.

[29] Jan Tinbergen, "Do Communist and Free Economies Show a Converging Pattern?," *Soviet Studies*, 12, no. 4 (April 1961), pp. 333-341.

[30] *Ibid.*, p. 338.

Chapter VI

[1] Philip Hanson, "Is there a Third Way between Capitalism and Socialism?", *Report on the USSR*, No. 35 (1991), p. 15-19.

[2] Steven Erlanger, "An Irresistible Force Moves a Few Objects in Moscow," *New York Times*, April 19, 1992.

[3] Keith Bradsher, "Trade Tie With Europe Frays Over Soybeans," *New York Times*, May 1, 1992.

[4] "EC Statement on US FDI Policy," *EURECOM*, March 1992.

[5] Stephen Engelberg, "With Some Misgivings, East Europe Snaps Up German Money," *New York Times*, Jan. 23, 1992.

[6] Jannine R. Wedel, "Getting It Right in Aid to Russia," *New York Times*, April 5, 1992.

[7] Michael Marrese, "Hungary Emphasizes Foreign Partners," *RFE/RL Research Report*, April 24, 1992, p. 25.

[8] *Ibid.*, p. 32.

[9] *Ibid.*, p.32.

[10] Roger Cohen, "Smaller Companies Grease the Wheels in Hungary," *RFE/RL Research Report*, May 3, 1992.

[11] Michael Marrese, "Hungary Emphasizes Foreign Partners," *RFE/RL Research Report*, April 24, 1992. p. 33.

[12] Victor Yasmann, "Murder Incorporated, Russian Style," *The Prism*, Jamestown Foundation, August 11, 1995.

[13] Thomas E. Weisskopf, "Challenges to Market Socialism: A response to Critics," *DISSENT* (Spring 1992), p. 250.

[14] Nicholas Georgescu-Roegen, *The Entropy Law and the Economic Process* (Cambridge: Harvard University Press, 1981), p. 279.

[15] Kevin Philips, *The Politics of Rich and Poor*, (New York: Random House, 1990), p. 73.

[16] "A Review of Economic Performance in 1992," *Research Bulletin*, RFE/RL Research Institute.

[17] *Open Media Research Institute's Daily Digest*, Feb. 24, 1995.

[18] Kevin Philips, p. 54.

[19] *Open Media Research Institute's Daily Digest*, Jan. 7, 1995.

[20] Kevin Philips, p. 60.

[21] *Ibid.*, p. 60-61.

[22] Paul Leinberger and Bruce Tucker, *The New Individualists* (New York: HarperCollins, 1991), p. 138.

[23] Quoted in Kevin Philips, p. 62.

[24] Lester Thurow, "The Spirit of Independence," *Inc.*, July 1988, p. 47, in Kevin Philips, p. 20.

[25] *New York Times*, Week in Review, 1992.

[26] *New York Times*, May 1992.

[27] Census Bureau, quoted in *New York Times*, 1992.

[28] Graef Crystal, "Cracking the Tax Whip on CEOs," *New York Times*, Sept. 23, 1990.

[29] "Thus, even a $50,000/year package is misleading. If you sit on the board of Texas Instruments, you receive $40,000 as an annual retainer. If you sit on the audit, corporate objectives, or finance committee, the retainer increases to $50,000. If you chair one of those committees, add another $2,000; and if you serve on a subsidiary of Texas Instruments add an additional $2,000. Every year, Texas Instruments holds a strategic planning conference. If you attend, you get $5,000. If you attend any special company events, you get another $1,000 per day. If you serve on the board for five years, you get a retirement package worth 60 percent of your retainer at the time of retirement for the number of years served as a director, up to 10 years. You also get life and travel accident insurance, as well as medical and dental coverage. Thus, you could receive in excess of $60,000 a year plus benefits and, upon retirement, receive roughly $24,000 a year." Robert A.G. Monks and Nell Minow, *Power and Accountability* (New York: HarperCollins, 1991), p. 175.

[30] Lester Thurow, *Head to Head*, p. 165.

[31] Laura D'Andrea Tyson, *Who's Bashing Whom?*, p. 46.

[32] Keith Bradsher, "Gap in Wealth In U.S. Called Widest in West," *New York Times*, April 17, 1995.

[33] Note the Japanese success at displacing the U.S. superconductor industry in less than ten years. From 75 percent of worldwide DRAM market share in 1978 the U.S. was down to under 20 percent in 1986, while the Japanese share increased from 28 percent to close to 80 percent during the same time. Also, a dramatic reversal on the worldwide EPROM market share: 1978 - 95 percent for the U.S. and 8 percent for Japan; 1986 - 40 percent for the U.S., 55 percent for Japan. In Laura D'Andrea Tyson, *Who's Bashing Whom?*, pp. 106-8.

[34] Alfred D. Chandler, Jr., p. 72.

[35] *Ibid.*, p. 72-73.

[36] Laura D'Andrea Tyson, p. 146.

[37] *Ibid.*, p. 146.

[38] This is the Chinese code word for the bureaucrat leaving secure state jobs for the lucrative undertaking of entrepreneurial money-making.

Chapter VII

[1] Quoted in William Greider, *Secrets of the Temple, How the Federal Reserve Runs the Country* (New York: Simon & Schuster, 1987), p. 270.

[2] Figures compiled by the Joint Economic Committee of Congress based on data furnished by the Federal Reserve Board, in Kevin Philips, *The Politics of Rich and Poor*, p. 241.

[3] Carolyn Kay Brancato and Patrick A. Gaughan, *Intitutional Investors and Capital Markets: 1991 Update* (New York: Center for Law and Economic Studies, Institutional Investor Project, Columbia University, Sept. 1991).

[4] Peter Drucker, *Post-Capitalist Society* (New York: HarperBusiness, 1993), p. 6.

[5] Henry Kaufman, "How Treasury's Reform Could Hurt Free Enterprise," in *Challenge*, May-June 1991.

[6] All data are from John Kenneth Galbraith, *The New Industrial State* (New York: Penguin Group, 1986), pp. 68-69, based on data from *Fortune*, May 1977, *Quarterly Financial Report for Manufacturing, Mining and Trade Corporations*, Fourth Quarter, 1976.

[7] James C. Knowles, *The Rockefeller Financial Group* (Andover, MA: Warner Modular Publications Inc., Module 343, 1973), also in an article in *Fortune*, May 1970.

[8] Ferdinand Lundberg, *The Rockefeller Syndrome* (New York: Carol Publishing Group, 1976), p. 40.

[9] *Ibid.*, pp. 40-41.

[10] Peter Collier and David Horowitz, *The Rockefellers* (New York: New American Library, 1976), p. 483.

[11] Peter Collier and David Horowitz, *The Rockefellers*, p. 596.

[12] Joseph Raphael Blasi and Douglas Lynn Kruse, *The New Owners* (New York: HarperCollins, 1992), p. 11.

[13] *Ibid.*, p. 112.

[14] *Ibid.*, p. 106.

[15] *Ibid.*, p. 133.

[16] I. M. Booth, president and CEO, Polaroid Corp. Quoted in J. R. Blasi, p. 194.

[17] Adam Bryant, "Betting the Farm On the Company Stock," *New York Times*, April 16, 1995..

[18] Cynthia A. Beltz, *High-Tech Maneuvers: Industrial Policy Lessons of HDTV* (Washington, D.C.: AEI Press, 1991), chapter 2.

[19] Alfred D. Chandler, Jr., p. 35.

[20] "The first attempt in this direction had already appeared at the beginning of the nineteenth century in a book by Johann Gottlieb Fichte, *Der geschlossene Handelsstaat* (The Closed Mercantilist State). It outlines the vision of an autarchic society in which the state is obliged to provide all citizens with employment and a minimal income as part of their natural rights." Avraham Barkai, *Nazi Economics: Ideology, Theory, and Policy* (New Haven: Yale University Press, 1990), p.74.

[21] G. Stolper, *German Economy, 1870-1940: Issues and Trends* (New York: 1940), p. 75.

[22] *Ibid.*, p. 77.

[23] A. Müller, "Elemente der Staatskunst," in *Vom Geiste der Gemeinschaft* (Leipzig: 1931 [1st ed. 1810]), p. 159, in Avraham Barkai, p. 76.

[24] *Ibid.*, p. 26, in Avraham Barkai, p. 76.

[25] *Ibid.*, p. 246, in Avraham Barkai, p. 76.

[26] *Ibid.*, p. 196, in Avraham Barkai, p. 76.

[27] A. Müller, "Von den Vorteilen welche die Errichtung einer Nationalbank für die kaiserlich-sterreichischen Staaten nach sich ziehen wirde," in *Asgewhlte Abhandlungen*, p. 52, in Avraham Barkai, p. 77.

[28] *Manufacturing Productivity* (Washington, D.C.: McKinsey Global Institute, 1993).

[29] *Ibid.*

[30] K. Knies, *Die politische konomievom geschchtlichen Standpunkte* (Braunschweig: 1883), p 329, in Avraham Barkai, p. 82.

[31] Jeffrey A. Hart, *Rival Capitalists: International Competitiveness in the United States, Japan, and Western Europe* (Ithaca, N.Y.: Cornell University Press, 1992), p. 112.

[32] *Ibid.*, p. 113.

[33] *Ibid.*, p. 118.

[34] *Ibid.*, p. 73.

[35] Laura D'Andrea Tyson, *Who's Bashing Whom?*, p. 99.

[36] Jeffrey A. Hart, *Rival Capitalists*, p. 79.

[37] *Ibid.*, p. 81.

[38] "Germany has a long tradition of world-class research, particularly in fields such as chemistry, physics, metallurgy, and medicine. Breakthroughs in important fields were the seeds of a number of German industries, notably in the chemical and optical sectors though far from limited to these fields (the X-ray tube and modern printing press were invented in Germany, for example)." Michael Porter, *The Competitive Advantage of Nations*, (New York: The Free Press, 1990), p. 370.

Chapter VIII

[1] Without engaging in a detailed examination of the following assertion in this paper, there is an obvious underlying validity in this pronouncement: regardless of how efficiently one nation manufactures cars or VCRs, there is more to its global status than economics. To define it, one must look at the concept of leadership, as vague as it might appear. In this sense, despite its undisputed manufacturing success, Japan is still circumscribed by its lack of world authority regardless of its factories' efficiency. It just has no stomach to assimilate a vast continent of the stature of the United States by resorting to the economics of consumer goods.

[2] Max Weber, in H.H. Gerth and C. Wright Mills, eds., *From Max Weber: Essays in Sociology* (New York: Oxford University Press, 1958), p. 214.

[3] Ryzhkov, *Time*,

[4] *New York Times*, March 4, 1992.

[5] *New York Times*, Feb. 5, 1992.

[6] D. Nigh and K.D. Smith, "The New US Joint Ventures in the USSR: Assessment and Management of the Political Risk," *Columbia Journal of World Business* (Summer, 1989).

[7] N. Ogarkov, *The Defence of Socialism: The Experience of History and the Present*, in Dale R. Herspring, p. 97.

[8] *Ibid.*, p. 97.

[9] Giambattista Vico, *The New Science* (Ithaca, N.Y.: Cornell University Press, 1968), §1008, §1026.

[10] Aristotle, *Politics*, V. 10, 1310^{b}9-16.

[11] There is a bizarre tendency nowadays to run a computer-aided regression analysis for every conceivable historical regularity. Hypotheses on the cyclic nature of the economic progression between booms and busts, international peace and war, and so on, abound. There are short-cycle (one- to two-year) models and long-cycle (fifty- to sixty-year) models, fixed-period- and varying-period-cycles. The common denominator is the expectation that there should be a time variable spanning over historical incompatible intermissions, spells of events, and nations - in total disregard for the detailed knowledge of what Hegel calls "the child of its time," which is the "concrete realization of the concept."

[12] G.E.M. de Ste. Croix, p. 281.

[13] Gustave Glotz, *The Greek City and its Institutions* (Eng. Trans. 1929, from *La Cité grecque*, Paris, 1928) in G.E.M. de Ste. Croix, p. 281.

[14] Immanuel Wallerstein, "The Rise and Future Demise of the World Capitalist System: Concepts for Comparative Analysis," in *Comparative Studies in Society and History*, vol. 16, no. 4 (1974), p. 389.

[15] Noam Chomsky, p. 106.

[16] Angelo M. Codevilla, "How the Missile Shield Was Sabotaged," *New York Times*, March 4, 1995.

INDEX

Also from Algora Publishing:

CLAUDIU A. SECARA
THE NEW COMMONWEALTH
From Bureaucratic Corporatism to Socialist Capitalism

The notion of an elite-driven worldwide perestroika has gained some credibility lately. The book examines in a historical perspective the most intriguing dialectic in the Soviet Union's "collapse" — from socialism to capitalism and back to socialist capitalism — and speculates on the global implications.

IGNACIO RAMONET
THE GEOPOLITICS OF CHAOS

The author, Director of Le Monde Diplomatique, presents an original, discriminating and lucid political matrix for understanding what he calls the "current disorder of the world" in terms of Internationalization, Cyberculture and Political Chaos.

TZVETAN TODOROV
A PASSION FOR DEMOCRACY –
Benjamin Constant

The French Revolution rang the death knell not only for a form of society, but also for a way of feeling and of living; and it is still not clear as yet what did we gain from the changes.

MICHEL PINÇON & MONIQUE PINÇON-CHARLOT
GRAND FORTUNES –
Dynasties of Wealth in France

Going back for generations, the fortunes of great families consist of far more than money—they are also symbols of culture and social interaction. In a nation known for democracy and meritocracy, piercing the secrets of the grand fortunes verges on a crime of lèse-majesté . . . Grand Fortunes succeeds at that.

CLAUDIU A. SECARA
TIME & EGO –
Judeo-Christian Egotheism and the Anglo-Saxon Industrial Revolution

The first question of abstract reflection that arouses controversy is the problem of Becoming. Being persists, beings constantly change; they are born and they pass away. How can Being change and yet be eternal? The quest for the logical and experimental answer has just taken off.

JEAN-MARIE ABGRALL
SOUL SNATCHERS: THE MECHANICS OF CULTS

Jean-Marie Abgrall, psychiatrist, criminologist, expert witness to the French Court of Appeals, and member of the Inter-Ministry Committee on Cults, is one of the experts most frequently consulted by the European judicial and legislative processes. The fruit of fifteen years of research, his book delivers the first methodical analysis of the sectarian phenomenon, decoding the mental manipulation on behalf of mystified observers as well as victims.

JEAN-CLAUDE GUILLEBAUD
THE TYRANNY OF PLEASURE

Guillebaud, a Sixties' radical, re-thinks liberation, taking a hard look at the question of sexual morals -- that is, the place of the forbidden -- in a modern society. For almost a whole generation, we have lived in the illusion that this question had ceased to exist. Today the illusion is faded, but a strange and tumultuous distress replaces it. No longer knowing very clearly where we stand, our societies painfully seek answers between unacceptable alternatives: bold-faced permissiveness or nostalgic moralism.

SOPHIE COIGNARD AND MARIE-THÉRÈSE GUICHARD
FRENCH CONNECTIONS –
The Secret History of Networks of Influence

They were born in the same region, went to the same schools, fought the same fights and made the same mistakes in youth. They share the same morals, the same fantasies of success and the same taste for money. They act behind the scenes to help each other, boosting careers, monopolizing business and information, making money, conspiring and, why not, becoming Presidents!

VLADIMIR PLOUGIN
RUSSIAN INTELLIGENCE SERVICES. Vol. I. Early Years

Mysterious episodes from Russia's past – alliances and betrayals, espionage and military feats – are unearthed and examined in this study, which is drawn from ancient chronicles and preserved documents from Russia, Greece, Byzantium and the Vatican Library. Scholarly analysis and narrative flair combine to give both the facts and the flavor of the battle scenes and the espionage milieu, including the establishment of secret services in Kievan rus, the heroes and the techniques of intelligence and counter-intelligence in the 10th-12th centuries, and the times of Vladimir.

JEAN-JACQUES ROSA
EURO ERROR

The European Superstate makes Jean-Jacques Rosa mad, for two reasons. First, actions taken to relieve unemployment have created inflation, but have not reduced unemployment. His second argument is even more intriguing: the 21st century will see the fragmentation of the U. S., not the unification of Europe.

ANDRÉ GAURON
EUROPEAN MISUNDERSTANDING

Few of the books decrying the European Monetary Union raise the level of the discussion to a higher plane. European Misunderstanding is one of these. Gauron gets it right, observing that the real problem facing Europe is its political future, not its economic future.

DOMINIQUE FERNANDEZ
PHOTOGRAPHER: FERRANTE FERRANTI
ROMANIAN RHAPSODY — An Overlooked Corner of Europe

"Romania doesn't get very good press." And so, renowned French travel writer Dominique Fernandez and top photographer Ferrante Ferranti head out to form their own images. In four long journeys over a 6-year span, they uncover a tantalizing blend of German efficiency and Latin nonchalance, French literature and Gypsy music, Western rationalism and Oriental mysteries. Fernandez reveals the rich Romanian essence. Attentive and precise, he digs beneath the somber heritage of communism to reach the deep roots of a European country that is so little-known.

PHILIPPE TRÉTIACK
ARE YOU AGITÉ? Treatise on Everyday Agitation

"A book filled with the exuberance of a new millennium, full of humor and relevance. Philippe Trétiack, a leading reporter for Elle, goes around the world and back, taking an interest in the futile as well as the essential. His flair for words, his undeniable culture, help us to catch on the fly what we really are: characters subject to the ballistic impulse of desires, fads and a click of the remote. His book invites us to take a healthy break from the breathless agitation in general." — Aujourd'hui le Parisien

"The 'Agité,' that human species that lives in international airports, jumps into taxis while dialing the cell phone, eats while clearing the table, reads the paper while watching TV and works during vacation – has just been given a new title." — Le Monde des Livres

PAUL LOMBARD
VICE & VIRTUE — Men of History, Great Crooks for the Greater Good

Personal passion has often guided powerful people more than the public interest. With what result? From the courtiers of Versailles to the back halls of Mitterand's government, from Danton — revealed to have been a paid agent for England — to the shady bankers of Mitterand's era, from the buddies of Mazarin to the builders of the Panama Canal, Paul Lombard unearths the secrets of the corridors of power. He reveals the vanity and the corruption, but also the grandeur and panache that characterize the great. This cavalcade over many centuries can be read as a subversive tract on how to lead.

RICHARD LABÉVIÈRE
DOLLARS FOR TERROR — The U.S. and Islam

"In this riveting, often shocking analysis, the U.S. is an accessory in the rise of Islam, because it manipulates and aids radical Moslem groups in its shortsighted pursuit of its economic interests, especially the energy resources of the Middle East and the oil- and mineral-rich former Soviet republics of Central Asia. Labévière shows how radical Islamic fundamentalism spreads its influence on two levels, above board, through investment firms, banks and shell companies, and clandestinely, though a network of drug dealing, weapons smuggling and money laundering. This important book sounds a wake-up call to U.S. policy-makers." — *Publishers Weekly*

JEANNINE VERDÈS-LEROUX
DECONSTRUCTING PIERRE BOURDIEU
Against Sociological Terrorism From the Left

Sociologist Pierre Bourdieu went from widely-criticized to widely-acclaimed, without adjusting his hastily constructed theories. Turning the guns of critical analysis on his own critics, he was happier jousting in the ring of (often quite undemocratic) political debate than reflecting and expanding upon his own propositions. Verdès-Leroux has spent 20 years researching the policy impact of intellectuals who play at the fringes of politics. She suggests that Bourdieu arrogated for himself the role of "total intellectual" and proved that a good offense is the best defense. A pessimistic Leninist bolstered by a ponderous scientific construct, Bourdieu stands out as the ultimate doctrinaire more concerned with self-promotion than with democratic intellectual engagements.

HENRI TROYAT
TERRIBLE TZARINAS

Who should succeed Peter the Great? Upon the death of this visionary and despotic reformer, the great families plotted to come up with a successor who would surpass everyone else — or at least, offend none. But there were only women — Catherine I, Anna Ivanovna, Anna Leopoldovna, Elizabeth I. These autocrats imposed their violent and dissolute natures upon the empire, along with their loves, their feuds, their cruelties. Born in 1911 in Moscow, Troyat is a member of the Académie française, recipient of Prix Goncourt.

JEAN-MARIE ABGRALL
HEALING OR STEALING — Medical Charlatans in the New Age

Jean-Marie Abgrall is Europe's foremost expert on cults and forensic medicine. He asks, are fear of illness and death the only reasons why people trust their fates to the wizards of the pseudo-revolutionary and the practitioners of pseudo-magic? We live in a bazaar of the bizarre, where everyday denial of rationality has turned many patients into ecstatic fools. While not all systems of nontraditional medicine are linked to cults, this is one of the surest avenues of recruitment, and the crisis of the modern world may be leading to a new mystique of medicine where patients check their powers of judgment at the door.

DR. DEBORAH SCHURMAN-KAUFLIN
THE NEW PREDATOR: WOMEN WHO KILL — Profiles of Female Serial Killers
This is the first book ever based on face-to-face interviews with women serial killers.

RÉMI KAUFFER
DISINFORMATION — US Multinationals at War with Europe
"Spreading rumors to damage a competitor, using 'tourists' for industrial espionage. . . Kauffer shows how the economic war is waged." — *Le Monde*
"A specialist in the secret services, he notes, 'In the era of CNN, with our skies full of satellites and the Internet expanding every nano-second, the techniques of mass persuasion that were developed during the Cold War are still very much in use – only their field of application has changed.' His analysis is shocking, and well-documented." — *La Tribune*